# Learning
## FROM
# Divorce

# Learning FROM Divorce

## How to
- ## Take Responsibility
- ## Stop the Blame
- ## Move On

Christine A. Coates, J.D.
E. Robert LaCrosse, Ph.D.

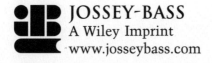

JOSSEY-BASS
A Wiley Imprint
www.josseybass.com

3 1257 01539 8992

Published by Jossey-Bass
A Wiley Imprint
989 Market Street, San Francisco, CA 94103-1741    www.josseybass.com

Jossey-Bass books and products are available through most bookstores. To contact
Jossey-Bass directly, call our Customer Care Department within the U.S. at 800-956-7739
or outside the U.S. at 317-572-3986, or fax to 317-572-4002.

Jossey-Bass also publishes its books in a variety of electronic formats. Some content that
appears in print may not be available in electronic books.

**Library of Congress Cataloging-in-Publication Data**

Coates, Christine A., date.
    Learning from divorce : how to take responsibility, stop the blame,
and move on / Christine A. Coates and E. Robert LaCrosse.–1st ed.
        p. cm.
Includes bibliographical references and index.
    ISBN 0-7879-6416-6 (alk. paper)
  1. Divorce.  I. LaCrosse, E. Robert. II. Title.
    HQ814.C63 2003
    306.89–dc21

                                                    2003002587

Printed in the United States of America
FIRST EDITION
*HB Printing*   10 9 8 7 6 5 4 3 2 1

# Contents

*To Howard and Jean—very, very special spouses*

*To all our clients over the years who lived this book and taught us how divorce could be successfully done and a new and better life begun*

*To our colleagues who have kept us thinking, helped us stay centered, and supported us when our professional lives seemed like steep uphill climbs*

# Preface

This book is proof that life intertwines, doubles back, and certainly is not a straight line. Christie, a family lawyer who now focuses on mediation rather than litigation, was divorced in the mid-1970s. While the executive director of a parent education organization, she started one of the first single-mother support groups in Houston, Texas. After moving to Colorado with her current husband, Howard Gordon, she went to law school. After practicing family law for some years, she now focuses her practice on mediation. Bob is a psychologist who was on the faculty at the Harvard Graduate School of Education, was a college president, and is now in private practice where he specializes in working with high-conflict post-divorce couples who eternally fight over their children. For both of us, writing a book about the concept of letting go of the blame game and moving on with your life was very appealing, even though it might put us out of business! Oh well, there is always running that B & B in Breckenridge.

We are fortunate to live and work in the state of Colorado, which is very progressive in its divorce laws and in the development of professional roles to help those who are having a difficult divorce. We both have received wonderful support from our friends, families, and colleagues in Colorado and around the country. There are a few people, however, whom we specifically wish to acknowledge. Our thanks to Sue Waters, the founder of Parenting after Divorce-Denver, and Arnold Swartz, its current director, for the materials they developed for their parent education course, which shaped our writing in the second half of Chapter Six. Further, Bob is indebted to Sue for a firsthand explanation of what it means to do your work after a divorce. Both of us have been influenced by the colleagues with whom we coauthored *Working with High-Conflict Families of Divorce: A Practitioner's Guide:* Elaine Johnson, Betsy Duvall, Carla Garrity, and Mitch Baris. We have also learned much from Janet Johnston, Ph.D., a premiere researcher and teacher in the field of divorce. We both received our mediation training at CDR Associates in Boulder, Colorado, and are grateful for our colleagues and friends there. One of Christie's greatest joys is training mediators with CDR and for other organizations and courts around the country. We are also very grateful to Alan Rinzler of Jossey-Bass for his belief in the project and his unerring and pointed direction and editing. He's the best!

Finally, we should say a word about our working relationship. We have been colleagues and friends for years and are each other's biggest fan! Writing a book together was stimulating, but also exhausting. We found that the hard part of writing a book is not in the initial writing but in the rewriting. We have different organization styles, writing methods, and ways of handling editorial criticism. However, we truly collaborated on this book and built on each other's strengths and backgrounds—we even flipped a coin to determine which name came first on the book. (Each of us offered the other top billing.) In this book we share as a team what we have learned and what we strongly believe is the path to an unencumbered post-divorce life.

We have been married for a combined seventy-three years. Christie writes from personal experience (including her mistakes) as well as professional knowledge. She wants to thank her ex-husband Russ Thompson for being such a terrific dad and a kind and gentle ex. She also wants to thank her current husband of twenty-five years for his patience and commitment to the marriage. Although we have drawn on the stories of our clients and friends, all names and identifying information have been changed totally to protect their identities and their actual life experiences.

We hope you will agree with the premise of this book and take it to heart. Moving on with your life is what life is all about.

Boulder, Colorado                              CHRISTINE A. COATES
Evergreen, Colorado                            E. ROBERT LaCROSSE

# Learning
## FROM
# Divorce

# Introduction

You can't sleep, lying wide awake, regretting the past and worrying about the future. You can hardly pull yourself out of bed in the morning, feeling totally depleted and de-energized. You go to work and find tears welling up over the smallest frustration, or you un-characteristically snap at a coworker. When you go home, you start to cook dinner, then break down sobbing in front of the kids. You know that your children shouldn't see you like this, a complete mess, but you can't help yourself.

Or you may be living alone in a rented apartment, the entire fabric of your life torn asunder. The family you loved is gone. You have to make appointments to see your children. The spouse on whom you depended, your one-time partner and lover, now lives in another home. You have never felt so isolated, so abandoned.

What has happened to you?

You are going through a divorce, and you are in indescribable pain. You never thought that your marriage would be over—and certainly not like this. Nothing in your life has prepared you for this kind of agony. Even if you initiated the separation and divorce, you still suffer deeply. You may be ridden with guilt for hurting your spouse and causing upheaval in your children's lives. You may be feeling angry, upset with your ex, upset with yourself. You may be losing self-confidence, wondering what kind of person you really are, feeling your identity shaken to its very core. Not only that, the financial burdens of the separation are immense, and you worry about making ends meet. The future looks bleak, gray, and dreary. What's going to happen to you, your children, your ex?

All your friends are telling you to hang in there, that things will get better. But how . . . and when?

1

# Life After Divorce

We are here to assure you that there is indeed life after divorce—and that your future can be incredibly rich and satisfying. We want you to know that you are not a terrible person or a failure, that you can learn from this divorce, that divorce isn't something shameful, crazy, or bad, but rather can be seen as a developmental process, a turning point, an opportunity.

But it won't be easy. Going through a divorce is a death—of your dreams, of a cherished relationship, of a home, of a desired social status, of financial stability, of a family. And you will grieve. You will be in agony. But your pain will diminish: the knifelike jolts of pain that bring you to your knees will ease to a dull ache. Your life will go on. You will survive, like most of the two million people who are divorced every year. In fact you may come out of this process in better shape than before: smarter, more mature, more secure in your identity, and ready for a new relationship. You may even look back to see this divorce as a turning point, a developmental milestone, when all kinds of new opportunities for growth and development first presented themselves.

The goal of our book is to help you not just to survive but to grow. Your divorce, this most painful of experiences, contains within it the key to a stronger, wiser, and more compassionate you. Most of us typically learn more from our problems than from our successes because we want to avoid the pain of the loss and garner the reward of doing things better next time. Most inventors would agree that failure provides valuable information for the next step. Once we know and understand what doesn't work, we can use our intelligence to do things differently. As the inventor of your life, tenderly nourish the seed of self-understanding so that you can harness this life force and use it to help you grow in a new direction.

The maxim ascribed to Socrates, "The unexamined life is not worth living," is one to which both of us subscribe. We know from personal and professional experience that self-examination is the key to understanding. And understanding is the door to a successful (in all of its many variations), happy life. Although not planned and certainly not desired, this painful experience of divorce is an opportunity for you to learn and grow as part of your adult development, and it can serve as the impetus to examining your life, your choices, your responses, and your motivations.

There is life after divorce! We know this, both personally and from working with thousands of divorcing and divorced people. But will your new life be more of the "same old, same old," or will it be more stable, satisfying, and fulfilling—thanks to the personal work you do to learn from this divorce? We promise that your life can be different, if you gain the self-knowledge crucial to the growth process that we discuss in this book. If you can look at yourself objectively and learn from what you see, warts and all:

- You will understand what caused your divorce: how your hidden needs, developmental struggles, and other unresolved conflicts may have interfered with sustaining a mature relationship.
- You will understand your defenses, dependencies, and unrealistic expectations that have gotten you in trouble in relationships in the past, and you will know what triggers them.
- You will be able to realize when you are about to repeat negative patterns, and to substitute healthier, more self-loving behavior.
- You will learn to focus on loving, rather than on being loved.
- You will understand that marriage is a long-term commitment requiring loyalty, compromise, devotion, perseverance, and selflessness—and that the rewards of love and family exceed for most of us all other joys and aspirations in our lives.

Considering that about 50 percent of all marriages currently end in divorce, you are not alone on this path. However, the work you need to do is self-exploration that only *you* can do. Of course, friends, support groups, books, and therapists all help—but if you're going to learn something from this divorce, you and you alone must do the work. By understanding who you are and how you contributed to what happened, you'll greatly increase the probability of not repeating this scenario with another partner.

We have seen many of our clients get divorced, then jump into a marriage that basically replicates the same situation and reaps the same painful results. Same song, second verse. This is one way to learn—but it is extremely painful and takes more time than giving yourself the gift of self-discovery. We don't have the luxury of Bill Murray's character in the film *Groundhog Day*, who repeated the same twenty-four hours over and over again until he perfected his actions, achieved his goals, and was transformed. Now is the time to write a new song, one with a beautiful melody that is hauntingly reminiscent of the past but with fresh lyrics and cadence that flow with energy and determination. You have a wonderful opportunity in your life to grow. Embrace it now!

## The Promise of This Book

We will help you look at your assumptions about marriage. What were your expectations? Why did you get married? What happened to those expectations? What do you believe about marriage?

Most of us are burdened by marital myths that keep us from having mature and dynamic relationships: marriages must be wonderful and happy all the time, marriage will satisfy all our emotional needs, marriage will resolve the pain and conflicts of our past, the job of our spouse should be to take good care of us unconditionally. We'll help you examine your own myths and expectations and see how they may have affected what actually happened in your relationship.

We'll also hold up a mirror and gently ask you to confront, honestly and bravely, the person you see there. We will push you to look at yourself, not just as you know yourself as an individual, but also as the person you are in relationship with another. We often behave very differently in our intimate relationships than we do in the workplace or with friends. Why is that? You will ask yourself, Can I truly be my best self in a marriage? If not, why not? How can I develop that capacity to truly shine in a relationship?

Your task, if you choose to accept it, is to understand who you are and what your contribution was to the unraveling of the marriage (we know you see your ex's contribution with utter clarity!), and to examine your basic assumptions about yourself and relationships.

As a crucial part of this process, we'll take a careful look at the many reasons we marry, the types of marriages we have, and the myths that misdirect our actions. Although everyone's intention in marrying is to live happily ever after, the reality is that we bring a lot of emotional baggage to marriage, most of which interferes with the true developmental tasks that we must complete to have a happy marriage and a contented life.

Although this knowledge may come too late to save your marriage, these insights should provide a much greater chance of success for the rest of your life. We will offer suggestions about how unreasonable expectations about divorce can be abandoned on this journey and warn you about unseen boulders and whirlpools that may obstruct your travels. We will attempt to keep you from the diversion of following the side streams that go nowhere, dead-ending in disappointment. We will help you begin charting the course for your future, one that incorporates the learning from the past with the self-discovery of today.

Too many divorced people never get past blaming their spouse for the demise of the marriage. And some people blame only themselves: "*If only I had been . . .*" *[fill in the blank with an unreasonable expectation of yourself]*. Unless you move through and past this stage of blaming others or yourself, you will not learn the lessons that are inherent in the divorce experience. Blame without understanding and forgiveness is futile and self-destructive. If you can turn the process of divorce into a rewarding game of self-discovery, you will glean the true gift from this very painful experience. Your work is to develop as a human being—to learn and grow so that you can be joyful, compassionate, and content with yourself.

We urge you to seize the day. Carpe diem! There is no better time than right now to get on with learning, growing, and understanding. Yes (as stated in the sanitized version of the infamous bumper sticker), Divorce Happens. But more important than the event of divorce is what happens after the divorce. You can do nothing but be miserable and blame your ex, yourself, or the fates, or you can choose to live your life in a fuller, more centered and insightful way. Rather than waiting for life to happen to you—make life happen!

The goal of this book is to guide you in asking the right questions about yourself, particularly about you in a relationship, to help you answer those questions, and then speed you toward applying your new knowledge in your life as a single person.

## What If You Have Kids?

If you have children, we know from our experience with thousands of parents that you are very concerned about them. This book will offer guidance and suggestions about how you as a parent can make this journey less painful and harmful to them. Yes, divorce does impact most children deeply. Yet parents can make the difference in big and small ways that help their children adjust, cope, and ultimately thrive.

There isn't a lot of information about the long-term effects of divorce on children. Dr. Judith Wallerstein, in *The Unexpected Legacy of Divorce,* tracked a small sample of California Bay Area children of divorce from childhood through adulthood. She believes that divorce is necessarily damaging to children and that the effects last into adulthood. However, a more comprehensive research study conducted by Dr. Mavis Hetherington had more hopeful results. As reported in *For Better or For Worse,* Hetherington found that 80 percent of children from divorced homes are reasonably well adjusted twenty years after their parents' divorce. Both researchers emphasize the role of parents in helping children adjust to divorce and develop into healthy, happy adults. Many children do fine with divorce *if* the parents handle things with love and sensitivity, don't use the children as pawns or surrogate spouses, and maintain reasonable boundaries and discipline. Such books as Edward Teyber's *Helping Children Cope with Divorce* and Issolina Ricci's classic, *Mom's House, Dad's House,* can offer practical suggestions about how to parent after divorce.

We also know that the single most harmful factor for children is unresolved conflict between their parents, whether the parents are divorced or married. There are many things about divorce you can't control, but you do have control over exposing your children to conflict with your ex-spouse. And you have a golden opportunity to create the environment with your ex that will nourish and promote your children's well-being. We will suggest some practical parenting ideas that you can follow and that we know from our experience will work to help your children survive divorce.

## How to Use This Book

We urge you to jump right in. Consider our thoughts—disagree if you like. But please, think about and play with these ideas. Abandon your preconceptions and be open to new ideas and insights. Read each chapter either consecutively or in order of preference, depending on your own situation and needs. Do the exercises; reflect on and examine your reactions and responses. Check out the

Resources section at the end of the book for additional reading suggestions. Although the book is aimed at divorcing adults, many of these suggestions will also apply to never-married heterosexual and same-sex couples, although we acknowledge that there are also different and additional challenges for unmarried couples who are splitting up.

Be fearless in your exploration. It takes courage to examine your life up to this point and to create the life you want for the future. The word *courage* is from the French *coeur,* "heart." We hope that you will not only read this book with your head and intellect but also engage with it from your heart. Some of your insights may be painful, but if you wrestle with them, like Jacob from the Old Testament, you'll find the angel in the struggle.

Ultimately, we think you will be delighted and heartened by the changes in your life and relationships that come about through self-examination and discovery. As Rollo May said in *The Courage to Create,* "Out of the encounter is born the work of art" (p. 97). You are that very special work of art. Through your work with this book, the "problem" of your divorce will be put into a new context and encountered so that you can learn from it, see it differently, and find within yourself the wisdom, intuition, and understanding to move forward with confidence and hope.

# Chapter One

# Why Did You Pick That Partner in the First Place?

In order to learn from our divorce, we must understand what led us to make the decisions we made and why we chose to behave the way we did. The idea is that the more we understand about ourselves, the better able we are to lead a life that pleases us and lives up to our image of the kind of person we want to be. The honest analysis of any failed relationship, even if we are better off without that person, provides us with an open window to our strengths and weaknesses.

There are many factors that influence the way we behave and the choices we make. Most of our interpersonal decisions are made with a focus on the here and now and the current facts before us. What we rarely think about is the "package" of life experiences within us that predisposes us to act one way rather than another or to make choice A rather than choice C.

Way back in 1807, the poet William Wordsworth wrote, "The child is father of the man." The insight is still valid today. As adults we are an amalgam of our temperament, our childhood experiences with our parents, our experiences with our peers, the values we absorb, and, finally, the way we put this together in our heads in order to define both our self as a person and our expectations as to what life should be. Our sense of self and our expectations of life are powerful determinants of the choices we make, particularly in love relationships. It is in a love relationship that we open our hearts in hope of finding oneness with another.

A silly example will show how our temperament, experiences with our parents and our peers, our values, and the way we chose to integrate it all into our sense of self all join and interact to influence our decisions and the way we present ourselves. Suppose you are a person who finds scented oil massages an incredible turn-on in sexual foreplay. Right off the bat, you have a constraint on you when you meet another person who interests you, because society is pretty clear that you don't open your first conversation with "Hello, my name is Sam Smith, and I find scented oil massages an incredible turn-on before sex." People would run screaming from the room. This is an external influence on your behavior. It is a socially imposed constraint on your behavior.

In addition, suppose your parents were absolutely silent on sex as you were growing up, so you gained your sexual information (or most likely misinformation) from your friends. Your parents quashed talking openly about sex, and your friends were always looking to tease you about some dumb question you asked, so you spoke very carefully in front of them. This is an internally imposed constraint. Long ago you learned to be very cautious about doing anything that would expose you to mockery.

Further, let us assume that your self-image is that of a not particularly attractive person—a sex object you're not. This kind of self-image would make it very hard to come forward with that piece of erotic self-revelation about the scented oil massage in sexual foreplay. Other people might misread you because they feel no sexual vibes coming from you, so they walk on by, convincing you even more that you are not a very desirable sexual partner. This is another internally imposed constraint. Because you don't think of yourself as sexy, you do not send out an erotic charge to other people. They don't respond erotically to you, which further convinces you that you are not a sexy person.

So the interaction of these constraints that have arisen from your life experiences all gang up on you, with minimum awareness on your part. As a result, you behave, without any conscious intention, in a way that signals you are not a very sexy person. Ironically, you have many sexual feelings, but your life experiences have joined to make this a very inhibited area for you. It would be very easy to miss the point by saying to oneself, I am rejected because I am not very attractive, so I will be very cautious because I don't like rejection. The real issue, however, is that you are ignored (which is very different from being rejected) because no one can read any sexual vibes coming from you. There is no encouragement for them to flirt or to approach you to test the waters.

To understand yourself you must first understand the internal and external influences on your life. Self-understanding is the first step in creating a new life for yourself after divorce. Once you understand your functioning and how it contributed to the breakup of your relationship, you can make conscious decisions as to how you will do things differently next time. An examined life offers many more degrees of freedom for the future.

## Internal Influences

There are many internal influences that affect our relationships and our success or failure in marriage, including temperament, values and morality, fears, and self-concept. So let's take a look at each of these and see how they work.

### Temperament

Temperament is one of those "inside" characteristics that we are all born with. Each of us has a particular style that shapes the way the world approaches us. For instance, you have heard the phrase, "He is a good baby." What that usually means is that as a baby, he doesn't give the adults around him much grief. He feeds well, doesn't spit up much, quickly learns to sleep through the night, and cries hardly at all. These characteristics reflect a temperament, an in-born style that has a powerful effect on the way the world interacts with the "good baby."

Compare the good baby to the high-strung child who is strongly reactive to things that happen around him. He startles easily, has a high energy level, sleeps little, and never whimpers when screaming will do! This child will often be labeled as a "difficult baby," and his world will be populated with people who are often frustrated or angry or resigned when dealing with him. How parents and others respond to the temperament a child is born with has much to do with the experiences a child has and how he eventually comes to see both himself and life.

Many years ago, when Bob was working in a child guidance clinic in North Carolina, he was asked by the mother and father of a one-year-old child to evaluate him for hyperactivity. They said their son was running them ragged. The mother and father were quite overweight. As they talked about their lives, it became clear that they were very focused on their own comfort and were very content to watch life from the sidelines as they took care of their needs.

A home visit was scheduled to see the child in his own environment, where he would be most comfortable. The child was observed with both of his parents, and he seemed very normal as he hooched around the house and played with his stack toys. The great "aha!" came when Bob went to say good-bye. Both parents were on the living room sofa watching TV. This was in the days before electronic zappers let people switch channels and turn the TV off by remote control. With great and laborious effort the dad got off the sofa and walked across the room to turn the TV off. Bob was struck that for the dad this was probably a form of violent exercise!

Obviously, the "aha!" was that a normally active baby in the context of two inactive, self-absorbed parents could be seen as hyperactive. The feedback the infant was getting, however, told him he was a handful and needed to slow down. The parents' passive temperament created a perception of the child that in another context— that is, among normally active people—would be quite different. Think then what might happen to this child over the years as he was told that he was too lively. He might cut back and try to emulate the passivity of his parents to gain their approval. He might think of himself as a misfit and decide that if he can't be good at being good, he will be good at being bad and actually become hyper. There are many paths he could take. The point is that the temperamental differences between his parents and him will be life-shaping.

In our search for a mate, temperament plays a role at the adult level as well. We have all met, and perhaps envied, the person who seems to have an easy, lively, and fairly energetic style. Such people are attractive in part because they can carry us over the lulls in the conversation or can be counted on to have ideas as to what to do when we are feeling bored. A person with a slower, more laid back temperament may need more time to connect with us and we with him or her.

For example, Ron and Skylar laugh about how they got together and fell in love. "We fell in love in an elevator stuck between the twenty-seventh and twenty-eighth floors of the Parker Building," laughs Skylar. She is a petite redhead with many freckles. Her tempo is bright and lively, and she tends to talk a mile a minute. She has a grand passion for dogs, and dreams of living on a ranch with dogs and horses. Ron is a great bear of a man. Although he is not handsome, his physical presence demands attention and respect. In high school his nickname on the football squad was Lurch. Ron was shy and low-key, but was a living example of "still waters run deep." He was very thoughtful, cared a great deal about the environment, and liked working as a volunteer at a boy's club near his apartment. He was a computer expert for his company; Skylar was an account manager in the advertising division of the same firm.

Ron and Skylar saw each other occasionally at company events and occasionally worked together if she needed some help putting together some artwork on her computer for one of her accounts or, worse, if her computer went down right in the middle of a project with a critical deadline. He thought she was flighty and hysterical, she thought he was pretty much a clod. Further, their sizes were so different. Ron's office mates would kid him about never dating her because one false move and she would be crushed to death. In sum, their size difference and their temperaments prevented them from considering each other as anything but coworkers in a large advertising firm. But then there was the day of the brownout, when, because of the intense heat, power failed in pockets throughout the city. Ron and Skylar were the only people in an elevator when it ground to a stop. She had gone to get him to come down to her office to check on a quirky computer program that was bedeviling her. They were trapped in the elevator for four hours.

As he recounts the story, Ron always laughingly says, "And when the doors finally opened we both shot off to the bathroom. Nobody would ever have thought we had started to fall in love." What had happened in the four hours that they were forced to be together was that Skylar, in her typical chatty, lively way, began to ask Ron about himself. After a while he felt it was OK to ask her about herself. Once they got beyond their initial impressions of one another (the Oaf and Miss Professionally Perky), they discovered that there lived a very intriguing person inside. The relationship developed from there, and in this case the initial impact of opposing temperaments melted away with further self-revelation.

## Values and Morality

In any relationship, be it with our children, our spouse, our parents, our work associates, or the plumber, our values and the level of our moral thinking have a great deal to do with how we treat people. In this book, we use the term *value* to mean any standard we hold that guides our behavior. Values can be major or minor, but the values we hold define us as human beings. For instance, we may hold the values of being honest and of not stealing, and as a result, we do not steal and we try to tell the truth. We may hold a value of cleanliness being next to godliness and so keep a clean house. We may hold the value that one must finish one's work before one plays. Moral behavior and moral values focus solely on how we feel we should behave in relationship with other people or how we should be in relationship to humankind. So whereas moral thinking is made up of moral values, we have many values that are not moral values because they don't impinge on how we feel we should be with our fellow humans. For instance, we may value low-calorie meals. This is not a moral value. We may value equal treatment of all races. This is a moral value.

*Ethical behavior* refers to how we apply our moral principles to our behavior toward others. When we behave ethically, we are taking our moral values and applying them to another human being or group of human beings in a manner that is consistent with our principles regardless of the particular human being. For instance, if we hold to the moral value that all people must be treated equally, then we apply that to all people. We do not say that some people can be treated "less equally" than others.

In an intimate marital relationship, our sense of the way humans should treat each other has great impact on how we treat our marital partner and on whether the relationship will be successful or not. How a person is treated in a relationship has a great deal to do with whether he or she is willing to remain in the relationship.

For example, George had been married to Colette for eight years. Over the eight years, he had put on about forty pounds of weight. His belly hung over his belt, and his legs tended to splay out at the knees as his body struggled to hold the extra pounds. His wife had told him, at first gently and then, over time, more forcefully, that sex with him was a super turnoff. His body was fat, flabby, and increasingly repulsive. She begged him to go on a diet. She packed him lunches for work that had a small individual can of tuna and a couple of pieces of fruit. George dutifully agreed to lose weight and eat the food she put in front of him, but he also had a secret stash of his favorite snacks in a locked file in his study at home. He would go into his study at night to "work" and pig out on his snacks, which he also sneaked in his sample case. While he gobbled down his goodies, he listened intently for his wife's footsteps in the hall. He was terrified of getting caught and facing her disappointment at his two-facedness.

He was lying to her, plain and simple. George was not behaving in an ethical manner—that is, in accordance with his moral principle that said he should not lie. He valued the feeling of a full belly more highly than behaving ethically, however. George was trying hard to offer the appearance of being a "good boy" when he knew he was not. He never did get caught, but his wife divorced him when he tipped the scales at 307 pounds.

Psychologists have been studying the development of moral thinking in children and adults for about the past seventy years and have come up with a developmental framework that attempts to describe the various stages through which our thinking evolves. As you will see, very few of us reach the highest stage of moral functioning. There is a certain irony here because it makes sense to want to reach the highest moral level, yet people who function at that level can be difficult to live with. You will have to decide for yourself whether being morally conventional is the better and ultimately kinder choice.

Psychologists who study the development of moral thinking and its translation into action have come up with three general levels of how people think about a person's proper relationship to others: pre-conventional morality, conventional morality, and post-conventional morality. Here, *conventional* means "everybody does it." It appears that moral functioning is distributed along a normal curve: the self-serving are at the far left, most of us cluster in the middle, and a few of us fall to the right, where moral behavior, doing what is right, always overrides our personal desires. Each level of moral functioning has been found to have two different *styles* of thinking, so, according to theory, there are six different ways to function morally.

### Pre-Conventional Morality

Pre-conventional moral behavior is motivated by one of two concerns, but the dominant operating principles are Don't Get in Trouble and Don't Get Punished, not some overarching principle such as Do Not Steal. In other words, a person who functions at the level of pre-conventional morality is constantly looking out for number one.

One style focuses on not getting caught and not getting punished. For instance, this is the sort of person who would shoplift or have an affair if there were only a minimal chance of getting caught. The person who functions at this level is strictly into pain avoidance. Such individuals would think nothing of having bank accounts that are kept secret from their partners or having a second wife and children in another country. The only value they espouse is that of not getting caught—as that will lead to their being in trouble—so for them moral behavior comes into play only when getting caught is highly probable. When Bob's twin sons were about four, one of their favorite admonishments to each other was, "Don't do that or you will get yelled at!" In other words, stay out of trouble.

The second style of functioning found in pre-conventional morality is that of choosing to act in a moral manner or behave ethically only when there is a trade-off. In other words, "I will do good for you if you will do good for me." For these people, making a choice to behave morally comes into play only when they see that there is something in it for them. For instance, consider a man who has several brief flings while his wife is in the last trimester of her pregnancy and then recovering from her episiotomy. His justification is, *Well, she is not making herself sexually available to me, so I will go elsewhere because I have a right to sex.* In this kind of thinking, moral behavior is worthwhile only if it is rewarded. At higher levels of functioning, behaving morally is satisfying in and of itself. The person does not need a cheering section or somebody handing out rewards whenever she completes a moral act. She knows she has done the right thing, and that thought alone is comforting and reinforcing.

Being in a relationship with a person who functions according to the rules of pre-conventional morality is very difficult because you are always in an unpredictable arena. The person does not act by a moral principle that would enable you to predict how he would behave if the particular moral principle were challenged. With the selfish practitioner, the answer to his moral behavior is always "It depends"; it depends on whether or not he will be caught and punished, or it depends on whether behaving morally has some very concrete reward in it for him.

A quick example will illustrate this type of moral functioning. Corey was a vice president for labor relations for a large international company. His job kept him traveling quite a bit overseas. He might be gone for five days at a time. When the job he had been sent for was over, on the last night of his stay Corey would go down to the hotel bar, where he would pick up a woman, have sex with her, and be on the plane back to the United States the next day.

He was shocked when his wife, informed by a coworker, was furious with him and asked for a divorce. His point was that he was not hurting anyone by what he did. He always had protected sex, he was not "getting any" at home because he was far from home, and his wife and kids were being supported well by his high salary. Corey also took some pride in his restraint: he had sex only after the job was done. This is how he rewarded himself. Plus, he had sex only once per trip. One could argue here that Corey behaved more morally toward his company than toward his wife in that he focused his energy on work and played only when the work was all done. You can get the sense that checking out the moral structure within which a potential partner functions is an important step when seeking a lasting relationship.

### Conventional Morality

This is the range in which most of us function. Conventional morality focuses on keeping society both peaceful and well functioning. At this level, a person accepts social conventions and rules because he believes that if society accepts them, he should adhere to them to preserve the social order. This is not just conformity to immediate authority to avoid punishment, or bartering with authority for reciprocity, as it is with pre-conventional morality; rather, it is conformity to sustain the broader social order. You will tend to act on and implement values if you see that by doing so, life goes on as you want it to.

One style of functioning in conventional morality is to be a nice person because it gets you accolades and keeps you included in a lot of activities. This is a morality based on staying in good standing with family and lovers so as to maintain their approval. When considering right and wrong, a person who functions at this level is heavily influenced by what people think of him. Note that there is a shift from the pre-conventional morality level where one does things to avoid pain or to get something in return. The focus in this stage is to be liked, so one makes the moral choice by assessing what the popular choice would be.

At this stage of moral development it is easy to hold that a political protester should be punished because the protester is a threat to the social order and the peacefulness of society. One can begin to sense the difference between conventional and higher-order moral functioning, which adheres to principle in the abstract. A person functioning at the highest level of moral development, which we will describe shortly, might view civil disobedience as acceptable in certain circumstances because, for example, the right to be treated equally could override the sanctity of property. Our society's reaction to civil rights protests gives a good illustration of how different levels of moral functioning can divide us.

A second style of functioning within conventional morality is that which totally accepts social convention and rules. Individuals with this style believe that society's rules should be maintained to protect society and the social fabric within which we function. This is the classic "law-and-order" mentality that unquestioningly accepts social regulations. Conformity to rules is applauded.

A marriage can become vulnerable when one partner evolves to a higher level of functioning and begins to hold beliefs that threaten the social order and people who hold that the social order must be protected at all costs. Here are two examples, one frivolous (at least now) and one more serious.

About ten years ago, both Christie and Bob had an influx of families in their caseloads, usually dads and sons, who were quarreling about who owned the son's left earlobe. The parents, particularly the fathers, were incensed that their sons wanted to pierce their ears and wear earrings. From our perspective today, when men with earrings—several in fact—are a fairly common phenomenon, this conflict may seem to be a tempest in a teapot, but at the time it was a hot-button issue.

The clash was, of course, over the boys' break from gender conformity: boys simply do not wear earrings! What will people think of you? You will be ostracized! Nice boys do not wear earrings! Most important, the fathers felt that their sons were not treating them with the respect that youngsters should offer their parents and elders. As far as they were concerned, their sons were making an immoral choice because it showed great disrespect and served as a corruption of the social fabric. The fathers were turning a value issue (do guys wear earrings?) into a moral issue. They elevated a fashion value into a moral issue because they were functioning at the conventional moral level of being concerned with following society's rules, even if the rules were never made into laws. Up to that time, society had ruled that boys don't wear earrings. We can note that the older generation often reacts to a younger generation's fashion statement in a moral context, such as when the flappers of the 1920s raised their skirts and rolled down their stockings.

On a more serious note, there is a split in this country over the death penalty. Those in favor see it as a deterrent to individuals who would consider taking another's life and just retribution by society toward a person who has taken a life. This is essentially the law-and-order position found in conventional morality. Others argue that "Thou shalt not kill." The taking of a human life by anyone, including the State, is immoral. No one is seen as being above that moral imperative. If this example gets your juices going, pro or con, you will begin to understand the chasms that moral differences can create between people and within a society.

### Post-Conventional Morality

The highest level of moral functioning conceptualizes morality in complex terms. Found at this level is the belief that moral behavior is based on a self-conscious social contract made between people. We agree to conform to norms that appear necessary to keep the social order and protect the rights of others. Because a social contract is a deliberate agreement between people, it can be modified if the participants rationally discuss alternatives that may benefit a greater percentage of the group than does the current social contract. So, unlike the conventional morality position that rigidly adheres to the social contract and sees it as cast in bronze, the next level of thinking holds that the contract can be changed if we can talk about it and agree. Change is valued if it benefits an increased number of people in a group. For instance, civil disobedience is acceptable under certain circumstances if it prompts people to examine and revise an entrenched belief or social convention.

Individuals who function at the highest level of this stage have an internalized set of values to which they conform. They do not worry so much about the criticism of others, but rather about their self-criticism should they betray a closely held moral value. Such individuals can be problematic in society and hard to live with on an intimate basis because they march to their own drummer, often against the mainstream of society. Little things that most of us would look away from stop them dead in their tracks as they take care that their principles are not breached. "Go along to get along" is certainly not their model of moral functioning. The very traditional Jains in India believe that "Thou shalt not kill" applies to insects; they sweep the path in front of them to prevent the accidental death of an ant. A Jain in this country would be difficult to live with given the attention that sweeping a path before them would draw as one approached the local ballpark.

A fairly benign example and a more serious one will help anchor the concept. When a young person hits adolescence, sometimes he or she will decide to become a vegetarian on the moral principle that eating the meat of an animal that can feel pain is inappropriate. The decision, if accepted by the family, can be a terrible inconvenience, as not everyone will sit down to the same meal, which places a burden on the cook. Further, adolescent converts to vegetarianism can be hearty and occasionally heartless in their proselytizing of other family members to join their ranks.

Here we have an adolescent moving to a higher-order value system that the majority of people do not worry about. The value is held close to the heart internally regardless of the inconvenience it causes for others or for the holder. It certainly can create uproar in a less than tolerant family and uproar for parents who disagree between themselves.

Another example concerns Arlene. She was married, with an eight-year-old son, and she worked for a large city paper. She was called to court to testify on a story she had done about a drug distribution ring that had its roots in Latin America and sales points all through the central United States. The prosecuting attorney wanted her notes on the interviews done for the story, and the judge ordered Arlene to turn them over. She refused, citing her prerogative as a reporter to protect her sources. She was jailed, where she sat for about six months.

Her absence from the family caused much hardship. Although the newspaper kept her on the payroll while Arlene was imprisoned, her husband was turned into an instant single parent, which was a struggle given his required evening work as the financial officer for a large car dealership in town. Her imprisonment was very costly to the family, it exposed her son to endless teasing at school, and as her husband Charlie put it, it kept him "busier than a one-armed paper hanger!"

Charlie was supportive of the position Arlene took, so although there was tension in the family because of the disruption and the absence of a loved one, there was cohesion among them as well, because morally they all thought she was doing the right thing. In this case, Arlene's moral stance brought everyone closer together emotionally, even though they were physically apart.

Where a person functions in his own moral development has a great influence on the kind of relationships he will have. In relationships, morality comes into play when a person has to decide how to handle a situation in terms of what is fair or, even better, what is morally right. An easy example is the decision to have or not have an affair. If one is functioning at the "getting caught" level of morality, then having an affair is a slam-dunk: just do it away from home where friends and spouse will not see you. Multiple affairs can be had under the umbrella of this kind of moral thinking. This is exactly what Corey did.

The line of reasoning is as follows: affairs are a little harder to justify when one operates at the conventional law-and-order level of morality. An affair flies against socially held convention, but convention can be easily rationalized away. Affairs are not legally forbidden; only social convention and religion frown on them. If a person combines the idea that she will not destroy society ("After all, I am only one person") with the idea that happiness is a goal, then she can overthrow convention.

At the highest level of moral functioning, secret affairs would be impossible. Either the spouses would negotiate for an open marriage in which other sexual partners were known and not hidden, or the affairs would not occur in the first place because they would be seen as harmful to a person who had placed his or her trust in you. Simply put, one does not deliberately harm the people one loves and, even better, does not harm people at all if one has a choice.

The choices we make given our level of moral functioning have much to do with the success of our interpersonal relationships.

## Self-Concept

Another internal part of ourselves that we bring to a relationship is our self-concept. Our self-concept is made up of the numerous ways we think of ourselves. For example, what do we think of ourselves as a lover, as an attractive person, as a cook, as a basketball player, as a story-teller, as a parent? The list can be very long. Hand in hand with self-concept is our level of self-esteem—that is, the favorableness with which we look upon ourselves. Also in the picture is our ideal self-concept, the image we hold of how we would like to be. We hope there is never too great a discrepancy between our actual self-concept and our ideal self-concept, or we are doomed to a life of discouragement.

How we think of ourselves and who we are has enormous power in shaping our behavior in terms of what we will be willing to risk and not risk doing. There are many shaping influences of self-concept that we will talk about when we deal with external factors. For the moment the question is, Given our self-concept, what do we bring to a relationship? Others often perceive aspects of our self-concept as personality quirks. For example, "George will just never go out on a dance floor no matter how hard I try to coax him. We tried it once when we were courting, and he had more than two left feet—there were three!" George saw himself as a bad dancer; he had convinced himself so thoroughly that he would "dumb down" when he tried it, so he was a picture of clumsiness. He defeated himself in his head by thinking he was a bad dancer.

Our self-concept, in both its positive and negative aspects, can heavily influence the person we choose as a partner. If for instance we feel we are terrible with names (as one of the authors does), we will select a partner who, among other things, is really good at names (as that author did). If we see ourselves as disorganized, we might seek a partner who is organized. This selection based on our self-concept is double edged, because in choosing an organized person, we are also probably choosing being nagged to get organized and being gotten angry with for being disorganized. Further, because we see ourselves in this way, we may consider ourselves hopeless (as did George) and not try to do anything differently. Be aware that what is initially attractive in a relationship ("She is so incredibly organized!") often becomes a strong negative in the unraveling of the relationship ("She is a compulsive bitch!"). The negative aspects of self-concept often hold us down and can become self-fulfilling prophecies, as we saw in George's case. *(I think I'm bad at dancing, so I won't try to dance. When I'm dragged onto the dance floor, my thoughts of being bad at it make me all left feet. See, I told you I was bad at dancing!)*

Name recall and dancing are pretty low-profile issues in the grand scheme of things in a marital relationship. The situation becomes more deadly when a person has a poor-self concept coupled with low self-esteem. This syndrome often shows up in abusive relationships. A woman comes to domestic abuse thinking very poorly of herself and often feeling she deserves the punishment she gets because, as a wife, she should please her husband. In addition, in her self-concept she sees herself as weak, ineffective, or damaged and in need of a man to make her life work. Because of these aspects of her self-concept, she stays in the abusive relationship and feels no power either to change it or move out of it. Abusing men are often described as having a very poor self-concept in that they do not believe, in their heart of hearts, that they are very attractive and loveable. As a result, they are very concerned about losing their spouse to another man who is more socially skilled, sexier, or more charming. His hypervigilance about the possible loss of the relationship is translated into obsessive control. He justifies beatings and verbal abuse as a method of teaching the wife a lesson and keeping her in line.

## Fears

Yet another internal issue that influences our functioning is fear. Sometimes we experience fear as a reaction to an obvious threat such as a snarling dog, a house fire, getting diagnosed with cancer, or seeing the stock market plunge when we are seventy and watching our retirement funds melt away. These we will call survival fears. They are normal reactions to threats to our existence. For most of us our response is direct: escape the dog, call the fire department, get medical treatment, pull out of the stock market. The cause of the fear is beyond our control, is typically unexpected, and prompts us to take a problem-solving approach.

There is a second kind of fear that is often more invisible and subtle, yet equally powerful: the fear that springs from any threat to our self-concept. It is the fear of appearing foolish or stupid or too smart or rude or a bumpkin or impolite or . . . The list is endless. The underlying issue is that our self-concept and thus our self-esteem will be undermined or assaulted. Everyone has these fears. How we choose to handle them often determines the level of efficiency with which we cope with life.

For example, Bonny and Zelda both have a fear of public speaking. The idea of getting up in front of a crowd and saying something is pretty scary for both. Each handles her fear differently, with very different results. Bonny decides that she will acknowledge the fear and take it on. She decides to try out for the high school play even though she knows she will be terrified at first. She shares her fear with a friend who has no trouble with public speaking. By externalizing her fear through telling a friend, Bonny opens herself up to coaching from the friend. Her friend Alice tells her that she too gets a little anxious when she gets up to perform, but the anxiety is not overwhelming and in fact sharpens her for her performance. Alice coaches Bonny and helps her with her lines, and Bonny is able to overcome her fear and perform. Like Alice she is not completely without fear, but she has learned to harness it to work for her rather than against her.

Zelda, in contrast, is ashamed of her fear of public speaking and worries that if anyone learns of it, she will be teased and put down. She copes with her fear through avoidance. She simply will not get up in front of a group and speak. This cost her a grade in school because she dodged making a classroom presentation by "being sick" each day she was scheduled and rescheduled to speak. When a person shuts down so as not deal with a problem, psychologists refer to it as ego restriction. Another example is of a person who does not believe she is good at math, so that when she is confronted with math she becomes "stupid" and simply can't deal with it.

Our fears related to self-concept can come from our experiences with our families. Several examples used later in this book have to do with individuals who are conflict avoidant. That is, they will do anything to avoid a fight because they see arguments and strong disagreements as harmful and dangerous. They fear "harming" their spouse if they do not agree with him or her and therefore give the person what he or she wants, and they are so fearful of being rejected if they disagree that they just go along to get along. In a marriage, the personal cost of this strategy can be enormous because the person can disappear as a separate individual with his or her own needs, which are fully as valid as those of the spouse. Often such timid souls come from families where parents did not tolerate deviation from what they wanted their children to do or where the parents fought long and hard and divorced. In these families, the child sees fighting as leading to abandonment. Disagree and you're dumped—so don't disagree.

Often the reason people enter psychotherapy is that they see themselves locked in self-defeating behavior but do not know why they are doing it. The recognition of self-defeating behavior is the first step toward a cure. That recognition is a central part of this book. For instance, if we can begin to recognize that our needs to be bossy and to micromanage, behaviors that are very annoying to their target, are based on our fear of being controlled (in other words, the best defense is a good offense), then we can begin to question formerly automatic responses. When we recognize we are about to micromanage, we can then ask ourselves, Is this micromanagement really necessary, or am I just being fearful?

Becoming aware of our fears and how they can run us is a great step toward personal freedom and smooth relationships.

## External Influences

One way to think of external factors is to appreciate that we live in an "atmosphere" that shapes our behavior often without our realizing it. We do not often think of the earth's atmosphere unless it is doing something dramatic, such as creating a thunderstorm or tornado. Yet the atmosphere is with us every day. Some people are quite sensitive to it. For example, when it gets very damp, those of us with arthritis can get creaky. When it gets very dry, we can get nosebleeds; when it gets hot, we can get very cranky.

Some elements of the psychological atmosphere that influence how we behave are parental expectations, societal factors, and peer pressure. In addition, there is a dynamic among the factors that further complicates things and often places us between a rock and a hard place, as when, for instance, our parents may press for one kind of decision and our friends another. We may impulsively make decisions just to get them made because of the pressures we feel from family, friends, and our own needs.

## Parental Expectations

Our parents' expectations have a strong influence on our choice of partner even though we may be unconscious of those expectations. Most of us do not fall very far from the family tree. There is the old joke about "Oh, my God! I have become my father [mother]!" For most of us that is not a bad thing to be. We love our parents and would be proud to emulate many aspects of their personalities. Sometimes, though, people purposely try to become the opposite of their parents in an attempt to break the "family curse."

Tom is a good example. He grew up in a "country club" family that was very prejudiced against Jews and African Americans. He went to a private school where neither group was admitted. He never really thought about the issue very much because he was so insulated from people of color and Jews. He went to a small private college where although both African Americans and Jews were in attendance, he remained isolated from both groups. He took ROTC in college and went into the army upon graduation.

In the army, isolation was no longer an option, nor was it something he desired. He chose a friend who was Jewish, almost as an antitoxin to his parents' worldview. Although Tom did not realize it at the time, the friend was an emotional target for Tom not only to work through his issues around prejudice but also to make amends or reparations for what he now saw as the bigotry of his parents and their social set.

Here are Tom's words: "There were so many signals coming from this guy that he was a user. But I was blind to that because every time he did something that my folks' prejudices would say he would do, I would say, 'No, that is just my prejudiced thinking, a gift from my folks.' I could not see him for what he really was as a human being because I was so busy battling my legacy from my folks. I could not see the man because the symbol got in the way. If he ever naturally fit one of my parent's Jewish stereotypes I reacted as if it were not there and it was not him." Tom and friend had a parting of the ways when the fellow borrowed a considerable sum of money from Tom over time and did not pay it back. The experience opened Tom's eyes in terms of seeing people as people regardless of the labels they come with. He now has friends who are Jewish and doesn't give it a thought. He does have a Christian wife and belongs to a country club that does not exclude people according to religion. His parents' world created a major struggle for Tom as he tried to come to his own terms about moral concepts.

Most of us wish to please our parents with our choice of a partner. Further, the cliché about marrying one's mother or father has a kernel of truth to it. Each of our parents has a style to which we become very accustomed as we grow up in their presence. For instance, if you have a mom who is bubbly and outgoing but with a quick, explosive temper—kaboom! and then it's over—you develop skills to cope with this. The lateral transfer to a wife who is bubbly with a quick temper is easy.

Unconsciously using the parental template to choose a mate can backfire and cause problems as well. If a woman grew up with a very domineering father, she might find herself attracted to a partner who has the same style. As life progresses, however, she might come into her own in terms of developing her own mind and preferences and, most important, begin to have the courage of her convictions. You can sense the pending conflict. If one's partner is used to being "alpha dog" and is suddenly challenged, some very powerful attitude adjustments may have to take place that a marriage may not be able to survive.

Besides the influence of our parents' value system or a personal style with which we have learned to cope, parental messages are probably the part of parenting that has the most impact on us. If you have children, you probably have directly experienced this. Kids love hearing family stories about themselves and their parents. In the stories are messages and assumptions about the person being talked about, and those messages can be life shaping. The messages can be quite negative, however, and exert influence over a person long after an event.

One of Bob's clients, Philip, came to therapy because his wife was divorcing him. He had come home from a sexual encounter with a woman who was a friend of his wife. The woman's signature perfume was Orchid Passion, a very heavy, powerful, and aggressive perfume. It made the wearer smell nice, but everybody in the room was very aware that the wearer was present. One evening, when Philip came home and leaned over to kiss his wife, who was sitting in a chair, the scent of Orchid Passion poured off his body. She guessed what had happened because she was well aware of the predatory nature of her friend who wore it. A confrontation ensued, and a separation quickly followed when Philip admitted to the affair.

In therapy, Philip admitted to numerous affairs, many of which he carried on simultaneously. He even had a Rolodex in which he kept track, for instance, of which woman got what kind of flower from him on Valentine's Day. He feared that if he did not write this sort of information down he would ask one girlfriend how she liked the roses when he had in fact given her daisies. Ah, the stresses of deceit!

As Philip's therapy progressed, several messages from his parents, particularly from his mother, surfaced that helped Philip understand why a stable of mistresses was a psychological necessity. His mother did not like sex. She did not like any evidence of sexual activity emanating from her son. Essentially the message was that nice boys did not think about sex; their thoughts were "pure" and "clean." You will note that through her choice of words, sex was obliquely labeled as dirty and impure. As an adolescent with normal (not exaggerated or extreme) sexual needs, Philip developed a second life outside his home. He sneaked dates, dances, and moonlit drives. He developed a parallel life where he could experience sex and keep a "pure" life with his mother during his adolescence. He never spoke of a girlfriend, and Mother never asked about one. The other part of the maternal message "took" as well. After Philip married (his mother could tolerate married sex), he developed a craving for unusual variations in sex. He liked sex toys such as handcuffs, whips, and battery clamps. He liked women who enjoyed being dominated and humiliated. So he took the message about sex being dirty and impure and turned it into something that would profoundly shock his mother if she only knew.

Parental messages can come in even subtler forms than the one Philip experienced. For instance, Tammy had spent her childhood helping her mother manage her father, who was an alcoholic. She helped him to bed some nights and covered for him on the phone when he was too drunk to talk. She was an expert in cleaning up his messes.

Tammy's mother was very grateful for Tammy's help, which made her caretaking for her father all the more meaningful. By the time she was twenty-seven, she had had a string of boyfriends who used her and dumped her. They were guys who had drug and alcohol problems, had a hard time keeping a job, and depended on her heavily to organize them and essentially make their lives work.

Tammy woke up one morning and asked herself why these men kept gravitating to her. Then she had the horrendous realization that it was she who was gravitating to them! Her whole childhood had taught her that in order to be loved and valued, she needed to dedicate herself to cleaning up other people's messes as she did for her father and her ever-grateful mother. She realized she was aiming symbolically toward marrying her father—a marriage she realized she did not want. At this point she entered psychotherapy and began to turn her life around. In Tammy's case, her mother never said anything directly to her. What was so powerful and rewarding was her mother's gratitude to her. Making Mother happy became very reinforcing.

Here's a final example. This is a story of two young men, George and Evan. George was Catholic, from a family whose parents were very active in the church. His father owned a very successful car dealership and was highly visible in the community on volunteer boards and at charity functions. It was here that his mother also shined. She had won many awards for her charitable good works for the local children's hospital, even to the point of having a hospital wing named in her honor.

George had four brothers. The family joke was that all Father had were Y chromosomes. As George began to seek a mate, he felt he was looking for a well-connected Catholic girl who wanted many children and who could help George rise in the corporate world by being a charming hostess. George's wife needed to be very capable and willing to promote her family's rise to eminence in the community.

Evan, in contrast, was an only child whose parents were teachers. His dad taught at a local community college, and his mother taught English as a second language at the high school. His parents had dedicated their lives to helping others. They lived modestly and drove their cars until they fell apart. They gave much of their nonwork time to young people's organizations, and for a time Evan's father was chairman of the local chapter of the ACLU. Evan went to the local state-supported college as a commuter, lived at home, and held a part-time job at a law office as a clerk and gofer. He was thinking of a law career in environmental protection.

As he began his search for a life partner, he thought not at all about her religious leanings or training. Instead he was looking for a woman who had an active interest in environmental issues. She could not be preoccupied with money and the toys it would buy, but she should want children and, most important, want a cause of her own, something that was quite separate from Evan's interests. Evan wanted a strong, independent woman who would through her interests bring a new dimension to his life.

Each of these young men was influenced by his background and his parents' expectations of him. Neither man, however, was consciously aware that he was imitating his parents' relationship and its messages. Their behavior and their choices were purely original with them, or so they thought.

As of this moment, one marriage has failed and the other appears to be working well. George and his wife are now divorced, while Evan and Louise continue to march along in relative harmony. Each man went about choosing a wife very differently. George chose a wife as he would choose a car from a crowded field of high-end sedans. He was methodical and focused. He made a list of characteristics he felt he needed in a wife. As mentioned before, he wanted a wife with good family connections in the business community, one who wanted children, liked to entertain, and was educated and polished enough to charm people and make them want to be with her. He had his parents check with family friends and inquired of people in his circle to see if they knew of anyone who filled the bill.

After many dead ends, he finally found Betsy. She fit the requirements perfectly. She was Catholic, she wanted children, her father was president of the town's largest privately owned bank, and she really enjoyed people. What George did not realize was that he was buying a role. He saw Betsy as a bundle of potential for his life's dreams, but did not really have a good sense of her as a person. After about ten years of marriage, three children in quick succession, and George's acquisition of partnerships in two more car agencies, Betsy became restless and dissatisfied. She saw herself as constantly in George's shadow—his handmaiden, not his equal partner. Now that all the children were in school, she wanted to open an antique store. To put it simply, as she matured, she changed. Her changes did not fit the role that George had always had in his mind's eye. He could not let go of the image of what he needed when he married her. He began to nag at her for not being a team player. She grew increasingly resentful and finally wanted out. She asked for a separation that is now leaning toward divorce.

In contrast, Evan and Louise are still going strong. If anything, they complain about not having enough time together. Louise works very hard, but not for money. Evan's law career in water rights brings in a generous income. Louise has devoted herself to the cause of acquiring more open space for her city and the surrounding counties. She has chaired several drives to obtain private funds to acquire plots of land contiguous to already existing open space owned by the county. She points with some pride to the fact that she, with the help of others, has added 1,239 additional acres to preexisting open space. Evan is extraordinarily proud of her. She is widely known in the community, and he often jokes that he is known as "Mr. Louise" rather than as Evan. Evan sought a person with a set of beliefs, not a role-filler. He takes as much pleasure from Louise's successes as he does from his own.

What both Evan's and George's marriages represent is a search for a partner who fulfilled certain expectations about what they felt life should be. Those expectations are guided, in part, by what parents say we are supposed to be and do.

## Societal Factors

U.S. society expects people in their twenties and thirties to find an intimate relationship with another person. The pressure is great to do so, although there is some evidence that people are marrying later, after they have established themselves as a viable economic unit in the relationship marketplace. Actually, during this time period we are assigned three tasks:

- To have an intimate relationship with another person
- To accept adult role commitments such as a job or a career (or further education for such)
- To begin to acquire things that will reflect increased stability, commitment, and participation in society

The outcomes of these decisions define the rest of our adult life. Once on a chosen path it is very hard to change direction, so these decisions are quite crucial for one's future life. The person who has trained to be a medical doctor much of her adult life and then decides she wants to leave medicine and become a novelist has a long, upward climb to convince people that she is not being foolish. The assumption will be "What a terrible waste of time and money. What took you so long to decide what you want to do when you grow up?" Similarly, when we make the choice of a husband or a wife, it's very painful and difficult later to have to explain to all our family and friends that we are getting divorced. "What a terrible waste of time and money," they may say. "Such a nice girl . . . and what about the children?"

Many societal factors we take for granted. They become so ingrained that they are absorbed into our unconscious and became part of our assumptions about how the world is. Trying to deal with these influences if we become aware of them and don't like them can be quite difficult and anxiety provoking. Travel to a foreign country can be a cultural eye-opener because one's ingrained assumptions are not taken for granted elsewhere. On a first visit to England, Bob found that he kept bumping into people coming toward him on the sidewalk. It was embarrassing. One day, light dawned. In the United States we pass on the right, so if someone is coming toward us on the sidewalk, we drift right to avoid a collision. It is absolutely unconscious and ingrained. In England people pass on the left, so when an American and a Brit come at each other, they veer in the same direction because their culture has told them to, and unless they are agile, collision occurs.

In selecting a mate, societal influences press in from all sides. In the United States, thin is in. Our concept of beauty has evolved from the rather voluptuous, hourglass-waisted woman of the turn of the century to a thin woman with small, high breasts. In the 1990s, the male body began to be held up as an icon as the female's had for a long time. Now men are concerned with having hairless, well-defined chests with "six-pack abs." Popular films glorify the ugly duckling (as in chubby, pimples, and dingy brown hair) becoming the swan, and here you can fill in your version of the swan. Beauty is culturally determined, and it sorts people along a continuum from desirable to very undesirable. Research indicates that people marry someone similar to them in physical attractiveness, although the very wealthy can break the curse of plain by knowing that beauty likes money more than looks. We have jokes about "but she has a nice personality" that underline our cultural obsession with good looks. The old bromide about beauty being only skin deep recognizes that the search for external beauty is ultimately shallow. It merely represents an external set of physical characteristics that has nothing to do with what is inside a person. It is what is inside that will form the basis for a friendship and lasting companionship.

Our search for beauty can make it difficult for us to seek people other than the very attractive person for a partner. It is hard for Americans to believe that in some societies fat is considered beautiful because it means that a person is wealthy enough to afford food in large quantity and rich in fat. We do have ways of making ourselves miserable!

Through its assumptions and imperatives, society closes us off from thinking outside the proverbial box. That is what society is supposed to do, so as to preserve a viable social organization. In any society we lose degrees of freedom of choice when we live by its rules. An occasional challenge to a societal imperative opens all kinds of new opportunities. For instance, a recent article in a Denver newspaper reported the "news" that more and more older women are taking on men ten to fifteen years their junior as lovers and partners. This was seen as a radical departure from society's unwritten rule that men can have relationships with younger women, but older women are cradle robbing if they choose a "boy toy." If, as you read this, you find yourself disapproving of the concept of younger men with older women, while feeling comfortable with older men and younger women, you are signaling that you have bought society's hidden rule.

Over the long haul, whether you marry someone plain or beautiful or handsome, fat or thin, younger or older does not matter if you believe that a relationship is between two people and no one else. When you consider all the forces and people outside with their noses pressed against the glass looking in, you can begin to grasp how difficult it is to maintain a relationship and how much more successful at relationships we can be if we are fully aware of what drives us to make the choices we do.

## Peer Influences

We often hear of peer pressure making adolescents take drugs, indulge in sex too early, and drink to the point of drunkenness and, in general, being the major propellant down the primrose path. The power of peer pressure does not weaken as we grow older, however; it just becomes more subtle because we no longer have our parents demanding an explanation for what we've done. Your peer group is likely to fall into one of three categories. Some of us choose peers as a kind of family antitoxin. "My family was preppy and yacht-clubby, so my friends are all counterculture types." By choosing such a peer group, a person can actively reject the lifestyle in which he was raised and surround himself with people who tell him that his new choice of lifestyle and values is preferable. Your peer group, as a second choice, could largely be your family, perhaps your extended family. Your cousins, aunts and uncles, and grandparents can essentially be the crowd you run with. It means, in all likelihood, that your family is a tight and cohesive group and that you share their values and ideals. A third choice you could make, partly to distance yourself from family dynamics or to create a greater sense of privacy in your own life, is of peers who reflect the values of your family but put a younger, more up-to-date twist on things.

A profitable question to ask and answer is, Why did I choose the peer group I did? For many it will not seem like a choice, but something that just happened. It really is a choice, however. Note that even in your peer group or circle of friends, there are some whom you will seek out more readily and frequently.

Our friends have power over us to the extent that with them we do not feel lonely if there is a true connection. As adults we must accept loneliness as part of the human condition. For most, however, loneliness is not a good feeling. The more satisfied we are with our friendships, the less lonely we will be. We also use friends to gain feedback and reduce uncertainty about how to behave. There are very few certainties in life, and we can use friends as sounding boards and reality testers to help place our feelings in perspective. It can be extraordinarily helpful to have a friend to talk to about a situation. Often the best friends are those who will simply listen and let us bounce ideas off of them.

Given the reasons you have friends, it is easy to see how terribly influential they can be in your choice of a partner. First, it is probably with friends that you will want to check out a potential lover. What will your friends think? Will they approve? Will they more than approve and think it a perfect match? Will they pull away from you because they do not want to hurt your feelings by saying what a loser your partner is?

It is difficult to say exactly what role your friends play in your selection of a partner, other than to say that their approval or disapproval will be influential. A couple of examples will demonstrate the point.

Tony had grown up in a family that was indifferent to organized religion. They did not take him to any form of religious service, did not pray or say grace, and did not own a Bible. Religion and spirituality just did not exist in the context of his family. When he got to college, he took a course titled "The Bible as History." He thought it would keep his parents calm because it was not about the Bible as religion, but it would also expose him to the Bible. He did not know the story of Jonah and the whale, for instance, and he thought that if nothing else, at least he would understand some of the biblical references he had been hearing much of his life.

The course was a revelation. He found a part of himself, the spiritual part, that was untapped and hungry for expression. For the next three years in college, Tony took numerous religion courses even though his major was chemistry. He joined an on-campus church youth group. Partly in reaction to his parent's liberal viewpoint, he chose a church that was quite conservative. His friends from the church's Youth Fellowship were quite conservative. They felt the Bible was law.

At the beginning of his senior year, Tony met Alma, who seemed the girl of his dreams. He fell head over heels for her, and Alma seemed to reciprocate his feelings. They began to plan to get married at the end of Tony's senior year and then go off to graduate school in chemical engineering. As Tony and Alma were having one of their many soul-baring, heart-to-heart talks, Alma, with some hesitation, told Tony that she had had an abortion when she was sixteen. Tony was shocked and, wanting to do some reality testing, spoke to his friends in his church group. They too were very shocked and held that abortion was a sin and an abomination. Ironically, Tony was painfully aware that Alma's abortion would mean nothing to his liberal family, but to his friends at church it was a major negative issue. Tony talked with his friends. Although he did not feel as strongly about abortion as they did, he did feel more strongly than he imagined his parents would have. Tony finally decided to break off the relationship with Alma. His friends strongly supported his decision, as they saw Alma as having taken a life, which was morally repugnant to them regardless of other factors such as her age and her goals for herself in life.

Here's another example with a happier ending. Peter, in his mid-twenties, was in open rebellion against his mother and father, who were wealthy, straitlaced, upper-middle-class professionals. Peter's father was a physician, his mother a lawyer who specialized in representing women in their divorces. Peter was brought up being told he should save for a rainy day, walk the straight and narrow, and above all, behave responsibly. Using the proper fork at a formal dinner and wearing the correct clothes at every function were also part of the rules.

To escape these powerful parents and be his own person, Peter took on an antimother, antifather philosophy. He did not save money and lived on the fringes in a bohemian lifestyle. He was into heavy metal concerts, mosh pits, and marijuana. A mattress on the floor and boxes in which to keep his clean clothes were all he needed for furnishings. He worked at a used CD and record store and hung out with his friends when he was not working.

One day a girl, Samantha, came into the store looking for some old hard rock CDs with an emphasis on Pink Floyd and AC/DC. She and Peter, who was the store's resident expert on heavy metal music, struck up a conversation. He was very helpful to her, and she asked him if he would join her for coffee when he got off work to continue the conversation. Samantha attended the local music school, and for her M.A. she was doing a comparative paper on African influences on rock music of the 1970s. The two of them hit it off over coffee, and in the next few months the relationship began to bloom.

Although her tastes in music were right up-to-date, Samantha came from a background similar to Peter's when he was growing up. He could relate to her easily, because they had had so many similar experiences. The girl had left her past without the flamboyance that Peter did his. She had somehow come to terms with her past, but had remodeled herself to be someone in the here and now. Peter was where he was because he could not accommodate to his past.

Peter found himself intensely attracted to Samantha. He was surprised at himself because she came from a background that was similar to his, one he was angry at for its rules. Samantha pointed out to him in one of their all-night marathon "Let's get to know each other" sessions that he seemed hung up on the *rules* of his parents' social class, but had he thought about the values? Her comment opened a door for Peter. "I realized that I was throwing out the baby with the bathwater. My parents were very controlling through their rules for everything. I hated that, but their values, such as anticipating the future, being responsible to others, and being a good citizen, I did not have trouble with. I had confused the packaging with the gift."

Peter began to move slowly into the mainstream *on his terms*. He still doesn't own a tie, but he does have a job with a record producer and, God help him, a house in the suburbs with Samantha.

## The Interactional Factor

The *interactional factor* is an amalgam of the messages we have received from friends and parents, plus our own life experiences and feelings about ourselves. It forms the template through which we look at ourselves and the world. This factor includes the interaction between our conscious view of ourselves based on experience and what we have been told and our unconscious assumptions about our lovability, our ability to survive, our sense of wholeness, and our need for closeness or distance. It also comprises the effects of the Greek chorus in our lives made up of the oughts, shoulds, and musts that our peers and society tell us are important.

As stated before, what we think we need is influenced by our parental input and how we dealt with it, input from friends and the times we live in, and how we arrange this information into a decision-making system. The interaction between our internal and external issues is what determines the choices we make. Choosing between what we want and what society says it is okay to have is often a struggle. Yet the transactions between our internal world and our external world as we perceive it define us in the eyes of others and consequently give us feedback about who we are as people.

Sharla and Gordon were attracted to each other because they had such a fun time together. Each was professionally employed with a good salary, so they had much discretionary income with which to buy "toys" and travel to the four corners of the earth. After a time, Sharla wanted children. Gordon did not, because children would tie them down and drain their discretionary resources. Actually Gordon was very fearful of being a father. His father had abandoned him before he could be aware of who his father was. In the thirty-four years of his life he had never met the man, as far as his memory could recall. He chose a "fun and games" wife because he did not want to be confronted with his fears about his adequacy as a human being.

If you asked Gordon, he would never be able to say, "I married my wife because I did not want to have children." Children simply had not come up as an issue because his wife, initially, was not interested in children either; she wanted a life where she was not tied down and so could behave as the moment seized her. In this example, Gordon's father never said anything to him at all. By abandoning him, however, Gordon's father "said" much in terms of what Gordon heard as his lovability and his capacity to father without a primary model. Gordon's unconscious fears about his adequacy as a father drove him to emphasize a fun-and-games approach to life. He could not let go of that attitude when his wife approached him with her request to have a child. His fear kept the door shut. He handled the predicament by blaming his wife: she had suddenly changed; she had suddenly turned serious on him. By blaming her, he could remain blind to his own issues. Yet he did feel some pressure from society in terms of such questions as "Got any kids?" or "When are you going to get pregnant?" He became annoyed at these questions because they reminded him of his sense of himself as a flawed person, so he gravitated to having single or divorced friends rather than married friends.

Pamela had been raised to believe that sex was an unpleasant but necessary activity to create children. She was raised in a religious community with very restrictive sexual messages. Her mother and father never kissed or touched in front of her. Birth control was forbidden, and girls and boys were never unchaperoned and were forbidden to touch until they were married. Upon graduation from high school, Pamela rebelled against her upbringing, moved to a major city, and began a new lifestyle with the enthusiasm of someone who had just discovered sex. She chose young men who were very interested in sex and who demanded that of their dates.

But soon Pamela found that her partners quickly dumped her. They called her unresponsive, frigid, and sexually inhibited. For Pamela there was a will but there did not seem to be a way. The messages she had received from her parents and her friends were too powerful. She could overthrow them up to the point where she could consciously decide to be sexually active, but her feelings could not let go of the messages of her upbringing, so she remained her parents' child and was sexually unresponsive.

Her struggle was between her family's messages in the past and her own physical desires. She could not permit herself to enjoy sex, something she desperately wanted to do, because of the struggles with the messages from external sources that had now become a part of her.

Andrew was a fit, bright, and very boyish man of about forty-eight. He looked like he was on a crew team from an Ivy League school: handsome, clean-cut, and dressed in a preppy style. He came to therapy as his third marriage was unraveling. He had what is labeled a Don Juan complex, named after the eighteenth-century seducer of many women. Andrew had never been without a romantic relationship since he left home. He moved from home at age nineteen into the apartment of his first girlfriend. While he was with her, he started a number of affairs and one-night stands.

As the relationship started to fail, he began another "permanent" relationship that overlapped his first by about four months.

So when he left his first love, he was firmly ensconced in the relationship with his second. This was characteristic of all his relationships. They all overlapped and all contained affairs with other women while he was living with his current partner. Andrew complained that the chase was very exciting, but the sex, though nice, was not terrific. What was striking was how impermanent his conquests were, exhibiting the proverbial Chinese meal effect. He would be thinking about his next conquest as he lay beside his most recent. This pattern of behavior continued through his three marriages. Each time, once he married he was looking out for the next lover.

By the time he came to therapy he was filled with self-loathing. He realized he was using women and hurting them, but he could not stop. The thrill was in the hunt, and the woman offering herself to him helped convince him that he was loveable. He had no internal way of generating a personal knowledge that he was loveable, and he always had to rely on sources outside himself for reassurance. He needed conquests to reassure himself.

His therapist reframed the issue by asking why he had no internal "battery" with which to store the strokes he was getting from his conquests to tell himself he was OK, whether or not there was a woman in his life. This refocusing enabled Andrew to begin to think about his relationship with his mother, who was an undemonstrative drug-dependent woman who was always unpredictable and slightly out of control.

Andrew laughed when he said, "Oh no, not my mother, that is such a cliché!" Going back to Mother, however, was crucial for him: he needed to understand how he had been shaped by that relationship in terms of his lack of self-esteem and his constant need for reassurance that he was an attractive, loveable guy. His conquests never satisfied his hunger because his mother's cold, self-centered, drug-driven, erratic way of raising him left him unable to believe that he was OK. He was never able to store away enough positive strokes from that initial relationship with his mother. His perceived (yet unconscious) lack drove him to successive situations in which women, by giving themselves to him sexually, said he was just fine, thank you!

Andrew is still a work in progress. He is now divorced and without a permanent relationship, which is a brave break from his old pattern. He is struggling with his fears that if he does not lie to a woman to get her into bed by telling her that this will be a permanent relationship, he will get no sex whatsoever. He and his thera-pist have made a deal that Andrew will now be as honest as he can with women and see where it gets him. He is confronting one of his major fears: I must lie and tell a woman what she wants to hear because she will never want me in her bed on my terms. With some trepidation, he is now going to try to say that he wants sex and fun but that marriage is not in the picture.

In each of these examples, the characters make choices based on their perceptions of themselves. These perceptions arise out of their experiences with their parents and their friends, and society's expectations of them. But their perceptions of themselves are also influenced by their fears, their sense of their own moral behavior, and their self-concept.

As you can imagine, this chapter cannot paint a tidy picture of the influences that shape our lives and our decisions. It is impos-sible to focus on all of them at once. But if we can gain some un-derstanding of which influences tend to dominate the decisions we make, we can narrow down what we look at when we try to un-derstand our behavior. It is as if you have a closet full of clothes, but you choose only two or three items to wear to a given function. All the clothes remain in your possession, but only a few define you at this particular event in this particular instance. So it is with all the factors we carry with us in life. Given the situation, some are more salient than others. The problem, however, is that unlike silent clothes, internal and external factors can suddenly cry out for attention and for influence over our decision-making process.

One such factor is the myths we buy into about what a mar-riage is all about. Our society says that marriage is the norm. It is expected. As a result, we attribute a great many things to marriage, particularly as to how it will meet our needs as adults. If we buy a myth and it doesn't describe our particular marriage, our disap-pointment can be bitter. The next chapter sheds light on marital myths so that you can better understand if they blinded you to the reality of your marriage.

# Chapter Two

# Overcoming the Myths About Marriage

Mary Jane met Joe on a blind date the weekend after her high school graduation. He was the man of her dreams—tall, blond, blue-eyed, and handsome—everything that she had decided her husband should be. They had an instant connection and professed their love for each other less than two weeks after their blind date. They lived in the same town, had the same religion, and wanted to marry, have two children, and live happily ever after. She was extremely attracted to him sexually and yearned to be his.

They married after Mary Jane's sophomore year in college, and both continued their education, living the hand-to-mouth existence of young married students. This was what she had always wanted—her knight in shining armor had rescued her from being alone.

But Mary Jane wasn't happy, and she didn't even know why. She had always dreamed that marriage meant romantic dinners together, elegantly prepared by her for her husband, with roses and candlelight. She also thought that being in love and married meant that Joe would always know her needs—that his only mission in life would be to make her happy and to create the homey little love nest that she had always envisioned. She had expected him to want to talk with her for hours—really communicate—but he resisted. Try as hard as he could, he didn't always want to talk about things with her and would even ignore her sometimes when he couldn't figure out why she was sulking. They graduated, had a child, and bought a house in suburbia with both of them working, but neither was happy. One night they had a fight about who would take the child to the doctor the next day, and Joe stormed out of the house. He never returned.

Mary Jane was devastated: the love of her life, the man whom she loved beyond all others, had left her. Why had he done this? How *could* he have done this? What went wrong? Joe had been the perfect choice of a mate for her in all respects.

What happened to Mary Jane and Joe has happened to thousands, even millions of couples. They were victims of the myths of marital dreams. They had no idea of what it really takes to create a loving relationship. Most of us in Western society grew up with the fantasy of "they married and lived happily ever after." Every romantic movie, novel, and fairy tale climaxed with the music swelling in the background and the couple gazing into each other's eyes, knowing that they had found their one true, lasting love.

In high school and college we dated until we had that zing in our heart (and zing in our loins, too) that told us that this was the person for us. Some of us married these first loves, only to learn that the happily ever after didn't happen the way we thought it would. Even though our parents didn't have happily-ever-after romantic relationships, we thought that *we* would be different. We would be the couple that was fantastically in love and in sync with each other every moment of every day. And too many of us thought that it was some personal flaw or flaw in our mate that kept us from experiencing this kind of day-to-day bliss. The disillusionment that we felt with married life was dramatic and, too often, led to blaming our spouses for the less than perfect relationship. Paraphrasing Carly Simon, it wasn't the way it was supposed to be.

## The Myths of Romantic Love

To learn from divorce, we need to examine the myths, fantasies, and stereotypes about marital love that exist in our society, extolled by the film, television, and print media and in popular music. These myths actually keep us from doing the work that we need to do for us to be successful at marriage. Marriage is so much more than an intense romantic relationship and divine, passionate sex. To be both long-lived and satisfying, it requires loyalty, selflessness, commitment, patience, compromise, respect, forgiveness, and two emotionally healthy partners. The following are some of the myths that we will examine in this chapter:

- My spouse will satisfy all my emotional needs; without my having to express my feelings or explain what I want, he or she will provide unconditional love and support—anticipating my moods, idiosyncratic desires, and strengths and weaknesses—and put me above all other individuals and priorities in his or her life.
- Our sex together will always be frequent, spontaneous, gratifying, and totally thrilling.
- My spouse will conform to the role model established by my mother or father, because my parents were so happy together—or, in some cases, the converse: my spouse will be nothing like my mother or father, as my parents were so obviously unhappy together.
- Marriage will heal all my wounds, solve the unresolved conflicts of my family of origin or troubled youth, and remain a stable source of comfort and safety from the rest of the hostile world.

We must recognize our own beliefs about marriage and how those myths got us in trouble in our marriage, or we will be doomed to repeat the past. So let's take a look at those myths that led us into marriage and perhaps into divorce when they were not fulfilled.

## My Spouse Will Satisfy All My Emotional Needs

In the classic book *The Art of Loving*, Erich Fromm declares that love is an art that requires knowledge and effort. "Most people see the problem of love primarily as that of being loved, rather than that of loving, of one's capacity to love. Hence the problem to them is how to be loved, how to be loveable" (p. 1). The fallacy of enduring romantic love—that flutter in your stomach when she touches you, the feeling of timelessness when listening to him talk—has distracted us from examining what love really is. It has also kept us from learning how to truly love the person we have chosen to marry.

Being "in love" is a connection to another person that seems to take away loneliness and human separation. Sex becomes the connection to the Other—often the only method of achieving intimacy for many people. Feeling sexually attracted to another person is considered part and parcel of falling "in love" with him or her. That ecstatic state of emotional and physical intimacy in the early stages of a new relationship is such a high that one would do anything to maintain it.

But as anyone who has fallen in love can tell us, romantic love has a flip side. Romantic love can not only bring excitement and a physical and emotional rush but also drive us to the deepest despair and anxiety. Desperate, angry, yearning, overwhelming thoughts and feelings flood our minds, and we seem powerless to stop them:

*Why didn't he call when he said he would? He must not love me anymore.*

*What will I do? I need him. . . . He completes me.*

*I'm nothing without her. When she smiles at other men, I just go crazy with jealousy.*

*She's going to leave me.*

We are obsessed with the object of our love and with keeping love. We constantly take the pulse of the relationship and take nothing for granted. The feeling of being in love has been described as temporary insanity. It hurts so good!

Thank goodness that the experience of falling in love is short lived. Although the adrenaline and endorphin rushes make us feel alive, we are also very distracted. It's hard to think of anything or anyone else, and the object of our love consumes our thoughts. We seem to know that we can't stay in that initial state forever, but we nevertheless expect life to be so much better with our new partner. This person will love me for myself, overlook my faults, and know and meet my every need and desire—forever.

One of the unfortunate by-products of our obsession and self-absorption when "in love" is that we try to be what we think is "loving" when in fact we are actually demanding constant attention to fill up our empty selves. This kind of loving often comes out of our being in a totally "me-centered" state. For example, when Joy was in college, she was very much in love with Lyman, who was to be her first husband. He was her dream man. Two weeks before Valentine's Day one year, she went through her entire set of Great Books given to her by her parents, and every other book she had in her dorm room, looking for references to love. She wrote each quotation on a small card, with the goal of having 365 so that Lyman could pick a card every day and think about love, about their relationship, and, of course, about her. She only found about 100, so she filled in the other 265 cards with "Joy loves you," "I love you," and so on. She thought that this gift was the perfect expression of her love.

Her intended was pleased, but didn't gush with joy. He enjoyed being loved, but didn't need anyone to tell him multiple times a day that he was loved and a good person. He was also a little embarrassed to have this much attention and did not want the other guys in the dorm to find out. And, to tell the truth, he felt somewhat suffocated.

Joy was disappointed. She began crying when she didn't receive the reaction she had expected. She sulked for days and was unresponsive to his attention. After all, she told herself, she had given him a gift that she would have loved to receive—one which showed that he had taken a lot of time to make for her and that he loved her above all others. She also wanted him to be just like her, to enjoy the same books and movies, to react the way she would react, and to have the same needs and desires. She felt that his different beliefs, perceptions, and ways of responding were flaws. How could he truly love her if he held an opinion different from hers? This scenario of disappointment was repeated time after time throughout their marriage. Joy's unrealistic expectations about love and what it meant—her fantasy of a total symbiosis with her lover that emphasized meeting *her* needs and agreeing with her views—ultimately drove him away, at first emotionally and then later into separation and divorce.

We all have our individual emotional needs that we expect a mate to fill and hope that marriage will satisfy. As we saw in Chapter Three, we search for mates who can provide the nurturing that we as adults no longer get from our parents—or maybe that we never received from our parents. Both men and women need warm and nurturing mothering and strong, protective fathering. In marriage, we can offer these qualities to our mates.

We want spouses to love us unconditionally but to give us the space we need when we need it. We want to be able to let down our hair and be vulnerable, sharing our anxieties and insecurities with our spouse. We want our spouse to bolster our self-confidence when we need it and to compensate for the failures we experience elsewhere in our personal or professional lives. We want perfect mates who will satisfy all our many neurotic needs. But to expect that our mates will always be there and give us just what we need at the right moment is unrealistic. Marriage and our spouse simply cannot satisfy all our many emotional needs.

- Have you ever expected your partner to know what you needed and to offer it to you without your asking?
- Were you disappointed when the romance left your marriage? Did you decide that your spouse must not love you anymore?
- Did you expect your spouse to always adjust and compensate for your weaknesses and idiosyncrasies?
- Was your spouse expected to smooth the way through the world for you, much as parents do for a small child?

If you answered yes to any of these questions, you have bought into this myth of romantic love.

## Sex Will Always Be Fabulous

Our society has convinced us that one of the signs of being in love is to be intensely and perpetually attracted to the other person sexually. It's true: at first our hearts literally beat faster when we see that person, and even thoughts about the object of our affections produce sexual arousal. It's fun to be in love. If our affection is returned, we feel attractive and loveable. However, over time, even though our love for the other person may grow stronger and deeper, the emotional and sexual highs that we felt during those early days of our relationship will ultimately decrease.

Sex may even become infrequent or boring. We can do things to improve our sexual relationship, but it is inevitable that we will not remain in the same state of sexual arousal over time. Sometimes we really do have a headache! Ebbs and flows will occur, caused by the normal challenges of marriage and living together. If we base the choice of a partner solely on the sexual excitement we feel in the early stages of our relationship, we will assuredly be disappointed over time.

Sexual attraction is not a basis for lifetime commitment. Jim and Luann's story illustrates this point. Jim met Luann when she was a senior in college. The first time he looked at her, his stomach did a flip-flop. As he gazed into Luann's green eyes and admired her long, raven hair, he felt that he was viewing a goddess. He determined that she would be his, no matter what it took. He pursued her with flowers and poetry, and ultimately she agreed to marry him. They experimented sexually, and both were convinced that the other was the perfect sexual partner for them. Sex was exciting, passionate, and validating. After they were married they made love every day and even more than once a day on weekends. But after several months, Jim noticed that Luann didn't seem as interested as she once was, and the frequency of their lovemaking reduced to once a week or so. They also began bickering over small things that each would do or say.

When Luann became pregnant, she begged off from having sex, saying that she was tired and felt fat. After the birth of their son, Billy, Luann began refusing sex more and more often. Jim also realized that he wasn't attracted to Luann with her twenty extra pounds and the frazzled, unkempt look of a new mother. She only vaguely resembled that svelte college co-ed that he lusted after and fell in love with. As his sexual interest waned, Jim began having an affair with a coworker. *She* made him feel alive and sexy. When Luann discovered his affair, she filed for divorce.

The sexual attraction we feel for a spouse changes over time. Urgent lust is difficult to maintain throughout pregnancy, illness, intense work schedules, and children. The myth of unlimited, fabulous sex cannot be the basis for a satisfying marriage. Typically sex moves from being the major thing to being only one of many things you love about your partner, which means that other factors can support the relationship when sex occasionally pales. For a marriage to survive and thrive, you must select your mate for more than his or her sex appeal and your mutual lust. The deeper love that you will feel toward a mate whom you love as a person, and not just as a sex object to satisfy your sexual needs, can contribute to an even more satisfying love life.

Nevertheless, we also want to emphasize that in a long-term relationship that has loyalty, devotion, respect, intimacy, openness, friendship, appreciation, and commitment, sex can become deeper, more meaningful, more profound, and more enjoyable than ever before. We have often seen couples in our clinical practice who demonstrate how there's nothing like that familiar, open, and uninhibited sex between partners who have been lovers through so much, for so long.

- Did you fall out of love with your partner because the sex just wasn't as good or as exciting as when you first met or became sexually intimate?
- Was your or your partner's lack of sexual desire a reason given for the divorce?

If you answered yes to either of these questions, you have bought into this myth of romantic love.

## My Spouse Will Be Just Like (or the Exact Opposite of) My Mother or Father

"I want a girl, just like the girl, who married dear old Dad." Many people do try to find a spouse who is just like their mother or father and has all their parents' positive traits. There are also many people who search for a mate who would be the opposite of their parents. "I would never marry a spendthrift like my mother." "No way am I marrying an alcoholic like my dad." They see the faults in their parents and want their spouse to be better, smarter, kinder, more organized, sweeter—you name it—than the parent of the opposite sex. Although it is important to think about what traits our parents have that we believe would be valuable in a mate as well as those that we want to avoid, each of us also has unconscious motivations operating when we select potential mates.

Harville Hendrix, the author of *Getting the Love You Want: A Guide for Couples,* has designed a very successful group therapy and workshop process that is based on the concept that as we search for mates we are unconsciously looking for caretakers. We want mates who will love us as our parents never did. We are attracted to mates who have both the positive and negative traits of our parents or early caretakers.

As we get deeper into the relationship, we often react to the spouse, not because of who he is but because he behaves like our parent and stirs up the old feelings of dependence, anger, frustration, and the like. Neither spouse understands why arguments and hurt feelings are occurring because both spouses are responding to their parents rather than to their spouses. Although it is highly simplistic to attribute all the problems of a marriage to this unconscious search for our parents (which Hendrix does not do!), an understanding of this process can help us understand our choices. Why do some women always select emotionally unavailable men? Why do some men always select caretaking women?

If you expect to repeat your parents' successful marriage ("After all, look how long they've been married") by looking for potential mates who seem to be just like them, you will fail. After all, you are not your parent. A marital match for you must take into account your unique needs, traits, history, and values. If you hope to avoid the unpleasant results of your parents' choice of partners, simply looking for opposite characteristics in potential mates will not guarantee success. No person will embody all of your parents' positive traits and be free of all their negative traits.

Look at what happened to Joanne when she tried to find the opposite of her father. She was thrilled with her new husband, Fred. He was so perfect! She was attracted to Fred because he had a steady job, unlike her father, who during her childhood could never stay employed. Fred was an accountant with one of the largest accounting firms in the country and had a comfortable income. She knew that their stability was guaranteed. She was so grateful to have someone to handle their checkbook and investments.

However, about one year after they married, she began to notice that they were getting late notices on their credit cards and other bills in the mail. When she questioned Fred, he accused her of not trusting his ability to manage the home accounts or said that the companies had made mistakes. Only when she found a credit card receipt from a nearby casino did she begin to suspect that he had a gambling problem. When Joanne investigated further, she learned that they were overdrawn at the bank. Other bills were months behind in payment.

Fred would not admit that he had a problem, saying that he used small-stakes gambling as recreation. He told Joanne that he was entitled to some fun since he worked so hard for her and the family. Unable to accept Fred's behavior and his unwillingness to change, Joanne moved out and filed for divorce. If Fred had been willing to acknowledge that he had a problem, and if Joanne had been able to stand by him through his recovery, the outcome might have been different. This would have taken time to sort out. But because Joanne was totally disillusioned by Fred's behavior, which resembled her father's unreliability, she was unable to see past the present situation to what would be needed by both of them to correct it. The pain of her childhood was rekindled, and the only way she was able to handle it was to leave.

- Did you expect your spouse to behave in all the positive ways of your parents?
- Did your expect your marriage to look just like your parents' marriage?
- Were you surprised that in spite of your conscious search for a person who did not have the negative traits of your parent, your mate behaved just like that parent?

If you answered yes to any of these questions, you have bought into this myth of romantic love.

## I Will Be Healed by My Marriage

We enter the search for a mate looking for Mr. or Ms. Right, whose love will instantly heal and complete us. We believe that our negative traits that so haunted the last relationship will be mitigated by a different type of person. After all, we tell ourselves, it is our former partner's fault that I reacted so badly. She wasn't a saint either, so why should I be?

It is a fallacy to believe that just being in a committed relationship with someone who loves us will cure our emotional distress, heal all the wounds of our childhood, or erase the weaknesses of our personalities. We may also expect that if we just love our partner enough, our love will heal him or her. We may not realize that although love can be the most powerful energy in this universe, it is usually not enough to make an alcoholic stop drinking, a gossip stop bearing tales, or a depressed person feel happy. Nor do we understand that our marriage will not automatically provide an unending source of solace from the assaults on our selves that we experience in our daily lives. We wrongly think of marriage as the antidote for any unhappiness that has plagued us during our lives. It is not. Marriage alone is not the magic elixir for personal happiness.

Chuck's story illustrates this search for wholeness through another person. As a child, Chuck was abused by his mentally ill mother. She would lock him in a closet when he was disobedient and withhold food as a punishment for the slightest malfeasance. She hit him for no reason and without warning. Chuck eventually told a teacher what was happening to him, and he was taken from his mother's home and put into a succession of foster homes. When he met Muriel, he was struck by her ability to smooth his rough edges and calmly wait out his bad moods.

Over the seven years of their marriage, Chuck began to expect Muriel to acquiesce to all of his desires. If she had an opinion different from his, he felt it as a direct attack on his manhood. When they fought, he would tell her how unloving and castrating she was and how he would leave her if she didn't shape up. She would cry, and he would feel guilty for making her cry. He would beg for her forgiveness, and she would forgive him. They attempted couples therapy, but Chuck used the sessions to blame Muriel for the problems in the marriage. She entered individual therapy and came to realize that she would never be able to heal Chuck, as he was not trying to heal himself in any way. He expected her to make him whole and healthy.

One evening they had a fight, the two of them following the usual script. When Chuck said, "Shape up or ship out," Muriel replied, "Fine," and left. Even though Chuck begged her to come back, crying that he needed her to be whole, they divorced shortly thereafter. Because Chuck was unwilling to look at his own motivations and reasons for his abusive behavior, the marriage was not viable unless Muriel was willing to subjugate her own health and well-being to his unreasonable demands.

- Did you believe that marrying your spouse would solve all your problems?
- Did you divorce because the marriage didn't heal your wounds from childhood?

If you answered yes to either of these questions, you have bought into this myth of romantic love.

## Beyond the Myths

If we looked for a mate with these myths about romantic love guiding the search, we inevitably became disillusioned with the spouse we selected. At one time our spouse met all our criteria: we were so in love with him and felt an intense sexual attraction; he seemed to meet all our needs, and we felt so whole when we were with him. What went wrong? We didn't realize that romantic love was not enough, that marriage depended on our own maturity, emotional self-reliance, selflessness, commitment, and loyalty—our ability to be more selfless and to devote ourselves to someone else.

What happens to the couple that bases their marriage on the myths of romantic love? The good feelings about the other spouse diminish. The couple may stay married but continue to live "lives of quiet desperation." Although they feel committed to the marriage, the marital relationship itself provides little satisfaction any longer. They are no longer "in love" with their spouse, and they may not even like their spouse. Every little thing that he or she does irritates them. They chronically bicker over inconsequential issues. Or they may go for days without even talking together, living more like roommates than intimate partners.

Sexual contact is infrequent and less enjoyable. Each feels terribly and totally alone. They may stay together "for the kids," but one or the other partner may seek outside the marriage for emotional and physical connection, engaging in serial affairs that recreate the excitement of first love. The couple may try marital therapy, but make little lasting progress. Each blames the other for the problems in the marriage. Finally, one or both spouses decide that divorce may be the only answer to the malaise or conflict.

If romantic love is not an adequate basis for a marriage, what is? If your marriage failed because you were swept up by the myths, then what follows is important for you to know.

## Loving Yourself

Strange as it may sound at first, you must love yourself before you can love another. This kind of self-love is similar to what people have often called self-esteem. By *self-love* we do not mean narcissism or self-absorption, whereby the person believes that the world revolves around him and that everyone and everything is secondary to meeting his individual needs. That type of self-absorption is very different from self-love.

The person with a healthy amount of self-appreciation, self-confidence, and self-love has high self-esteem and is able to care about others. Until we care about ourselves and believe that we are worthy of our own love, we will not believe that we are truly worthy of another person's love and cannot truly love another.

Learning to love oneself is not easy if such love wasn't nurtured as a child. Even many adults who had a wonderful childhood and feel blessed to have the love of their parents experience some difficulty loving themselves. The parents may have thought that it was too self-congratulatory to praise their children or to tell them that they were proud of them. Or parents might have unconsciously showed appreciation for their child only for his or her accomplishments, not simply for being a good person. However, a task of growing up, not just in age but also in maturity as an adult, is to come to the place of acceptance of oneself, warts and all. If you can't accept your own weirdness, failings, and delightful uniqueness, you won't be able to accept those qualities in another.

In our practices we often see couples in which one person has very low self-esteem. For example, Jed fell in love with Mariah the minute he saw her at the political meeting. He thought that she was the most intriguing woman he had ever seen: blonde hair cropped short, fiery brown eyes, and skin the shade of honey. He loved the way she walked with long, purposeful strides. He exalted in the way she talked with her strong opinions on every subject. He determined then and there to get to know her, woo her, and win her.

Mariah was fascinated by Jed's attentions to her. He was so romantic. She had found that most men were put off by her assertive personality, but Jed seemed to revel in it. He would listen to her talk and hardly talked about himself. She was a lobbyist for children's issues and spent most of her workday speaking with politicians and foundation executives. A new associate in an architectural firm, Jed was very quiet and laid-back. But when he did talk about his dreams of becoming a world-class architect, Mariah caught a glimpse of his passion and decided that the adage "still waters run deep" must apply to him.

After a whirlwind courtship, Jed and Mariah married. Their relationship did not flourish, however. Jed resented the time that she spent traveling for work and attending meetings. Mariah was disappointed that they had a lot of trouble talking about anything that she considered important. Jed began resenting Mariah's outspokenness, telling her that she didn't know what she was talking about. He called her stupid and uninformed.

What Mariah didn't know about Jed, and what he barely remembered himself, was that when he was a small child, his father would yell at him, telling him to be quiet and go away. When he chattered eagerly about something he had seen or done that day, his father would stop him midsentence, telling him he was stupid and to shut up. Of course, Jed learned to be quiet around his father, and other people as well. He worked very hard to please his father, excelling in school. He received praise from his teacher for being a conscientious student. But he always felt anxious about expressing opinions and expected others to put him down.

Jed was initially attracted to Mariah's obvious comfort with expressing her opinions. However, this same trait became irritating in their relationship because she behaved in ways he could not. Her ease in expressing herself and her feeling of competence became a rebuke to him of his inadequacies in the same areas. Further, her outspokenness triggered a ghost of a childhood fear: "Speak up and get told you are stupid." Mariah not only reminded Jed of his limitations but also tripped a childhood alarm of "not safe" when she spoke up. Because Jed didn't love and value himself, he was unable to love Mariah and to accept the traits that made her uniquely Mariah.

If Jed had appreciated his own worth and felt competent and smart, he would have been able to accept Mariah's opinions, respond with his own, and shrug and laugh off the times that Mariah went over the top in expressing herself. Instead of thinking fondly, "Oh, that's just Mariah," he converted his negative feelings about himself to negative feelings about her. Jed and Mariah had the potential for a happy marriage. If Jed had been willing to look at his own reactions to Mariah in terms of *himself* rather than in terms of her, he might have uncovered his underlying insecurity and low self-esteem as the reason for his criticism. Although it would have been painful, he could have examined the legacy of his father's rejections and their effect on his self-confidence and ability to express himself and seen how it was affecting his relationship with Mariah. He could have grieved for the acceptance that he didn't receive from his father and then learned to give himself the love he didn't receive as a child. His relationship with Mariah could have been transformed by self-awareness. Before he attempts a new relationship, Jed has much to learn about himself from the old.

All of us are drawn to people who have traits that we would like to have ourselves, but we often ultimately reject those people because of the very traits that were once appealing. Conversely, we find that the negative traits in others that push our buttons are the same traits that we actually have ourselves but have not acknowledged. What we loathe in ourselves we most hate in others. This duality of attraction and repulsion leads us into relationships with people with whom we may not have anything else in common, and then may drive us apart.

The key to understanding this dynamic is to ask yourself some questions whenever you become drawn to someone else or irritated by another's behavior. Rather than focusing on the other person, focus on your own reaction. Ask yourself, Why am I reacting this way? and What am I telling myself about this other person's behavior? Also ask, What am I really feeling—what are my unrealized desires or fears? These questions will help you understand your true motivations.

If Mariah had also asked herself these questions when Jed became angry at her, she might have realized that sometimes she did, indeed, talk too much and too forcefully. She knew that her behavior irritated other people. She also would have realized that Jed's anger erupted when he was feeling small and insecure—when something had gone wrong at work and he felt incompetent or, at the core, unloved. She could have become more attuned to the causes of his behavior and have told herself that it wasn't she, it was he. Jed's work was to understand his own process. But if the two of them were more self-observant, through counseling, self-discovery, and self-disclosure to the other, their marriage could have survived and flourished.

Knowing and understanding yourself is a lifelong process of peeling the onion of self, layer by layer. Until you can say, "I'm OK," and truly mean it, you won't be able to say, "You're OK" to your loved ones.

## Loving Someone Else

We would ask you to think about love as something you *do*, not something you *have*. Another person may love you, but the goal of a committed relationship is not to *have* love but to *give* love. Consider that love is a verb, an action word.

Loving is not easy. Erich Fromm said that it takes discipline, concentration, and patience. Another popular expert on love, Leo Buscaglia, said, "If one wishes to know love, one must live love, in action" (p. 91).

Surely we want to be loved back. We all need love that is selfless, supportive, accepting, constant, and forgiving. But the first step to receiving that kind of love is to give that kind of love to another person in a committed relationship. How do we bring love as an action to a marriage? In this chapter, we discuss a few ways to give love; in Chapter Three, we recommend more ideas when we talk about love for the long haul.

### Be a Friend to Your Spouse

We believe that spouses must be friends first and foremost. Basing your choice of spouse solely on romantic love is a backwards approach to one of the most important decisions in your life. As we said earlier, the "in love" state is essentially a me-centered state—it's about experiencing the exciting and intense feelings that accompany being loved.

As adults, however, we cannot maintain that symbiosis and thrive. The goal of adulthood is to actualize fully as a separate human being, not to remain dependent on parents or a spouse. Loving is the key to that independence and growth.

What does it take to be a friend to your partner? Friendship is built on mutual respect and trust. You must truly like each other as people, not just as lovers. You must be willing to allow your spouse the opportunity to confide in you, and not mock, jest, or divulge her deepest secrets to others. You must not use your spouse's vulnerabilities against her. Once words are spoken, they cannot be retrieved or taken back.

An old adage comes to mind that Christie was taught as a child: "If you can't say something nice about someone, don't say anything at all." Bob was taught, "They can't hang you for things you don't say."

These sayings still ring true today. Although friends can be honest with each other, "brutal honesty" destroys friendships (and marriages). There are always ways to be truthful and at the same time tactful. We don't always treat our spouse with the same gentleness and courtesy that we would give our best friend or even strangers. Although at times it seems impossible to keep your mouth shut, it is usually the best policy and the "friendly" thing to do.

For example, Gina was appalled by her boyfriend George's lack of fashion sense. His clothes were never color coordinated, and she found them old-fashioned and dowdy. She often joked, "George dresses as if he were fleeing a burning building." After their marriage, she determined to upgrade his wardrobe. She began insisting on shopping with him and would ridicule his clothing selections and insist that they purchase her picks. But rather than compliment him on his sexy, handsome look in his new clothes, she continued to point out his physical flaws ("You can't wear horizontal stripes because you're so pudgy," "You walk like a duck in those shoes") until he felt that he never looked good enough for her. He resented her constant attempts to improve him. He began spending more time with his male friends, whom she resented, and the two of them decided to call it quits after only one year of marriage.

Gina needed to realize that the outward package is much less important than the person inside. She fell in love with George as he was (or so he thought), and her constant need to change him indicated that she didn't truly love him for himself. She wouldn't have been so blunt and critical with a good friend and would have assisted with a friend's wardrobe only if asked. We don't expect our friends to be fashion plates or perfect in other ways; we shouldn't expect our spouse to be perfect either. And certainly a constant verbal barrage of our spouse's failings is destined to drive the spouse away. Gina could have achieved her goal of a well-dressed spouse who complemented her own stylishness by complimenting George. And even if George relapsed into his frumpy ways, she could still appreciate him for the good man that he was and not just expect him to be her fashion appendage.

Another aspect of friendship is having fun together and enjoying each other's company. Usually couples spend a lot of time together as they are getting to know each other before marriage, but then devote less time to doing things together after the marriage. Mary, a veteran of a thirty-five-year marriage, advocates that married couples have a "date night" every week. She urges couples to take turns planning the evening out and to forget the kids and other work and family obligations to focus just on each other.

"You just have to have some fun together that you can count on. It doesn't have to be expensive—a moonlight walk in the woods, a picnic and concert in the park—anything that gets you out of your routine and reminds you of why you married that ornery cuss," she laughingly advises. Having fun together is also a tension reducer. Look for the humor in the problems that arise. Sharing a belly laugh with your spouse will always smooth the way over rough passages in a marriage.

### Compromise, Compromise!

If you always have to be right, don't get married. No one is always right—and even if she were, she wouldn't have any friends. Christie had a first big fight with her spouse when he became angry that she had put the catsup bottle in the refrigerator. Her husband's parents had run several successful restaurants in Los Angeles and never refrigerated the condiments.

He couldn't believe that she was putting the catsup in the refrigerator rather than in the cupboard. She had been raised in the hot and muggy South, where people refrigerated everything. She responded that she had always put the catsup in the refrigerator, everyone refrigerates catsup, and it was really petty of him to suggest that she do it another way. The label on the catsup bottle offered no guidance as to the method of storage. Neither was able to convince the other of the rightness of their position, and the argument escalated beyond the topic of catsup to the flaws of each spouse.

Although Christie and her husband laugh about it today (the catsup is now refrigerated, but was not for quite some time after the argument), it was a painful moment of discovery of how disputes about little issues can grow out of proportion unless one spouse is willing to just give in.

Now isn't this the way it often goes? The argument is about something relatively inconsequential, but without one person being able to say, "Well, I may not agree, but I'll go along with your viewpoint because it makes as much sense as mine," the conflict becomes much greater than the original situation that stimulated it.

But, you might say, "My wife always had to be right, in everything. I wanted to be right sometimes, too. It felt weak to always give in." Yes, it does. Particularly if you or your spouse had a strong need to be in control of your environment and the things that affect you. But ask yourself the following questions:

- Do you find yourself arguing with friends and coworkers about your beliefs or the way things are done?
- Do you hold on to an argument like a dog with a bone until the other person backs off from the discussion or admits defeat?
- Do other people often avoid discussing anything with you with which you may disagree?
- Has anyone ever called you a control freak?

Perhaps your need to control others and your environment contributes to difficulties in relationships. Or maybe your spouse needed to be in control of every situation to feel comfortable. However, regardless of which of you was at fault, think about the fights that accompanied these power struggles. Were they worth the anger and frustration and disharmony in the relationship? Would you rather be right or be happy? Save being right for the issues that are most important to your core values and principles. A crucial mind-set in marriage is to insist on being right only when the issue relates to one of your core values. For example, if your spouse wants you to fudge deductions on your income taxes or discipline your child in a dangerous way, of course you should refuse and hold your ground. However, if the issue is a small one, let your spouse have his way. We're not suggesting peace at any price, but pick your battles.

Ideally, both spouses will be willing to give in occasionally so that balance exists in the relationship. However, you can only control your own behavior, not the behavior of the other spouse. In Chapter Five we will discuss ways of effectively managing conflict and communicating in a relationship so that both partners feel validated and empowered.

## Keeping the Reservoir Full

Marital love can occasionally seem like a one-way street. Although most of the time the relationship feels warm, inviting, and loving, with support flowing between the partners, it may occasionally feel confining, conflictual, and lonely. There is no relationship, in or out of marriage, that is always a perfect cycle of giving and receiving. We often go through times of anger, distrust, distance, and loneliness with our spouse. We feel as if the other has withdrawn all the sustenance on which the relationship thrives. You may wonder, Why me? What did I do to deserve such treatment?

It may be that a spouse is ill or involved in a major project at work that is consuming all his time and energy. Or the needs of a child may be taking priority over the relationship. What do you do during these difficult times to keep the relationship alive and not give up on it?

Here in Colorado where the authors reside, summer droughts are a common occurrence. Although spring is lush with rain and new growth, the summers, which are exquisitely beautiful, can bring the devastation of forest fires. The quantity of winter snowpack and its melt in the spring and summer make the difference between a normal summer and a drought. In the West, the adequacy of the water supply is a life-and-death matter. We rely on filling the reservoirs with water in the spring to get us through the dry summers.

Just as all living creatures depend on water to thrive and grow, a relationship is the free-flow of love between the partners. When that flow of love from your partner is blocked, you feel lonely and discounted. It is important to take care of yourself when this happens and to make it through this "drought."

Christie remembers one couple with whom she worked in mediation, Anne and John, who had not been able to keep their reservoir of love full. They met as college seniors, dated for six months, and married two weeks after they both graduated. John and his two best friends from college, who had graduated at the same time, immediately started a high-technology company, pooling their meager savings and borrowing from friends, family, and the bank to finance the start-up. Anne obtained an accounting job, but missed John, who was working sixteen- to eighteen-hour days. She told herself that when the company got going he'd have more time for her and their marriage. She immersed herself in her work and began going out after work with her coworkers. Over the next year, John's company became wildly successful during the dot-com heyday, and more employees were hired.

But John continued to work long hours and was rarely home except to sleep. The three friends' plan was to build the company, sell it for millions of dollars, and retire. When a larger firm ultimately did buy the company, Anne and John were ecstatic. Anne hoped that now John would have time for the marriage. However, before John received the majority of the proceeds from the sale, the purchasing company filed for bankruptcy. John and his partners lost everything.

Anne was still working, so Anne and John could pay their monthly bills. But John became despondent. He rejected Anne's attempts to support and comfort him, went to bed, and stayed there for two months. During this time, Anne tried to get him to see a counselor or even his family doctor, but John refused. He totally withdrew from Anne. She decided that she did not want to deal with him anymore and left.

When Christie saw them, John was still depressed, and he blamed the demise of the marriage on Anne, saying that she was deserting him during his hour of need. Anne told him that she had loved him, but that because he hadn't shown that she was important to him over the past year, she was no longer in love with him. He had distanced himself from her during the building of the company, and there was no reservoir of love and commitment to draw from to sustain them. They ultimately divorced, but with great sadness and cynicism about marriage. As newlyweds, Anne and John had not built a history of loving acts, sharing, and communication on which they could draw in the dry times. They had been entirely focused on their individual needs, so when they needed to draw from the reservoir of love to keep the marriage watered and growing, they found it had run dry. Both needed to realize that to survive the hard times, each partner must be willing to give more than he or she receives.

What must you do to fill this reservoir of love? First you must consciously take advantage of and enjoy those wonderful moments and good times you have together over the years. You must set aside time and make specific plans to keep your relationship filled with meaningful experiences and great memories. Then you must be prepared to weather the drought. It is one of the most difficult things to do because you have to forgo having your needs met by the other.

During the dry spell, you must remember that the other is going through a difficult time in his or her life. You may not totally understand it, but you must realize that your partner is not normally this unloving, unhealthy, or unavailable. You must keep busy and try not to dwell on the negative feelings about your spouse and about yourself that come up. The little ego inside you will try to convince you that you need to withdraw too, or that you can punish the other into becoming loving again: "I'm not going to speak to him again until he is totally present with me."

This reciprocal behavior—tit for tat—never works. Instead, offer compassion and empathy. "I know you're having a hard time [are sick, distracted, angry, depressed], and I love you. What can I do to help?" Maybe you will be spending a great deal of emotional and physical energy taking care of your spouse. But during this time, know that the rains will return to bless the parched earth. (If they don't, the normal relationship cycle is in real trouble, and the two of you need professional help.)

Stay involved with friends and family. Participate in individual activities that bring you the greatest joy. For Christie, her favorite activities that restart the cycle of joy and love in her life are music, singing, meditating, reading a well-written mystery novel, and playing with her two dogs. For Bob, it is cooking a really good meal (the waistline will bear witness), reading and getting lost in a good novel, and working in the garden. Know what gives you joy and do it, whether it's baking bread, fiddling with your computer, or building model airplanes.

Volunteer work also connects us with the universal flow of love. Putting aside your own problems for a while and doing something helpful for others is a proven way to lift your spirits. Volunteer in a soup kitchen, read stories to children at the low-income day-care center, or walk the dogs at your local animal shelter. When you are the most selfless, you actually receive the most in return. What an amazing principle! Without even trying, you will feel better about yourself, and your life will look a bit more manageable. In order to receive love, you must first give it. Keep your love flowing to your spouse and to the world around you. You will receive love in return.

As we have seen, marriage requires new skills, attitudes, and motivations that are developed only when one is in a relationship with another person. The myths about romance and marriage that have been handed us by our culture must be discarded in favor of mature, realistic expectations about committed relationships. Although divorce is painful and immensely sad, you must examine the impact of these myths on your relationship with your spouse. In the next chapter, we continue looking at what you must be willing and able to do in the future to sustain a long-term relationship. With this knowledge, you can do better the next time.

# Chapter Three

# The Nuts and Bolts of Maintaining a Long-Term Relationship

How do we sustain love in a marital relationship? How do we keep the relationship alive and well? When the bloom is off the rose, how does one stay in a monogamous relationship and in love for life? As you read this you may be thinking, How corny! A monogamous relationship for life? In this day and age! Yet most people enter marriage with the hope and expectation that marriage is for life. With the new marriage failure rate at about 50 percent, there are a lot of disappointed and disillusioned people out there. Something did not work. How can we get it to work?

This chapter is about what couples must do to sustain a relationship over time and some of the things that tend to sabotage it. In the previous sentence we purposely did not use the word *love* and used *relationship* instead, because in any "love relationship," love ebbs and flows. It never goes away, but it can be strained at times. How then does one survive the strain without love dying and the relationship snapping?

## Replacing Unconditional Love

Our first love relationship with our parents has a built-in hazard for our later years. For most people, a parent's love is unconditional. As children we don't have to do anything back—we are loved because we exist. As children we can become rather self-centered because there is nothing we have to do to obtain a parent's love.

65

(Love is different from approval. There is much we must do to gain approval: "Don't hit, use words; don't run indoors; use your napkin not your sleeve; put down the toilet seat; don't spit; don't loll on the sofa; don't you roll your eyes at me, young man," and so on.) The child takes being loved for granted. It is like a deep underground stream that is always there.

When child psychologists talk about the withdrawal of love as a disciplinary technique, it is really a misnomer. Psychologically healthy parents do not withdraw love; they withdraw *approval*. In fact, the withdrawal of approval as a disciplinary technique will work only if there is a strong sense of love between parent and child. The child wants to get back into the love relationship that is so comforting, but the lack of approval shuts the door on feeling loved.

## Loving Dangerously

In a marital relationship, one must break out of the self-centered thinking of childhood—"I am always loved, no matter what I do"— and take the often terrifying risk of loving without a guarantee of being loved back. In our first love relationship, that with our parents, we don't have to do anything to be loved except exist, but subsequent love relationships require that we do have to do some things to stay loveable. The working assumption must be, If I am alive, open, and loving, the same feeling will be created in another who will give it back to me. Thus, although each of us remains separate, we each give to the relationship and to each other.

We join in marriage to become partners. In that partnership should come the ability to give meaning to life and meaning to what is important in the world. By becoming partners we transcend the solitary *I* and join to become a *We*. Mind you, we don't do that every living moment of the relationship; nevertheless, when we come together, the whole is greater than the sum of the parts. If we come together only to have our needs and fantasies met, then we are not transcending the *I* into a *We* but are instead emphasizing *Me*.

What do people mean when they refer to the "perfect couple"? It is that complementarity, that oneness that people find themselves remarking on. It is interesting that the "perfect couple" comment is often made when the couple splits up, as in, "Oh, they seemed such a perfect couple." By being a perfect couple, or appearing to be so, their coming apart is a shock. In fact, a good exercise is to look at a couple you call perfect and define perfection for yourself. What makes that couple perfect? Do they never get mad at each other? Do they laugh a lot? Do they share the burden of housework? Does each have agreed-on jobs in the relationship and do them well? The words and phrases you use to define them create a wonderful picture of what *you* value and hope for in a relationship!

Perfect couples are made, not born. What shapes two people into a team? How do two people become a "we"? Research tells us that the most powerful form of reward to induce or change behavior is what psychologists call intermittent reinforcement. In simple terms, it means that the more often you are rewarded at times you least expect it, the longer you will keep at something, hoping madly for a reward. Gambling capitalizes on this phenomenon. The more you play, the more likely you are to win (that is, you can't win if you're not in), so you keep playing. When you win, you keep on playing because you hope to win again, but you don't know when. Needless to say, this is the same reinforcement pattern that keeps guys hitting on girls!

The concept of intermittent reinforcement is true for a relationship like marriage. If you work at it consistently and are occasionally reinforced by hitting pay-dirt, the more likely you are to continue. The more predictable things are, the more likely you will lose interest when the same old pattern doesn't work. For instance, people who have great sex all the time are more likely to walk away when the great sex stops. People who have OK sex most of the time but glorious sex occasionally are more likely to hang in there waiting for the next truly blissful moment. People who have bad sex or no sex most of the time are very unlikely to wait around too long for good sex to happen.

Perhaps you have had a moment, or we hope many moments, when the feeling in your relationship was glorious. You felt alive, madly happy, madly in love with another person, and free and powerful. The feeling is as much dependent on the other person as it is on you. Some sort of transaction has occurred between the two of you that raises you to that feeling of oneness. This commonly happens when one has a child and is confronted with the miracle of having created this living thing with your partner. It can happen at the end of a really good vacation, when you and your spouse are sitting on the beach watching the sunset as you lean against each other. You feel the warmth of the body next to you and are one. These moments do not come frequently, but when they do, they are incredibly rewarding and keep us going through the next round of the ordinary. We have to speak carefully here, because *ordinary* does not mean boring or dull, it just means routine or everyday.

## Trust and Self-Disclosure

Marriage is an exercise in defining priorities and the building of "a life." Many couples spend hours with each other talking about their hopes and dreams, what they want for the future, and what they want to shed from the past. Such conversations build intimacy because they are honest and self-revealing.

Research indicates that tracing the degree of self-disclosure is to trace the progress of a relationship. The better you know someone, the more likely you are to disclose things about yourself. The more you disclose about yourself, the more available you are to the insights and feedback of others. People who do not disclose about themselves are blocked from knowing themselves fully. One can see that in a relationship, the more open and honest we are in our self-revelation, the more pleased both parties will be. I know more about me, and you know more about me! And I know more about you, and you know more about you too.

We do have to be sensitive to issues of timing in self-disclosure. Intimate details of your life told too early in a relationship can prompt your partner to leave your vicinity very quickly. Intimate details told too early put great pressure on the other person to be intimate too. He or she may not be ready to self-reveal and so may flee. So timing and relevance both are criteria to be watched.

Some individuals in a relationship are, of course, not always honest and self-revealing. People can be manipulated and tricked by being told what they want to hear. This is the con artist's way of getting into the inner sanctum by offering the appearance of intimacy and then in some self-serving fashion using the person whose guard has been lowered or turned off. This is a tool that our man Andrew (in Chapter One) used to get women in bed with him. As another example, Bob worked with a gentleman in therapy who was a trust baby. He had a very large fortune, left to him by his parents, which was held in trusts, each with a different trustee. He had been quite protected growing up, as his parents were deathly afraid of his being kidnapped and held for ransom, and was consequently not terribly wise to the ways of the world. When his parents died suddenly, he was essentially alone with his fortune, and he plunged into all the things that had been previously forbidden. He frequented strip clubs and ultimately met a stripper who sensed him as an easy mark. Her story was that she was a college student who wanted to go to law school. Her parents were dead, she said, and stripping paid her a lot of money for very little work on a schedule she could control. She could live, pay for school, and plan for her future.

As their relationship developed, they talked about both of them desiring children. She was charmed by his large family ranch in Western Colorado and revealed that she had always liked working with animals. What she did not share was that she had a long-standing drug habit. He took drugs recreationally but not habitually. She did them every day and hid her drug use from him. They married, and she soon became pregnant but continued to use drugs and alcohol. Her triplets were born with fetal alcohol syndrome, were intellectually limited, and would need to have care all their lives. The husband did not know she was abusing drugs while she was pregnant and was suddenly confronted by three infants whose condition revealed that her abuse had been terrible.

This father was in therapy because he blamed himself for being so naive and so blind to what was going on. He was right on both counts, but he needed to recognize that he was not on a level playing field with his wife, who withheld aspects of herself from him. Their divorce was front-page material as she went after his fortune as the mother of his three children. A prenuptial agreement kept her at bay to some extent, but he still had to live with the results of her nondisclosure.

A less dramatic but equally corrosive form of lack of self-disclosure is exhibited by the person who functions at the level of pre-conventional morality (as discussed in Chapter One), who sees moral behavior as a tit-for-tat transaction. You do something nice for me, I'll do something nice for you.

George was abruptly and unceremoniously made aware of his wife's barter mentality when one day she, in a fit of temper, screamed at him: "I hate fishing! I hate fishing camps off in the boonies! I hate the smell of fish! I am never again going to sit on the shore of some God-forsaken Canadian lake while you commune with nature and bond with your smelly buddies!"

George was flabbergasted. He had always thought Annie enjoyed the wilderness and the peacefulness of a mountain lake or stream. It turns out that she had merely gone along to get along. She was a city girl and thought that the only way she could get George to do the things she liked—opera, theatre, ethnic restaurants, and the like—was to capitulate to his desire for the great outdoors and fishing. Fear of being deserted prevented her from revealing her dislike of fishing. At her level of functioning, she believed that if she did not do what George wanted, he would never do what she wanted. In fact, when her feelings were out on the table, George realized that he did not need her along fishing. He liked her chosen activities as well as his and was more than willing to leave her behind when he went off stalking trout. He did not think in barter terms—one fishing trip entitles you, dear wife, to two operas and a play. She had been needlessly suffering for the first seven years of their marriage because she said yes when she did not really mean it.

With self-revelation and honesty there is a richness in a relationship that grows over time. There is no better friend than an old friend. Why? Because there is a huge foundation of shared experiences from which one builds a profound sense of empathy. One can understand a friend because you have been there too. There is so much that does not have to be said because you already know. By already knowing, you can cross over the gap that separates you and join with the other. This is what one hopes for in a marriage. This is why we espouse this progression: first be friends, then lovers, and ultimately spouses.

## Creating Institutional Goals

As two people build a marriage, or any relationship, they share mutually agreed-upon goals and areas of interest. For example, we might choose to raise children and be the very best parents we can be, or go into a family business that will make the family prosper, or become teachers so no young brain is wasted. It is the joining together in holding and trying to achieve these mutual goals that is the key to a lasting marriage. When we as a couple have these spoken or unspoken agreements, achieving for oneself is also giving to each other because my or your success adds to our success as a couple.

In a sense, being married is like building a little company. One goal of this institution is to provide for economic security through work, financial planning, and perhaps even running a business together. Another goal is to provide for domestic comfort with a good home, a vacation condo, vacations, and things to make life easier and more enjoyable, such as a better car or a great full-screen video system or a sailboat. A third goal might be raising children and having a larger family, although of course not all couples choose this. A fourth goal might be to perform community service so as to leave the world in a better place than you found it. A fifth goal might be to share in other causes, such as a spiritual life, politics, or public or private education.

The list can be endless, but there must be a list of agreed-upon goals of some sort, spoken or unspoken, for a marriage to survive. Any marriage, like any corporation, has to have a statement of purpose and goals that are known to the members, be they bosses or workers. When this is accomplished, everyone can pull in the same direction; the couple can achieve its goals much more easily and avoid executive battles or aimless drift. We are not implying that there has to be a flowchart of goals on the refrigerator door, but there does need to be some sense of mission and direction as a couple.

If you are a dyed-in-the-wool romantic, our talk about organization-style mission statements and goals will seem dismissive of true love. We believe that a marriage must have both. But no matter how you prefer to think about marriage, one of the things you do in a successful marriage is create an institution devoted to the comfort and success of the participants.

In a marriage there are three sets of goals: the personal goals of the husband, the personal goals of the wife, and their joint goals as a couple. If I love you and want you to succeed, then when you reach those goals that are of value to you, I am enhanced because I wish you well, and your success becomes my pleasure. When you serve yourself by reaching your goals, you serve us as well because we are a team with common or overlapping goals. And when you serve yourself, then I am enhanced, too, because we are one. Marriage is not a box or a static place, but a place where one works and grows with the one who is loved. Marriage is a process, and the transactions in the process help us further define our goals, our selves, our values, and our love for one another.

## Building Character

As trite as it may sound, marriage builds character. A long-term relationship that is reciprocal requires us to step outside ourselves and think of the other. One forsakes narcissism, self-centeredness, and self-absorption for loyalty, devotion, compromise, and selflessness.

No, none of us is going to become a saint. Sometimes we use our partner mainly for our own satisfaction, such as by pressing for sex when she is not wildly interested or convincing him that true happiness will be found by owning a BMW when he thinks of a car in terms of "it goes–it doesn't go." We do, however, try to be altruistic and make sure the needs of our partner are satisfied. We move from our one-way infantile relationship with our parents to a relationship between equals that is not a barter relationship but one in which the other counts at least as much as we do, if not more.

If we think of character as the sum of all our psychological parts, we understand when we hear, "She has great strength of character" that she is sure of her values and her sense of herself and that she is not afraid to stand up for her convictions. In other words, her sense of self is strong enough that she will not be deterred by personal assaults, she is not totally selfish and self-absorbed, she has an innate sense of fairness, she stands by her friends, and she knows how to deal with people fairly without abandoning her own standards.

A marriage for most people is the crucible in which character is built, refined, and strengthened. If one accepts that character building leads to loyalty, compassion, compromise, and deep concern for the well-being of the partner, then the greater the mutual growth in character, the less likely the marriage is to fail.

The story of Gretchen and Stanley will underscore our point. Both of them came from ranching families in the eastern part of Colorado. They went to school in a one-room schoolhouse until high school, when they transferred to a consolidated high school that served several sparsely populated counties. School bus rides in the winter took more than an hour. Both were active in extracurricular activities, so they often found themselves on the late bus that got them home about 5:30 in the afternoon. They were drawn to each other because of their physical proximity, the friendship between their families, their equal popularity at school, and their common background as ranchers' children.

Gretchen and Stanley married out of high school and came to Denver. Stan wanted to go to college and on to graduate school to become a veterinarian for large animals. He hoped ultimately to return to the plains and set himself up as a vet to ranch animals and continue the ranch life he had so loved as a boy and as a youth. Gretchen wanted to be a mother and a helpmate to her husband. She had been raised in a family with very traditional notions about the role of women in a marriage and was quite content with the role prescribed for her since birth.

The only way Stan could make it through college was by going to night school and working during the day. Gretchen had to work, too, to help cover college tuition and simple living expenses. She landed an entry-level job as an accountant for the state, but the hours were good, the benefits were solid, and the pay was regular and not that bad. Gretchen, in fact, earned more than Stan, who, drawing on his ranch experience with machines, worked as a car mechanic during the day and took classes at night.

Looking back to that time in their lives, Gretchen said, "The glue that held us together was our dreams of the future. Stan was antsy about my earning more money than he did because he was supposed to be the breadwinner. I told him this was just temporary. I wanted babies so bad, but we agreed that we were not ready for them yet financially. We had to get Stan through school, then bring on the babies!"

Thinking about the same time in their lives, Stan said, "I hated it. I always had grease under my nails and in the lines on my hands. I worked all day and then went to school at night from seven to ten. I was doing premed courses, which were hard. We did not have much time for fun, but I just kept my eye on the future and what it would be like when I was a vet. Gretchen helped a lot, I mean a lot, in my keeping my eye on the prize."

Here, in the initial stage of their marriage, Stan and Gretchen had a common goal, his becoming a vet and their returning to the plains to a life they knew and loved. Keeping their eye on the prize, as Stan said, was what helped them endure the hardships of working, school, and the role reversal of Gretchen's earning more money than Stan.

Stan graduated from the University of Colorado at Denver and went on to apply to the University of Northern Colorado, which had one of the top ten graduate programs in veterinary medicine. This meant another four years of genteel student poverty, but Gretchen figured they could pull it off with some student loans and her continuing to work for the state. It meant that she would have to stay in Denver during the week and be with Stan on the weekends. If he lived in a house with other graduate students to keep costs down and Gretchen really pinched pennies, they figured they could swing it.

Consequently, the first eight years of their marriage were an exercise in the delay of gratification, particularly for Gretchen. Stan was moving ever closer to his dream of becoming a doctor of veterinary medicine. Gretchen was in a helper role, as she had been brought up to be by her family, but the missing ingredient for her was children. Her clock was ticking, but she loved Stan and felt the sacrifice was worth it for the end goal. During Stan's years in vet school, Gretchen worked and commuted to Greeley on weekends. "I told Stan that on the day he walked up and got his sheepskin, I would throw my birth control pill dispenser high into the air."

Life had other plans. Stan had been an outstanding student and had been mentored by a professor who was developing new cancer treatments for both large and small animals. The professor asked Stan to stay on for a two-year postdoc to help him with his research. It did not pay much, but the experience would put Stan into any veterinary school faculty in the country because he would be at the cutting edge of animal treatment. After the experience of a top vet school and a first-class academic environment, Stan was leaning strongly toward a research-focused academic career. He had not told Gretchen because he knew what her dreams were and did not want to spoil them.

So we see that what had been Gretchen and Stan's joint goal, the marital glue that had held things together through a period of quite a bit of sacrificing by both of them, had weakened for Stan. Because he had never talked about the change with Gretchen as it was happening to him, his delay created a binary situation: yes or no, now! He had been afraid to talk about it as it happened because he did not want to burn the dream, and he was afraid Gretchen would say no to something he really wanted. He recounted, "I came home from my last class with the postdoc offer from Professor Katz. I told Gretchen cold turkey that I had accepted and that we would have two more years of graduate student life with no possibility of kids or going back to the plains. In fact, I said I thought I wanted to find a slot as a faculty member at a vet school that would mean, in all probability, a city life for the two of us. I felt so guilty, but I really wanted this. I have never seen Gretchen so mad and so miserable. She screamed at me that she had not sacrificed eight years of her life so that I could continue to be selfish. She felt like I was treating her like an automatic teller machine that just burped out cash and had no feelings. When did she get to have her needs met in this relationship? I stuck to my guns. I was devastated when she left and went back to her mom and dad's ranch in La Junta."

Gretchen's comment was, "I felt so used and tricked. Here we had a dream that we had kept alive and had kept us alive for eight years, and he just up and dumped it without even talking to me about it. I felt so betrayed. Up to this point our marriage had been one where we talked about everything. We did not deal in ultimatums. All of a sudden he turns it into a 'Me Tarzan, you Jane' kind of a marriage. There was no way I was going to put up with that! With one unilateral decision, he had crushed all that we had worked for. I felt so used!"

Stan was being fearful and conflict avoidant. He knew what he wanted and knew that it flew counter to their dreams up to that point. He was afraid she would say no, so he avoided any opportunity to negotiate and in his fear simply pulled a power play. What should also be noted is that Gretchen reacted to the betrayal of trust, not to the issue of whether they should stay in graduate school for two more years or even whether they should ultimately aim to be city-dwelling academics rather than country folk.

Gretchen fled back to the farm and ranch community in which she was raised, leaving Stan in Greeley. In her hurt and anger, as well as in her self-pity for all the sacrifices she had made to enable

Stan's career, she had an affair with an old high school fellow who had always been on the visible sidelines when she and Stan were a high school "item." She noted, "Actually sex was not much fun with Art. I kept thinking of Stan and how mad I was at him. If a person can use sex to get even with someone, then I was the poster girl!"

Stan became depressed—so much so that after about four months, Dr. Katz asked him if the postdoc was really what Stan wanted to do, because his heart didn't seem to be in it. He really seemed to have dumbed down in the past few months. Stan broke down, and in tears told his mentor how his career decisions had apparently destroyed his marriage. Dr. Katz was noncommittal and emotionally somewhat aloof. He said that this was not the first time that career and marriage collided; Stan needed to make a clear decision and then get on with his life. Going home after this conversation, Stan remembered a motto he had seen on the side of a Eddie Bauer shopping bag that weekend: "Never confuse having a career with having a life."

The following weekend he hopped into his car and drove to his parents' ranch in La Junta. On Saturday morning he appeared unannounced on Gretchen's porch. Her parents were glad to see him because they were troubled by the turn in his and Gretchen's relationship. They called Gretchen and then gracefully disappeared into the barn. Gretchen said, "When I saw him standing there in the living room in his old Wranglers and holding his Stetson in his hands I nearly died of the pain. I missed him so, I loved him so, and I was so mad and hurt. What feeling should I pay attention to? I was so afraid of making things worse." Stan said, "When I saw her coming down the stairs, first ankles, then those nonstop legs, her body, her breasts, and her face, I knew my life was with her, my children should be with her, and I had made a terrible mistake. My first words were, 'Can you forgive me for being so selfish?' She burst into tears, and I thought at first, 'Guy, you have really, really blown it!' That fear just ran away when she came over and hugged me."

Gretchen and Stan had a lot to work through. She decided she had to tell him about the brief affair, not knowing what his reaction would be, and he had to tell her how sorry he was for his "my way or the highway" attitude about his career. He realized how self-centered he had become in the pursuit of his career, but realizing it was only the first step; the really hard part was confessing to her that he had been selfish and pigheaded. They decided they were not ready to move back in together quite yet. Stan was stunned and hurt that Gretchen had had an affair, yet a little part of himself said that he was as much a part of the cause of it as Gretchen. Gretchen felt gun-shy because her trust had been betrayed. She was very worried about Stan coming in with another ultimatum once he felt safe with her again. Meanwhile Stan continued with his postdoc, and Gretchen moved back to Greeley to live with an old girlfriend. She and Stan saw a counselor and had weekly dates as they cautiously reengaged with each other.

Gretchen laughed and said, "The first time we had sex it was like nothing either of us had experienced before. It was a mad mix of anger, lust, longing, loneliness, hunger, and just pure pleasure. When we were finished, Stan took the top off a film canister that was on my nightstand and said he was going to capture some of the air in the room and save it because he wanted to be able to do this again! You know, I still have that canister in my top bureau drawer."

Stan and Gretchen decided that they would get back together and would not wait any longer to have a child. Stan said, "We've had macaroni and cheese four days running at the end of the month; I guess we can do it again and survive. Kids like macaroni and cheese anyway."

## Building a Life

Happiness is a by-product of doing what we like to do. We can't get directly to happiness without going through some sort of activity that will, by its doing, bring us happiness. A lasting marriage is a by-product of shared goals and a shared investment in or passion about those goals. From this comes happiness and contentment in the relationship because there is a shared pleasure if one or both parties reach those goals. If the goals change, then both partners must be on board for the change. Often in divorces you hear the cause as being "We just drifted apart" or "We just stopped communicating."

Stan and Gretchen stopped communicating when Stan, out of fear, laid an ultimatum on Gretchen about his doing a postdoc. The goals of the marriage had been unilaterally changed; Gretchen was not even given a chance to participate in the change, and happiness fled (as did Gretchen). When they went to the counselor, the best they could do to describe what they needed was to ask for help in learning how to "communicate." The therapist wisely refrained from teaching them "communication skills." They both knew how to articulate their concerns. What Stan did not know how to do was deal with his fear of being told he could not have what he wanted. Gretchen couldn't deal with her fear of what her anger would do if she did communicate it, so she "communicated" by fleeing Stan and the marriage. She further "communicated" by having an affair to act out her sense of betrayal by Stan. They were both fearful of sharing feelings of vulnerability and anger. Those feelings prompted both of them to abandon the *We* of their relationship and isolate the two of them as very separate *I*'s. What Stan and Gretchen needed to do was reestablish intimacy by regaining a sense of joint emotional safety. They needed also to evolve as people to be more mature, devoted, and compromising, and they needed to make a commitment to building a life together.

In Stan and Gretchen's story, Stan "blinked first." Somebody had to make the first move to reestablish intimacy. For anyone this is often a difficult move because one's feelings are hurt, and there is a sense of sniveling and groveling, sort of like the cocker spaniel who crawls toward you on its belly when it thinks it has done something wrong. Apologizing and saving face often do not go hand in hand! It takes a fairly strong, mature person to make the first overture. Stan was driven by his need for his wife. It was not a dependency need in the neurotic sense, but a need to make life whole by having a helpmate at his side to make the future happen. He was seeking the intimacy with Gretchen that had been his source of happiness. Gretchen moved cautiously back to him because she sought the same. Both of them grew up a great deal as they moved to reestablish intimacy and negotiate over what their common goals would be.

## Growing Up

As you may have guessed from our discussion of sustaining love in a marriage, we are talking about each partner growing up. In fact, Harville Hendrix, author of *Getting the Love You Want,* has said that the purpose of marriage is to finish childhood. A mature person must have a great deal of self-knowledge and self-acceptance. In other words, she needs to see herself warts and all. In addition, she must be willing to admit mistakes, take corrective action, and move on with life.

One of the things that happens to us in childhood is that we learn to deal with the world from a relatively powerless position. We have to do what our parents tell us to do, we have to behave in school, and we have to mind our manners. So, as relatively powerless children we learn ways to cope that, if carried into adulthood, again remind us of how powerless we are. A neurotic cycle is begun that keeps us, as adults, in the mind-set that we are powerless children.

Take Stan, who steamrollered Gretchen with his choice of a postdoc. He feared that he would not get his way. He acted as if he had no negotiation skills. Most important, he acted as if he knew what Gretchen would do (say no!) and as if her no would override his desires. In fact he did *not* know what Gretchen would do, but he had a childhood-based fear that led him to assume he could predict the future about what would happen when his needs conflicted with those of someone he loved. He was raised by parents who were loving but conservative, so they often said no to something for which he was arguing, "But all the other parents are letting their kids do it!" As a teen he would sometimes sneak behind their backs to do what the other kids were doing. It made him feel guilty, but the doing was a lot more powerful than the guilt. His method of handling his desire for the postdoc was derived from his childhood beliefs and experiences. Stan was not being mature; he was being childlike. He was taking his experience as a powerless child and carrying it into his adulthood.

Gretchen was deeply hurt, and, instead of staying and dealing with the issue, she fled. Further, she took her anger and frustration out on Stan by having an affair, which was her way of hurting him. Her behavior was passive-aggressive in that she did not deal with Stan directly, but instead attacked him indirectly by breaking their marital agreement of monogamy.

Gretchen was the youngest of four children. The only girl in the family, she grew up with brothers who dominated her. Because she could not win fights either physically or verbally, she would simply withdraw, go to her room, or, in later years, flee the house. Her parents developed the technique of sending quarreling children to their rooms rather than trying to play judge and jury to the accusations and counteraccusations of a sibling quarrel, so tattling simply did not work in her family. As a child without power, she learned to withdraw when a conflict occurred, so she too was conflict avoidant. She acted immaturely in concert with Stan. In Chapter Five we discuss the importance of resolving conflict in a marriage and the best way to approach "fighting" with our spouse.

## Dealing with Our Fears

What is clear from Stan and Gretchen's story is that our fears cause us to do things that are harmful to ourselves and others. Fears nearly always stand in the way of intimacy. The mature person knows what his fears are and tries to grapple with them, no matter how hard that may be. People enter therapy to try to understand their fears and develop ways of handling them in a non-self-destructive way.

When we do not want to face a fear, we develop defenses that help us say, "I am not being run by fear, I am simply reacting to something outside me that I can't control." Often people fear something in a relationship, when the fear in fact really lies within themselves. When they cannot acknowledge that the fear is theirs alone, growth is prevented because what they fear is seen as "out there" and beyond their control.

Defenses are necessary to cope with the world. They become problems only when they so blind us from seeing ourselves realistically that we cease to grow, and we become frozen in our quest for maturity. Projection of blame is one of the most common defenses people use when a relationship begins to lose intimacy. With a little concentration we can catch ourselves before we use this tactic.

Here is a little test for you intended to raise your awareness. Suppose you are in the grocery store and reach into the freezer chest for a package of frozen corn, toss it into your cart, and take it with all the other stuff you have selected to the checkout stand. When you get home, as you unpack, you notice that you have picked up a package of peas, not the corn you had intended. Whom do you blame? Do you say, "I wish that darn store could get its stockers to shelve things properly!" or do you say, "Darn, I should have looked before I grabbed. I'll have to check more carefully next time." If you blame the stockers, you are projecting blame.

Let's say, underneath it all, that you feel like a jerk for not having been more meticulous. Feeling like a jerk is not a welcome or pleasant experience. Let's also say that "You jerk!" was your father's favorite expression whenever you did something that annoyed him. Feeling like a jerk would be something you would rather avoid. It is not a good feeling to begin with, and if it is layered over with childhood humiliation, it stings all the more. So, instead of ruefully admitting, "Yes, I was a jerk," you blame the store instead. "It's the shelver's fault. If the store did not pay such low wages to shelvers they might be able to hire somebody who was able to *think and pay attention!*" And now you are off to the races blaming the store and avoiding the painful recognition that you were the jerk. In fact you are using the very words "think and pay attention" that you should be applying to yourself.

In an intimate relationship, projecting blame becomes an easy choice when we are in a situation where we do not want to assume fault or responsibility. For instance, Gretchen could have blamed Stan for her affair and said it was his fault: "If you had not just cut me dead as a partner, I would not have had to go seek affection somewhere else! My affair was your fault!"

Fortunately, Gretchen was able to be more mature when she looked at what happened in the cold light of day and asked herself some hard questions and attempted to come up with honest answers. She learned a lot about her tendency to flee conflict and to express her anger in passive-aggressive ways to avoid dealing directly with the person who was making her angry. It was a hard truth and a major lesson when she accepted that the affair was her choice and her responsibility, not Stan's.

Stan could have blamed Gretchen for his unilateral decision by saying, "If you were more open and not so rigid, then I could deal with you, but you have such a closed mind. There's no reasoning with you!" Fortunately he did not project the blame for his choice of behavior onto Gretchen. He took responsibility for his choices, even though his choice made him feel ashamed.

When you hear yourself blaming the other person for the problems in your relationship, let it be a red flag for you. Ask the question, Is he really responsible, or am I just passing the buck because there is a side of myself I do not wish to see? One helpful strategy is to listen carefully to what your partner is accusing *you* of. He too may be projecting blame. Or he may be telling the truth and seeing things accurately. By facing ourselves warts and all and trying to recognize the fears that launch our defenses into action, we are taking a long step toward the achievement of character and maturity.

## Reaching Maturity in Relationships

Relationships are a wonderful crucible in which to learn maturity. To learn from our experiences we must care about something, and caring about another person is a connection that matters. Because it matters, it is something we want to preserve. Raising children is a case in point.

Most of us learn to choose our battles when our children reach adolescence because we realize that they are becoming increasingly independent and we can control them much less than when they were three. We can no longer take control for granted. So we learn where to stand our ground and where to say some variation of "Well, if he doesn't know it now, he'll have to learn it on his own." In other words, we stop trying to control and start to accept the other person's differences.

Control in marriage is the same way. For 99 percent of us, the relationship matters from the outset. We build it by sharing dreams, developing common goals, and functioning as a team in certain parts of the marriage. We make an attempt to treat each other decently, but a great corrupter of decency is our fears. Feeling safe enough and being mature enough to recognize our fears is a major task of a well-lived life and certainly a necessity in a love relationship. If our fears remain hidden or if we can't talk about them, then defenses kick in, the most popular of which are to blame our spouse for the bad choices we make and to try to control them rather than ourselves. With blame comes a cessation of growth, because by thus failing to accept responsibility for our behavior, we block our path toward maturity.

A common definition of a wise person is a person who is well educated and knows a lot. That, in our opinion, is not a wise person but a "learned" person. In our opinion, a wise person is one who understands the strengths and weaknesses of humans as a group and of the individuals he or she loves (and, most of all, of himself or herself), and uses that understanding to create meaningful, safe connections between people.

A wise person moves through life without self-delusions or distortions based on fear. In the next chapter we invite you to look at your marriage and divorce and see what went wrong. The goal, of course, is to learn from this examination, not to beat yourself up and feel that you failed. What you learn will help you become wiser in the ways of intimacy and relationships.

When you join your spouse in marriage, you are joining another on a journey on which both of you build character and learn to place your partner above all others. Marriage also requires joint goals, spoken or unspoken. Finally, it requires that you both risk being open. The risk in being open is the vulnerability that comes with it. When a relationship fails, the first thing we rush to do is to shore ourselves up against our sense of vulnerability. We can be crystal clear about the faults of our ex-partner, but it is much harder to be clear about our own contribution. Until we know and can accept what we contributed, we are doomed to repeat the same mistakes. In the next chapter are questions to ask yourself about your responsibility for the failure of the relationship.

# Chapter Four

# | What Went Wrong?

Whenever Bob does custody evaluations, he always sees both parents together for an intake interview. When they are both in the same room together, they offer him an excellent opportunity to see how they interact and what kinds of tactics they use with each other to persuade or intimidate. On those rare occasions when one of the parents is from out of town and a simultaneous intake can't be scheduled, Bob must see the parents separately. When this happens, Bob always finds himself thinking, at least briefly, *My goodness, how did this poor woman ever endure seven years with such a beast!* Then he'll see the other parent a week later and have an initial reaction of, *Good grief! How did this poor man survive seven years with the Woman from Hell?*

When a marriage breaks up, it is very easy to blame the other person because we see his or her faults with utter clarity. It's much harder to look at the contribution we have made, particularly if we feel we have failed or if we are being told in no uncertain terms that we are at fault. In a divorce, to protect yourself from pain, you tend to blame the other guy. Yet, as the joint intake interview proves, it takes two, not just one, to make a marriage fail. Sometimes, of course, one partner might carry the larger responsibility for a failed marriage (in cases of alcoholism or philandering, for instance), but you *did* choose him or her. Understanding why this kind of personality was attractive to you in the first place might help you not to marry another alcoholic or "man [or woman] of affairs" next time.

If you are still frothing at the mouth about that S.O.B. and what he did to you, this chapter may not be for you—yet. Self-examination can be painful when there is a failure of any kind, but particularly so when you look at your love life. Taking responsibility for your contribution requires a level of maturity that we hope you will eventually reach if you are still at the S.O.B. stage. Half the battle, however, is knowing what questions to ask of yourself. If you are uninformed, you can't behave intelligently. What we hope to do is offer you ways to think about what causes marriages to unravel and to ask yourself focused *Is this me?* questions.

## Seven Types of Breakups

Over our years in practice we've often encountered the following general types of breaking up.

### Gradually Drifting Apart

You wake up one Sunday morning and look over at your sleeping partner and realize that this is a really nice person, but you have no sense of attachment to him or her. It's as though you are living with a roommate. You share the same space and feel responsible for it, but as Gertrude Stein said, "There is no there there." It appears as if you have just drifted away from each other. The light went out with a whimper, not a bang. There is little sense of connection, but there is still caring. When a couple like this divorces, the reason they often state is, "We just stopped communicating." There is not so much hostility as there is a sense of emptiness and a lack of connectedness.

### Affair

Some marriages end through one of the partner's becoming dissatisfied and acting out rather than dealing with the problem directly. Acting out is a defensive technique in which a person takes action in response to something without ever talking about it. The spouse who consistently "forgets" to call when she will be late coming home from work is acting out her frustration and anger. The spouse who has an affair is similarly acting out all sorts of unresolved conflicts—including insecurity, alienation, a need for more intimate connection, contempt and hostility, even the desire to inflict pain. When a person is dissatisfied in a marriage, an affair can reassure him that he is still attractive and desirable. It is also a wonderful acting-out way of showing how incredibly angry he is at the other spouse for not meeting his needs—without having to confront her directly. Many people who use affairs to act out ache to be caught, because then the topic of their dissatisfaction is brought forth by the discovery, without their having to say to their spouse, "We need to talk."

## Trauma

In some marriages, the precipitant for a divorce is an unexpected tragedy that drives the spouses apart. Usually it is something that they are not prepared for and have different ways of dealing with; their differences over the crisis gradually pull them apart. A child's death can be a catalyst for such a marital unraveling. Multiple sclerosis can take a terrible toll on a relationship as one partner becomes more incapacitated. Moving, getting fired, earthquakes and fires, all sorts of unexpected trauma can totally disrupt and destroy a fragile relationship.

## Dysfunctional Spouse

In some marriages one spouse either becomes dysfunctional or was always dysfunctional and hid it well until the marriage ceremony was over. Although there are always premarital signs if you know what to look for, domestic abuse often does not emerge until after the marriage has been in place for a while. During a marriage, a spouse may slowly slide into drug abuse or severe depression, or can be chronically unemployed. Usually whatever the dysfunction is, it gradually takes over the marital relationship so that it seems as though one's entire waking life is spent dealing with it.

## Gay Spouse

Ours is a heterosexual culture that places a great many pressures on people who are gay or who suspect they might be. In U.S. society, the worst thing that one boy can say to another is "What a fag you are," and the like. "You are such a dyke!" is spoken as a cutting sneer. Because of the pressures and assumptions in the culture, people are often afraid and unwilling to identify themselves as gay.

They stay hidden in the closet, sometimes so far hidden that they marry. A spouse's gay orientation often leads to sexual problems and frustrations on both sides. And if a spouse decides to come out of the closet, it is usually a shock to the other spouse, who often feels betrayed. Often that spouse also perceives the situation as an assault on his self-esteem: *Why didn't I know that I was making love to a gay person for the past five years? How dumb can I get? What is wrong with my sexual radar?* Further, by announcing his or her true orientation, the homosexual spouse is also usually announcing that the sexual relationship is over. Aside from other difficulties this change may cause, it can also trigger fear (usually unwarranted) on the non-gay parent's part that the gay parent will be surrounded by sexual predators who will groom that parent's children for a sexual encounter. Custody issues can become incendiary.

## Growing Away

This is different from drifting away, but just as compelling a cause in the ending of a marriage. It refers to a relationship in which one spouse grows and the other spouse does not. Usually the realization is sudden. "Jon is so boring; he just wants to fish and bowl. He is so blue collar. My college degree opened doors to me in culture and the arts, and he'll have nothing to do with it. He'll *fish* in Swan Lake, but he'll never go to see it." Whereas drifting away is accomplished by both partners, growing away is one sided. It often happens in marriages where the parties married young, when they were still half-formed in terms of their identity. As they mature, their interests become better defined, and because of the intellectual or personal growth of one of the partners, the original basis for the marriage holds no more. Psychotherapy can also move people to divorce when they realize they entered a marriage for all the wrong reasons. Their personal growth can distance them from the person who stays the same.

## Victimization by a Predator

Occasionally a marriage really does fail because of the "other woman" or "other man." (Think for a minute, though. How often do you hear stories about the "other man" as compared to the "other woman"? We'll bet you hear about the "other woman" ten times more often than the "other man." Does that say something about predatory women, or does that say something about the nature of men and their weakness for sexual enticement? We think it is probably the latter, although the "other woman," not the wandering man, gets the blame.) In this scenario, a spouse is seduced from one relationship into another by whatever offers for bliss hook him. A highly focused, manipulative person who has a single goal, your spouse, often causes the marriage to unravel. This is different from an ordinary affair because in an affair, one spouse goes seeking a relationship. In this case, the spouse is found by someone else and succumbs to his or her blandishments.

The seven scenarios we've discussed here comprise the majority of the apparent reasons for divorce. In the next part of this chapter are vignettes that present each of the scenarios in much greater detail.

## Analyzing Your Role in the Failure of the Relationship

What we would like you to do is ask yourself the following master questions and answer them as they apply to you and your marriage. We also want you to practice by asking the same questions of the vignettes we will give to you shortly. To answer the master questions well, you will have to ask a lot of additional questions.

1. What was the problem?
2. How intense or serious was the problem? Use a scale from one to ten, one being very minor and ten being very, very serious.
3. How did you judge or weigh the problem behavior?
4. How did you interpret the problem behavior?

Now let's see how those questions play out in the following examples taken from our practice.

## Gradually Drifting Apart

Stuart and Grace were married in 1990, and they separated in 1999 after about eight-and-a-half years of marriage. They have two children, Heather, age four, and Carolyn, age eight. Stuart and Grace met in college. She was captain of the girl's volleyball team and took some pride in her partial athletic scholarship in volleyball. She also ran women's track. Stuart played college-level lacrosse and was very active on the college newspaper, where he rose to the position of assistant editor. They met at a freshman mixer and were immediately attracted to each other. People said they were made for each other and that they would have beautiful children. Both were aware of their good looks and used them to advance themselves whenever they could. They were drawn to each other by their enjoyment of people's admiration of them as the "beautiful couple." Both were athletic, Grace more so than Stuart, and both wanted to have careers in publishing.

The beautiful couple had a beautiful wedding, went on a beautiful honeymoon to Yellowstone, and came back to a beautiful little house in Topanga Canyon in Los Angeles. If you think we are overusing the word *beautiful* as we describe these people, you're right—we're doing it on purpose. Stuart and Grace were drawn together by their own narcissism, or self-love. Each saw the other as the reflection of themselves: beautiful, reasonably talented, and pretty successful in what they undertook. Their relationship was based less on a real connection and more on their sense of complementarity. Each saw the other as the black velvet to his or her diamond.

When Stuart filed for divorce, he told his therapist, "I don't know what happened. We just drifted apart." When asked to elaborate, he continued, "I can't say when it began, but I became aware of it when we were giving a dinner party for a couple of authors my company represents. They were in town for a writers' conference, and we had them over for dinner with a few people from the firm. I was sitting at my place at the table and looked down at the other end and saw Grace. It seemed like I was looking at her through the wrong end of the telescope, so small and so far away. Who is she, I thought. I felt no more attached to her than I did to any of the guests at the table. It was like she was no longer my wife but just a friend, and a distant one at that."

In therapy sessions, Stuart further explored what he came to call the Drift. He asked, "How do you drift away from each other? It is so subtle. I think it began when I started with my new publishing house. There was a lot of evening stuff I had to go to, like dinners and meetings with authors, and when the big guys came in from the New York headquarters they expected attention. I started spending many evenings away from home. Grace works for another publisher, so many times she had to stay away from my meetings. Somewhere along the line we just became roommates who had occasional sex. She went her way and I went mine, until we both realized that there was no connection or passion in the relationship."

Stuart could not be more forthcoming than he already was. It was a relationship he had never examined very closely. It was a connection like many others in his life—serviceable, forward moving, but no more important than any other in his life. He loved his girls, but they were largely raised by their mom. In many ways, the cause of his divorce was vague in his own mind, a nothing event. He was reminded of the lyrics of Peggy Lee's song, "Is that all there is?"

Stuart had his defenses up really high when he tried to grapple with the four questions we listed earlier. Each of the four questions will require many other questions to reach an answer. The issue he could not see was that he was so self-absorbed in his own activities and life that he could not see outside of himself to what happened in his relationships with anyone. He did not see people as distinct entities in their own right with thoughts and needs. He viewed them more as characters in a play with scripted parts. They were actors in his play, authored by him. It took several years of intense therapy before Stuart could see that his contribution to the divorce was that he was so self-absorbed that he took from people and could not give.

His wife was programmed the same way; she never protested when he went off to lead his life, because his doing so let her lead her own life with minimal interference yet keep the appearance of the "beautiful couple." Stuart's part in the demise of the marriage was not dramatic; he was no roaring alcoholic or wife beater. It was simply one of self-absorption. Often in cases where the explanation is "We just drifted apart," the root lies with partners who are self-absorbed, narcissistic, and unable to see anyone else's point of view. In Stuart's marriage, both parties were so "me-centered" that they could see nothing beyond their own needs.

Here are some questions Stuart needed to ask and answer about himself to see if the self-absorbed label fits (and these would have to happen fairly frequently, not just once in a while):

- When you get called to dinner or something else, do you respond, "Just a minute, dear," and then arrive ten minutes later?
- Do you want to be the one to name the movie, the restaurant, the concert, the type of car you'll own?
- Do you usually get your way?
- When running family errands, do you go to your places first?
- Do you correct your spouse in public—a lot?
- Do you often fail to hear what the other person is saying because your mind is elsewhere?
- Because you are loved, do you feel entitled to be served in certain ways by your lover?

## Affair

Archie and Sandy had been married about eight years. Sandy was a very dependent woman who relied on Archie for all her needs. Often over breakfast she would ask him what of several things she should do on a Saturday. He would tell her, and she would do them. He approved of all her clothes. He bought all her jewelry as gifts for her, and he set the week's menu at her request. Sandy was a timid soul whom Archie married because she needed him. He grew up being needed, so this was a role for which he was superbly trained.

When Archie was eight, his parents divorced. Actually, his father walked out without a word and disappeared. Mother finally moved for a divorce, but it was some years after her husband had abandoned them. With Dad gone, Archie took on the role of parent. He became his mother's confidant and helpmate. She walked him to and from elementary school before she left for work as a cleaning lady. Until he was ten, he and his mother shared the same bedroom, although not the same bed. Mother said that it was comforting to her to have him close at night because she was a woman living alone. Archie was his mother's best friend. They would go everywhere together and would watch TV together at night. Life was undiluted Mom. As he grew older and reached his teen years, Archie became very ambivalent about his relationship with his mother. She kept him from sports because of a lack of time and money on her part. He became a computer whiz both because it gave him something to do and it did not take him from home where his mother needed and wanted him. He loved her dearly, but he felt he was being suffocated.

At college Archie met Sandy and eventually married her. Sandy fit perfectly into the mold of Archie's mother. She was a timid girl, frightened and overwhelmed by her move from a small farming community into a rather raucous college town. It was with great ease that Archie began to be there for her, helping her out and doing things for her to make her life easier. Sandy was amazed and gratified, for instance, at Archie's cooking abilities. He had cooked for his mom all during his high school. She would come home after a long day of house cleaning, and he would lighten her load by having dinner nearly ready.

With a group of college friends, Archie decided to start a software development company that would make software for small companies. The idea was that the software would walk a naive entrepreneur through all the steps of data collection and bookkeeping that would have to be done to get a small company up and running. Together with his three best friends as major officers in the firm, they hired a young woman with marketing expertise to interpret the company to investors. Anna was a stunning woman, probably perfect for marketing. She dressed fashionably and sharply, had huge violet eyes, and a very articulate way of speaking. After working together awhile, she and Archie began an affair. She was so unlike his wife and his mother. She was independent; she would fit him into her busy schedule for an occasional "roll in the hay" and asked little of him outside of sex. They had fun in that they would do lunch and rent a room, or do after-work drinks and a room, but it never went further than that. Archie had a mistress, and he reveled in it! As Archie put it, "With Sandy I lived life in a very small closet. With Anna it was like living life in a stadium."

Sandy discovered the affair when she glanced at a charge card bill that Archie had thrown out in his study wastebasket. She had begun to suspect something was not right when Archie was often home late, much later than when the company was first starting up and everybody was frantic. There was a cell phone bill. She noticed that there were many calls to a single number, usually just after Archie got out of work. There were also consistent lunch charges at an amount that meant that someone else had lunch too. The clincher for Sandy was that there were restaurant charges to local restaurants one weekend when Archie said he would be on a go-Friday-return-Saturday business trip.

Sandy confronted Archie. She did not order him out of the house or say she wanted a divorce. Her way of handling it was to burst into tears and complain mightily about her victimization. Here she had given him the best years of her life, had trusted him and been faithful to him, and then he destroyed her trust by going behind her back with another woman.

Archie felt very guilty for having been caught, but he was more disturbed about another, equally powerful feeling. He enjoyed seeing Sandy in pain. There was pleasure in seeing her anguish. "What kind of a sicko am I?" was about the third sentence he got out to his therapist. He did not think of himself as a sadist and was made very uncomfortable by his reaction.

Over time, during the course of his therapy, Archie found out a number of things about himself. His affair was a statement of anger against his wife, but especially one against his mother. He felt smothered by these women and cloistered by their dependence and neediness. On the one hand, he liked being champion to a woman in distress, but on the other hand, he hated how smothered he always began to feel as they clung to him. In a sense he was a victim of his own excellence. He was a wonderful caretaker, and his caretaking reinforced and increased the passive dependence of the women in his life. Anna was a breath of fresh air because she made no demands. She just wanted sex and that was it. He did not need to care for her or "do" for her. (For her, he was a penis that happened to have a man attached.)

By having the affair, Archie was making a very angry statement against the smotherers. At one point he observed to his therapist, "Did you ever notice that the word *smother* is just *mother* with an *s* added? Are the gods trying to tell me something?" Although he had had no choice as to the kind of mother he got, he was unaware of the choice he had in terms of what wife he chose. He chose a relationship that mirrored that with his mother. He had been groomed for it, but he had repressed his angry feelings about his role; because his anger was thus unavailable to him, he did not consider alternative relationships. Without recognition of his anger, there was no recognition of how he hated being smothered.

Sandy was consistent throughout her relationship with him; it was he who changed, acting out his anger by the affair. He did not deal with the issue by approaching Sandy directly and saying, "I am feeling smothered in this relationship." He acted out those words and feelings by having an affair and getting caught.

Archie's issue was that he was unaware of his anger. He repressed his anger, so it did not exist. Except of course it did, but out of his conscious awareness. When the pressure became too great on the lid of his angry feelings, the feelings leaked out in the form of an activity, the affair. His actions rather than his words blew the lid off of the way he really felt and finally let him (and Sandy) see it.

Repression is a defense whereby we keep our threatening feelings out of conscious awareness by pushing them down into the unconscious. We protect ourselves when we repress, but the feelings do not go away, nor do they stop influencing our behavior.

If we had asked Archie our four questions, he would have *initially* said, "The problem was that I was bored and needed some excitement in my life without complications. Plain sex with no strings with Anna was wonderful! It was not a huge problem, maybe a 'four,' but it was just something I wanted to do to break the monotony of everyday life. I thought Sandy would never find out and that what she didn't know wouldn't hurt her. I am a very responsible husband and take care of my wife really well. This was just a bit of 'boys will be boys' that went awry."

As you read Archie's position right after the affair was discovered, you can clearly see his repression. If you consider boredom to be an indication that a person does not have the capability to generate his own behavior, then Archie's "boredom" stems from his stifling of his feelings. If he would allow himself to feel, he would be angry, so instead he shuts down and becomes bored. "Sex with no strings" is another giveaway, as it signals, "I want no commitment and no obligation in this relationship." His philosophy of "what Sandy doesn't know won't hurt her" is another sign that keeping things out of awareness is an effective tool in being able to do something without consequences. His "boys will be boys" cliché says, "I am not responsible, my biology is responsible." If we listen closely to what we say, there are clues everywhere as to how we defend against uncomfortable feelings.

With the help of a therapist who did not let Archie get away with his glib clichés and his repression of feelings, Archie would now answer our questions this way: "The problem was huge, a 'ten' because I was so shut off from the way I felt that I was dying a slow death. I did not feel, I just did. As I got in touch with my anger, I began to see how serious this was for me and how self-defeating. I could not deal with it because I would not let myself be aware of it. Talk about an ostrich with his head in the sand! Now I think I understand what I was doing. I needed my mom; she was all I had. The tax I paid for being her son was to find a way to endure her smothering neediness. I chose not to feel, particularly not to feel anger because anger would drive her away, or so I thought. So, to be safe growing up, I had to 'serve and stuff.' Be Mama's little man about the house and not have any feelings about not being allowed to be separate. I learned well because I easily took on the same role in my marriage. As the saying goes, I married my mother. With my new girlfriend I am trying hard to talk about feelings when I first have them. It is hard and I get anxious, but I'm doing it!"

Are you a stuffer of feelings? Here are some questions to ask yourself.

- Do I pride myself on not losing my temper, but when I do, it's a real lollapalooza?
- Do I ever cry at movies? At funerals? Stuffers rarely cry.
- Do I go crazy in the car when somebody cuts me off?
- Do I get acid indigestion or headaches after I have been in a tense situation?

- Do I tend to tell people when they have done wrong, but not when they have done right?
- Do I absorb my spouse's anger at me and withdraw rather than deal with it?
- Do I ever just let go and get silly, exuberant, and childlike?

## Trauma

Betsy and Phil met at an office party. They worked on different floors at work and, although they had occasionally seen each other on the elevator, they really did not know each other until the office party. After the party, it was raining hard, and Phil offered to take Betsy home in his car, as she normally took the bus. They were intrigued with each other; Phil asked Betsy for a date, and that was the beginning of their courtship, which lasted about eleven months.

What attracted Betsy to Phil was that he was the strong, silent type, rather like her father, with whom she had a good relationship. Phil was very attentive and clearly from the old school where men were supposed to take care of women. Betsy did not find this offensive, as did some of her girlfriends, who often said, "I am perfectly capable of opening doors for myself!" Betsy saw Phil's opening doors for her as honoring her, not demeaning her or sending her the message that she was a weakling. She rather liked her place on the pedestal where Phil put her. Further, he liked to hunt and fish and play golf. Betsy saw these as opportunities to be apart where she could have some alone time to do what she called "girly-girl" stuff. For her it was fortunate that canning season and hunting season coincided.

Phil was drawn to Betsy because she fit into his idea of what relationships between men and women should be. He was confused by women who bristled at what he thought was polite behavior on the part of a man. Where he felt he was honoring and showing respect to a woman by standing when they came into a room or holding a chair for them, many women read it as insulting of their ability to be independent. He also liked his freedom to do "guy stuff" without having to barter one fishing trip for one visit to Betsy's folks' place 150 miles from their house. Further, she enjoyed sex and never had a headache. She wanted children, as did he. Both came from large families and thought they had something to pass on, given the good ways in which they were raised.

Within three months of their marriage, Betsy was pregnant, and one year after they were married, Elizabeth Victoria was born, to her parents' great joy. Although Phil teased Betsy by saying that Beth looked like Winston Churchill, he thought she was the living image of her mother and was greatly pleased. Betsy reveled in motherhood, partly because Beth was a "good baby." She was cheerful, slept through the night at three months, and seemed to have no allergies or feeding problems. She felt they were off to a really good start as parents.

As Beth approached her seventh month, Betsy put her down one night and went off to a birthday party of a close high school friend. Phil came along. They left Beth with a sitter, a woman they had worked with in occasional child care for about three months. Betsy had refused to leave Beth with anyone the first three months of her time in the world. They got home around midnight, paid the sitter, and checked on Beth, who was peacefully sleeping on her stomach with thumb in her mouth as always. They went to bed and slept hard. They had had a few beers at the party, nothing extreme, but neither drank much, so when they did, they got a buzz much earlier than their drinking friends.

The next morning, Betsy went into Beth's room and called, "Wake up, Twinkle Toes," and fleetingly thought that Beth must have been tired out from the trip to the zoo the day before, because usually she was awake when Betsy came into the room. Beth did not stir as Betsy drew the blind up and flooded the room with sunlight. Betsy went to Beth and quickly noticed that Beth was slightly bluish in color and had not moved. She bent down to pick her up and realized Beth was not breathing. Her screams brought Phil into the room. "She's stopped breathing!" Betsy cried, and she tried the infant CPR that she had learned as part of her Lamaze class. Phil called 911, and in about ten minutes the house was filled with emergency medical technicians and police. It was the presence of the police that stunned Phil and Betsy. Why the police when they had done nothing wrong?

Beth was dead. It was later determined to be Sudden Infant Death Syndrome. Whenever a child dies, the issue of abuse must be clarified. The baby-sitter was interviewed, and according to her

Beth was alive when she left, which Betsy corroborated. Betsy was beside herself with grief. She blamed herself for having partied and drank. If she had not slept so soundly she might have heard her daughter cry out. No amount of education was ever able to pry her from her guilt that if she had been available, her daughter would not have died. Phil was deeply grieved also, but he and Betsy handled it very differently. Betsy wanted to talk about the death and to reminisce about Beth's short life. Phil withdrew into himself. He did not want to talk. In fact, he was driven off by Betsy's preoccupation with her daughter's death. Betsy felt no support from him. She felt very alone and isolated. In fact, she felt abandoned by Phil. Phil was saying to himself, "Betsy, get a life, get over it." He did not say this to Betsy, but he avoided her. Phil and Betsy divorced about a year after Beth died. They now have no contact with each other.

If Betsy were to answer our questions, she would state the problem as one of Phil's being totally unsupportive of her need to grieve the loss of their daughter. The problem was a "ten," the pain was overwhelming, and Betsy wanted to turn to her husband and the father of her child to grieve. He seemed to have no feelings and just went about his daily routine, sad, but hardly grieving. Betsy judged him as uncaring and unconcerned about her and probably unattached to Beth.

The real issue is not that Phil grieved differently than Betsy, because everyone has his or her own style. The real issue was Betsy's egocentric position that there was only one right way to grieve, which led her to deal with the situation nonconstructively. Perhaps if she had been more tolerant and less rigid about the right way to grieve, she might have been able to address these issues with Phil in a way that would have strengthened the marriage and honored his (and her) uniqueness.

What can Betsy find out from her attitude? If you look carefully, you can see that it's all about her and not about Phil. Phil is to be there to help her grieve. His stoic stance is seen as not grieving, as opposed to grieving in his own way that was different from that of Betsy. In her grief Betsy could not see what she was contributing to the situation. She had married a man's man. As such, Phil was not the type to cry and was much more likely to draw inward and do his grieving quietly and without drama. Betsy could not stop demanding that they grieve on her terms and by her rules rather than realizing that there were two parents with two ways of grieving. Betsy could have learned about herself that when she was under the stress of strong emotion, she tended to see only her side of the issue and her way of solving it.

Further, when Betsy was upset, she required the support of other people and, in that sense, she was dependent. This is not a problem in and of itself; many turn to others to grieve. What was problematic was that Betsy demanded that Phil be like her in his grief. She could not accept individual differences; in fact, she could not tolerate them when she was feeling needy. Phil felt blamed because he was not grieving the right way, and withdrew even further because around Betsy he felt as though he were a bad person.

The following are some questions to ask yourself if your marriage was destroyed by a trauma.

- Can you tolerate differences in handling feelings, or is your way the only right way?
- Do you force-fit your emotions into what you think your gender requires of you—real men don't cry, something is wrong with a woman if she doesn't?
- When you are feeling needy, how do you approach your partner? Do you ask directly for what you need, do you hint, or do you just hope he or she will notice you and read your mind?
- How do you handle strong emotions? Do you hide them, show them all at once, or let them out in bits and pieces?

## Dysfunctional Spouse

Trey and Vivi met in a bar at college. Trey was there with two of his buddies, and Vivi's roommates had coaxed her from her study of organic chemistry to a Saturday night out on the town. She did not do that very much, so it was a real event for her. Trey hit the bars every weekend. When Trey drank, he became Mr. Sociable. He was a good-looking fellow with a droll sense of humor. He was fun to be around. In college, where drinking was an accompaniment to any major form of recreation, Trey fit in with the crowd and drank no more than many of his buddies. Vivi also had a good sense of humor and a rather quick dry wit. She drank socially, but tended to nurse one drink all night long. She wanted to fit in, but as a premed student she needed her "beauty sleep" and an available, functioning brain the next morning. Trey wanted to be in advertising and was majoring in media and communications.

On that first meeting in the bar, Trey and Vivi were drawn together almost immediately. It was neither love nor lust at first sight, but rather a meeting of minds and a fascination with the elegance of each other's thinking. Vivi was a linear thinker. Logic was her strength. Trey, in contrast, was more poetic. He problem-solved by listening to his heart, Vivi by listening to her brain. They proved that opposites could attract.

A relationship developed, and they took an off-campus house with two other couples in their junior year. They decided to marry on the day after graduation in June. The wedding was a big affair. Vivi's parents wanted to "send their daughter off right!" They did so lavishly. Trey was in his element and drank quite a bit. He drank so much, in fact, that he collapsed into bed that night and was out like a light. Vivi had wanted a romantic evening where they could rehash the wedding and have sex to remember because Trey, as he put it, had just "made an honest woman of her." Vivi was forgiving because she knew Trey was happy and excited. There will be other nights, she told herself.

Trey had landed a plum of a job at an ad agency. He was a junior account executive, which he considered as getting a good foot in the door. What he really wanted to be was a creative director for accounts and develop national TV ads. He said his goal was to do a Super Bowl ad that people would talk about for weeks afterward. Vivi had given up her hopes of being a doctor, but had become interested in medical illustration and had landed a job at a company that produced medical books and training films. Hers was a quiet, steady job that she loved for both the solitude and the detail work that was required. Trey, in contrast, was in a world of expense accounts and sales. There were pressures about keeping current accounts happy and cultivating new accounts as well. Further, the company wanted their employees to be visible in the community to get the company name out and to create goodwill and thus possible referrals.

Trey was exposed to the proverbial two martini lunches fairly early in his career. He liked the gentle buzz he was left with after lunch. He also found that liquor really helped dissolve the tensions he experienced in trying to keep his boss and his clients happy. He soon started to stop off at a local upscale bar to "have one for the road." There were other young professionals at the bar, and Trey found himself liking the camaraderie of the other guys, just as he did in college.

Vivi noticed alcohol on his breath when he came home, but she didn't think too much of it because he didn't seem drunk and was usually pretty happy. They had a tradition of having a drink before the meal. Trey would pour, and they would stand around in the kitchen as Vivi prepared dinner and talk about the day. Trey soon added a nightcap before he went to bed.

Time passed, and about six years into the marriage, Vivi began to notice that Trey would have two drinks before dinner and two nightcaps. Essentially he was drinking from the moment he got home to the moment he went to bed. She noticed that he was slow and grumpy in the morning, and one Saturday caught him nipping from a bottle of cold vodka he always kept in the freezer. He just sheepishly laughed and said he needed a bit of the hair of the dog that bit him. Things went from bad to worse, as Trey started to be late for work in the morning and would ask Vivi to call in for him and make an excuse. She did at first, but then became increasingly uncomfortable about lying to cover for him. She begged Trey to cut back on his drinking, but he denied that there was a problem and warned her not to become a nagging bitch.

Vivi became so uncomfortable with her role in protecting Trey from his boss that she went to her doctor to find out more about alcohol abuse. He handed her over to one of his nurses who had previously worked in an alcohol treatment facility. She talked with Vivi a total of three hours over a couple of weeks. What Vivi came away with was that an alcoholic had to want to change. No one could force him. But Trey denied he had a problem. One night, driving home from the train station after his commute from the city, Trey ran off the road, hit a tree, and totaled the car, but escaped with only a few scratches and a bruise on his forehead. He was ticketed for driving under the influence and had his license suspended for three months. Now Vivi had to reorganize their commute so they could go into the city together. After the accident, Trey promised he would change and did for a while, but soon the sound of ice tinkling in a glass was again an all-evening accompaniment. Trey started to miss their 6:00 P.M. rendezvous at the train station, and Vivi would have to pick him up as late as 11:30 P.M. on a work night.

Vivi became desperate, and one night she poured out all the liquor she could find in the house. Trey came home late again in his new car. Vivi had gone to bed because she did not want to have a major fight about the alcohol's being gone. Trey discovered that the liquor cabinet was bare, but found the vodka in the freezer (Vivi had forgotten about that storage place) and drank it. He then went out to find more vodka. On the way back home he was speeding; he took a corner too wide, ran up on the sidewalk, and hit a couple who had just left a late-night diner to walk home. The couple was badly hurt, but no one was killed. Trey was again arrested, and his picture with his car on the sidewalk was on the front page of the local paper the next day.

Vivi was overwhelmed with guilt. *If I hadn't poured out the liquor, he would not have gone out for more and injured those people! I should have forced him to go to AA, but he always refused! I should have noticed things earlier. It's my fault they've been hurt.* In fact, Vivi was not responsible for their injuries. She did recognize that Trey, not she, was not driving the car, but in her heart she placed herself behind the wheel. Although she was not the driver, she felt she was the instigator, somewhat like the little snowball that starts the avalanche.

Vivi left her marriage. She was overcome with guilt about being a link in the chain of events that led to the injury of innocent people. She also saw herself trying to stop Trey from drinking even though doing so was his job, not hers. She felt helplessly responsible and could not stand the relationship any longer. If Vivi were to answer our questions, she would say that the problem was that Trey was an alcoholic and that as time progressed the problem became a "ten." If she were honest she would say that she did not see the problem of Trey's drinking as being particularly serious until the injury accident. She put blinders on because she did not want to deal with it. Trey could be charming, even when he drank, and she had her own life to lead and career to follow.

A truth about Vivi was that when she was confronted with a problem she tended to get passive. She was not simply being conflict avoidant, but problem avoidant. She would put up with a great deal just to get along and make life smooth. If she did this in her next relationship, there could be a repeat.

If you chose or let yourself be chosen by a dysfunctional spouse, here are some questions to ask yourself.

- What head-game did I play with myself so that I could not recognize the signs?
- Did I feel that my love could "cure" all my partner's weaknesses? Where did I get that idea?
- Am I a rescuer? Am I challenged by helping someone get better, particularly if I see him or her as weaker than me?
- Am I attracted to recklessness in other people, allowing me to continue to be good and also watch somebody else be bad?
- Do bad boys or girls intrigue me? Why?
- Do I let others create excitement for me because I would not dare do it for myself?

## Gay Partner

Sharon and Tim met at the Highland Dinner Playhouse. She was in the chorus of *South Pacific,* and he played Lieutenant Cable. Tim was a drop-dead gorgeous hunk of a fellow. He was actually fairly shy when he wasn't playing a role and having his lines scripted for him. Sharon was attractive, but not in the top 10 percent, so she was enormously flattered when Tim started to pay attention to her. As members of the cast, they spent a lot of down time together as they waited for others to rehearse their scenes. Sharon was struck with how well mannered Tim was and how he treated her as an equal rather than as a sexual target for the handsome stud. The relationship developed over the long run of the musical, and when it closed Tim asked her to marry him. It was a bit of a whirlwind courtship, Sharon admitted, but they just seemed made for each other.

They married, and Sharon dropped out of the theater to begin secretarial work. Tim continued in theater and soon moved from the playhouse to a more stable career in the city's repertory theater company, which had been in operation for fifteen years and was very successful.

They wanted children and had two, both boys about a year-and-a-half apart. Getting pregnant was a fairly slow process, partly because Sharon had some minor ovulation problems. She also noticed that Tim did not press for sex too much anyway. He was basically a good lover, but he did not want to make love that often.

When the boys were six and seven-and-a-half, Tim starred in a play in which he was a psychiatrist treating a young man who hallucinated running nude with horses. The young man's role was played by a twenty-eight-year-old newcomer who looked eighteen. They rehearsed fully clothed until close to the opening of the play, when the director said that they would close the set and begin rehearsals with the young man nude so that everyone could get used to the nudity. When they did this, Tim felt stirrings that he had not experienced since his early twenties, when he had experimented with several brief gay relationships for about a year. He had never mentioned that period in his life to Sharon.

The young man was gay, and he and Tim began an affair. Tim felt very wicked carrying on a gay relationship behind his wife's back. He became increasingly depressed and distraught. He stopped having sex with her altogether. She had no idea what was going on, except that she was aware that he was gone from the house more and more and seemed very withdrawn from her. As a father, Tim loved his boys, and was further distraught about what would happen to his relationship with them if his liaison were discovered. He became more involved in the after-hours gay world and became increasingly fearful about being discovered and "outed."

After much agonizing, Tim decided he would make a clean break with Sharon. He now was convinced he was gay. As he put it, "I love Sharon, but I can't make love to her." One evening, after the boys were in bed, he sat down and talked with her about his desire for a divorce and the discoveries that led him to make this request. Sharon was stunned and then outraged. She felt as if she had been duped and used in some sort of a breeding experiment that a gay man, who happened to have married her, wanted to conduct. She wanted him out of the house immediately, to which he agreed.

Sharon thought homosexuality was an abomination and a sin against God. She was particularly afraid that her boys would be seduced and taken advantage of by one of Tim's friends. The boys were confused and distressed by their mother's anger and fear, but still wanted to see their father. The divorce was very contentious and ugly. Sharon asked for Tim's parenting time to exclude any of his friends, but the court refused her request. Tim was very distressed by the sudden publicity his sexual preference was given and deeply hurt by Sharon's turning on him and vilifying him as someone who associated with child molesters.

Sharon and Tim's divorce was what some writers refer to as a developmental divorce. Tim married Sharon at a time in his life when he thought he was heterosexual and had to find out by trying a long-term relationship with a woman. As he got deeper into the relationship, he discovered he was not primarily heterosexual. Technically Tim was bisexual, because he could function with both sexes. It was only through his committed relationship to Sharon that he could discover important aspects of himself. His intent was not to use her as an experiment; at the time he genuinely thought he could make a go of it. The relationship helped him develop to a new level of understanding about himself. At the same time, Sharon was clueless as to what issues were being gradually resolved.

In a situation such as this, both Sharon and Tim could well ask themselves our four questions.

Tim's response was that "the problem was a sleeper. At first it was a zero and then it was a ten. I would have been just fine if I had not started that play with the young man who brought old memories and issues back that I thought were long dead. I guess instead of dead they were just dormant. The problem is that I like men, but I like women too. It just becomes an issue when I switch from one to the other. I should have been honest with Sharon up front before we got married. But then she would not have married me because of how she feels about homosexuality, and my boys would not exist."

You can see that Tim is doing quite a bit of rationalizing and self-justification. His job is to know himself much better, because he could be very hurtful again to someone if he leaves that person for a member of the opposite sex. His gay male partner could be just as devastated as Sharon was about being left. Psychotherapy would be very helpful in his finding his sexual preference.

Sharon's comments were, "I was blindsided! I never suspected he was gay. I was tricked and taken advantage of. The problem was the worst I have ever faced. It was so humiliating! He just used me to get himself children that now he wants to expose to his preda- tor friends, and they will be made gay as well. I don't think he'll personally harm the boys, but his friends will, and he'll be expos- ing them to an abomination in the eyes of God!"

Neither Sharon nor Tim is able to ask and answer the questions in a constructive way. Neither are ready, and both must do a great deal more grief work before they can let go of their "not me" atti- tudes. One hopes that some day Tim can say to himself, I never should have married until I was sure of my sexual orientation. I should have worked that through and then chosen a partner rather than choos- ing a partner and then experimenting. It was not fair to her, nor would it be fair to any children I might bring into the world.

Sharon paints herself as a victim. She is deeply wounded that she could not see that her husband was gay. In addition, her background leads her to think of homosexuality as a sin. This background blinds her to the fact that she had been married for a number of years to a man whom she loved and who loved her. Her reaction is an over- reaction based on her sense of woundedness. It will take her a long time to begin to see Tim as a man and the father of her children who also happens to be bisexual, rather than as a homosexual who used her.

If your marriage fell apart because of a sexual orientation issue, here are some questions you might ask yourself.

- Does anything about the person I loved change now that he or she enjoys sex with people of the same sex? Does the person change or just the target of his or her affection?

- Would I feel differently if my spouse had had an affair with a member of the opposite sex instead of one of the same sex?
- As I look back on our relationship, were there signs and signals I did not pick up on? Why did I not pick up on them?
- In truth, what concrete difference does it make now that my spouse is "out of the closet"?
- Will I ever be able to talk about this without embarrassment?
- How do my children feel? (Make sure that your answer is not just a projection of your own feelings onto them.)

## Growing Away

Louis and Hannah met when he was in his first year of medical school and she was a college senior in the same university. Hannah was in college because that was what her parents wanted her to do and she wanted to marry a college graduate, so going to college seemed sensible. Louis was from the wrong side of the tracks, with a driving ambition to succeed. His goal was to join a prestigious "carriage trade" medical practice in his home city of Chicago and rise quickly in the ranks. Hannah was focused on raising children. Although she was academically bright, Hannah loved kids, wanted a large family, and wanted to be an at-home mom. With Louis on the fast track at work, he would earn enough money for her to stay home and tend to the children. Louis wanted a wife who would be a good hostess and who did not want to work, because that underlined the fact that he was the sole provider.

They married and had three children in the first five years of their married life together. Hannah was in her element. As each of the children entered school, Hannah became involved in his or her classroom. As Louis was able to bring in more money, Hannah enrolled the kids in countless activities. She was the wonder of her friends because she was so involved and so "there" for her children. Louis worked long hours. The firm encouraged its members to become involved in community affairs, especially those that would bring visibility to the practice. Louis sat on the board of a local children's residential treatment center, which took up a few evenings a month; he was also very active in Young Republicans. As a rising pediatrician, he was welcomed to boards because of the expertise, particularly about children, that he brought free of charge.

It seemed almost as if the more Louis got involved in his practice and the community, the more Hannah became deeply invested in her children and their lives. Looking at the relationship, one had the sense that there was a written contract between them. Mom would do home and hearth and dad would go out and slay dragons and bring back large sums of money. As the years passed, each parent became quite skilled in their particular end of the marital bargain.

Once Louis reached partner in the practice, he had more time to devote to his own pursuits, but he found that Hannah was never available because she was so tied down to the children's lives and schedules of appointments. In fact, it was very difficult to do anything spontaneous at all with the family because of the streaming schedule run by one parent, Hannah. Further, Hannah would not accept a substitute for herself. She had given up on trying to hire nannies because they left out of boredom. Louis also began to notice that Hannah really did not follow current events, and even if they watched TV together (not his favorite pastime), she would fall asleep because she was chronically tired. He began to think that he did not have a wife or a helpmate. She was boring, and that is exactly what he said to her when he told her he wanted a divorce. "You are boring. All you do is take care of the children and do laundry. You don't know what is going on in the world, and our kids are so overscheduled we have to plan weeks in advance to go away for the weekend! You are nothing but a kitchen drudge! Our kids have every toy known to man and more designer label clothes than they'll ever need. Get a life!"

Hannah was stunned. She thought she had been doing what they had agreed would be their division of labor in the marriage, and she had done hers very well. Their children were straight-A students, active and popular with their peers, elected to various school posts, and good athletes. She got high praise from other moms for her level of commitment to her children and the product she was turning out—they were good kids!

She realized that Louis was serious. He filed for divorce and moved out of the home. She felt very vulnerable because he was well known and liked in town, and she was neither. Very quickly after the separation, he began to be seen around town at various charity events and social galas with different women, all much more glamorous than she. What turned out to be the catalyst in Hannah's transformation from a scared, shy housewife and mother into a combative, in-your-face mother bear was Louis's statement to her that he was going to ask for a 50-50 split of the children's time, one week with him and one week with her. Hannah's reaction was that Louis was stepping in to take the glory of all the hard work that she had put into raising the children the past ten years. She had poured her heart and soul into her children, and now he was trying to take them away from her. Not only was she being humiliated by being called boring, but her life's focus was being taken away from her. She began to play keep-away from Louis with the kids and made it very difficult for him to see them or to negotiate parenting time changes with her.

About a year-and-a-half after the divorce and three years after the separation, Hannah got to the point where she could begin to do her work. She began by asking questions about how she had contributed to the demise of her relationship with Louis and what mistakes she did not want to repeat with a new person, although there was no one in her life at the moment. She recognized that she and Louis had grown apart. Each had gotten so involved in his or her own life that when one of them wanted to change the rules (Louis), the other was too deeply entrenched in a set of tasks to be able to change quickly. She admitted to herself that there was a kernel of truth in Louis's accusation that she was boring. She was trim and fit, as she exercised frequently and ate right, but her brain focused only on the kids, and her social life revolved around school activities and volunteer work on behalf of her children.

Hannah began to see that she had been blind to the problem because she was subservient in her relationship with Louis. Theirs was a traditional marriage: he was the boss even though she ran the household and raised the kids. Maybe she should have been more outspoken and demanded that he spend time with the children even though he was working hard in the practice to rise in the ranks. She realized that if she had put demands on him related to her favorite task, the raising of the children, he would have pressed her to be more involved in his career development, such as by entertaining more, rather than just dumping her when he reached a new plateau. She had never kept up with him, and that was her fault.

In fact, some of Hannah's absorption in the children may have been driven by her sense of loneliness as Louis relentlessly pursued his career and left her to fend for herself. She told herself that next time she would be more assertive and would demand—nicely, but nonetheless demand—that her husband enter into her world and let her into his. She and Louis never achieved a *We* relationship. She was a prop to his career in that he could say he had a wife and wonderful children to complete the picture of the perfect pediatrician and family man. She raised the kids and liked what she did, but there was no connection with him. She let him use her as a prop. Hannah saw her subservience and her style of going along to get along as flaws within herself. She vowed that never again would she let "go along to get along" happen in her life.

Hannah had another insight. She became so deeply involved with her children because that was all she thought she could do well. By being a good mom, she had isolated herself from adult affairs. In a sense she was hiding from adult-adult contact because she did not see herself as a particularly good thinker or as an independent soul. Her problems stemmed from how she thought about herself as a woman. Where was the women's movement now that she was ready to deal with its issues? What was hard and what slowed her progress in asking and answering her questions was that what Louis had said about her was true. His statements were dripping with contempt and anger, so it took her a long time to deal with his emotional message and move on to looking at the facts.

If your marriage failed because you grew apart, here are some questions to ask so as to understand your role better:

- Did you invest in things outside the relationship to avoid having to deal with issues within the relationship?
- Even though your ex's statements may hurt your feelings, are they true? Why?

- Do you settle for consolation prizes in relationships because you believe you cannot have what you really want?
- Do you get so absorbed in what you like and what you need that you do not have the time or the inclination to participate in doing what your partner likes?
- If you were blindsided by your partner's request for a divorce, what did you do to make yourself blind? Look at yourself, not at your spouse.
- What was the payoff to you for not seeing how precarious things were?

## Victimization by a Predator

Ilona, thirty-seven, and Rory, forty, had been married about twelve years. By choice they had no children, as they felt they would not be good parents. They liked a life that was quiet, structured, and predictable, and having kids did not contribute to that. Both were positioned right about where they wanted to be in the trajectory of their careers, and all was progressing according to plan. They had a dual income that made travel and a beach house quite doable, and in the summer they shuttled back and forth every other weekend to the beach that they both loved. Essentially they were happy with their life and the measured pace at which they chose to live it.

Ilona worked in the risk management department of a large national fast-food chain. She worked on settling claims brought by customers against the company for real, imagined, or manufactured slights or failures to deliver. Along with the in-house attorney, she decided which claims they would settle and which they would fight. She got to do quite a bit of traveling as she conducted on-site investigations and risk management training for the operators of their franchises.

The company attorney she had worked with for about eight years retired. He was a man in his mid-sixties who was a very courtly southerner with a bit of an accent, even though he had not been in the South for thirty-six years. He and Ilona worked well together, and she was sorry to see him retire. To replace him, the founder and chairman of the company selected his own son, Orrin, thirty-four years old, who had majored in corporate law in law school.

When Ilona first met Orrin, she commented to herself, He is like a cat! Indeed he was. His movements were very fluid, almost languid at times. He had piercing blue eyes whose irises were ringed with a darker-colored blue that gave his eyes a rather exotic quality. He had a way of looking at Ilona that flustered her. She joked with herself that she was acting like a schoolgirl, but his stares (they really were not just glances) did unnerve her a bit. She laughingly said to herself, but not to her husband, There might be life in the old girl yet! But Ilona thought of the comment as a joke, because she would never stray from or betray Rory. She was happy with the life and the husband she had.

She and Orrin went on the road together to teach the risk management classes and occasionally to look at facilities where a really serious lawsuit had been filed. After they had been working together for about a year, there was an opportunity for a joint trip to Puerto Rico where some children were claimed to have been hurt on an in-store playground. Orrin teased her and said that she needed to bring her bathing suit because Puerto Rico is balmy in January. It was to be a four-day trip. As was their usual pattern, they arrived midday the day before any meeting just to get acclimated. They both worked quite hard the first three days, but on the fourth day and their last night there, Orrin suggested that to celebrate a job well done they swim either in the hotel pool or the ocean or both. Ilona agreed. They agreed to meet in the hotel lobby in bathrobes and go to the pool. When they got to the pool, Ilona was surprised to see that Orrin was in a very scanty Speedo swimsuit that left little to the imagination. He offered to put sun lotion on her back and the back of her legs. His touch was disturbing to Ilona, but she permitted it. It was very soft and sensual and fit right in with Orrin's other catlike qualities. While it was happening, Ilona's eyes glazed over, and she went limp. His touch was so sensual and relaxing. He suggested that they eat at poolside in their bathrobes and watch the sunset. Ilona asked herself, Is he coming on to me? She convinced herself that he was not and chided herself for getting lost in erotic daydreams, but she had to admit it was nice to know that she was still desirable.

After dinner, they had a nightcap and watched the sunset. Ilona said she had to go to bed to be rested for the trip home, and he agreed. She was a little tipsy, but nothing bad, just loose and re-laxed. Their rooms were across the hall from one another. As they said goodnight to one another, Orrin, still in his Speedo, grabbed her and kissed her full on the mouth. Ilona yielded in his arms while a small voice inside her head said, Don't do this! The voice continued, This is a scene from a really bad bodice-ripper novel. Stop! Something took over and did not permit Ilona to say no, and she and Orrin slept together that night.

The next morning she was filled with guilt and regret. Orrin seemed fine, but he was not married and so had no loyalty bind. Ilona was unsure as to why she let Orrin go so far and was very wor-ried about facing her husband. She felt she needed to tell him be-cause she had never had any secrets from him before and knew that no matter what the consequences of his knowing, she could not bear to hold this secret inside her.

They arrived in Atlanta at noon, and Ilona went straight home. When Rory got home, they exchanged the usual pleasantries, and Ilona shared the working part of the trip. By the end of the eve-ning, before going to bed, Rory sensed something was wrong and asked Ilona if something was bothering her. In response, Ilona's story spilled out like marbles out of a bag. She did not cry—she was too angry at herself. In a sense she had had an affair, but she was not the driving force, just the one who acquiesced. She hated her-self for it and, of course, was worried about Rory's reaction. He be-came very quiet, and teared up but did not cry. He asked for space and slept in the study.

Happily, the one-night stand did not lead to divorce, as both partners felt that it was a signal that something was wrong that they needed to take a look at. Ilona had to ask herself the four ques-tions to see how it had happened. She said, "I never thought there was a problem until I was confronted with the kiss. I guess I was in denial. At some level I knew what was going on, but I just kept won-dering and not making decisions. 'Is he making a pass at me?' is really a different position than 'He is making a pass at me, and I had better do something about it!' I interpreted Orrin's behavior as just flirting—safe flirting. I think I succumbed because I needed to reassure myself that I was still desirable, and frankly, there was a part of me that thought what we did was deliciously sinful! I am thirty-seven years old and still attractive to a younger man. My life was so measured and controlled and boring. I thought it was what

I wanted. I've got to build some spice into Rory's and my life, or I may fall off the fidelity wagon again."

Rory and Ilona were able to mend their marriage by themselves. At first Rory was skittish, Ilona guilty. Their initial talks were very brief. They agreed they would set aside Friday nights to talk with each other for an hour—Friday because it was the beginning of the weekend, so if there was emotional fallout they would have time to recover before work, and one hour because they knew it would not be an "eternity." Both agreed that married life had become pretty routine and dull. They were roommates rather than husband and wife. Their desire for routine and predictability had taken them too far into dullness. Both agreed they should "break out of the box." Each week they agreed to try something new, be it a restaurant, play, movie, or concert. They would not go to the beach this year, but rent a motor home and "do" Canada. It worked. Rory had been sexually remote, but after a particularly hilarious play one evening, they fell into bed and started fooling around. It was fun, and they welcomed each other back into the relationship.

If you have been vulnerable to seduction, ask yourself the following questions. First, however, make sure that you are the one being seduced and not the seducer as defined in the affair section of this chapter.

- What is missing in my life that I hunger for?
- Why do I need to be reassured that I am desirable? Why don't I believe that without a concrete demonstration?
- Why can't I believe myself when I say I'm OK?
- Is my life in a rut? If so, why, and what can I do about it?
- What stops me from doing things that please me and make me feel good about myself?

## Points to Ponder

Robert Burns said, "Oh would some power the gift give us to see ourselves as others see us." This lament written in 1786 is still valid today, and this chapter has attempted to address it. Never assume that your ex is seeing you totally accurately, but do assume that within his or her complaints and accusations there are kernels of truth. When issues are flung at you frosted with anger, loathing, or contempt, your natural tendency will be to dismiss them out of hand and protect yourself. We are asking you to look at the charges and find the kernels of truth. It may take some time for the sting to wear off before you can deal with the issues. That is why we said at the beginning of the chapter that you might not yet be ready for this task.

Many of the people in our illustrations dealt with their issues in psychotherapy. Not everyone will need to do that, but psychotherapy and divorce support groups can be very helpful in the task of asking the hard questions about your contribution to the unraveling of the relationship. Divorce hurts, and when we are hurt we protect ourselves by saying some variation of "I am fine. You are not fine!" Perspective comes when the hurt and its attendant emotions calm down, allowing us to see things more clearly.

If you finish this chapter and say, "I did nothing to contribute to the demise of the relationship," reread the chapter! Once you are able to identify your contribution to the unraveling of your relationship, you can learn to avoid making the same mistakes twice. One way to do so is to understand how to communicate and fight fair in future relationships. These skills are the topic of our next chapter.

# Chapter Five

# Talking and Fighting: Crucial Skills in a Marriage

The two most important skills you need to create and maintain a mutually satisfying relationship with another person are the ability to communicate successfully with each other and to use effective conflict resolution when you do not agree. Unfortunately these skills are not commonly taught in school, and many of us have not had them modeled for us by our parents. As we have seen in the previous chapters, our family background, expectations, and conscious and unconscious teaching greatly affect our attitudes and behaviors in marriage and relationships. Our conscious and unconscious needs motivate our choice of partners, our treatment of our spouse, and our reactions to the other person. Unless you have learned effective communication skills, you will probably talk to your partner in the same way that your parents talked with each other and to you.

Think about how your parents communicated. Was there nagging, sullen withdrawal, bickering, loud fighting and screaming at each other, or even physical violence? Have you experienced this same pattern in your marriage or in other relationships? We have found in our practices that a common cause of divorce is poor communication and the inability to resolve disputes in a principled and collaborative manner.

Many couples could have avoided divorce and might have created enriching marriages if they had only known how to talk with each other and to resolve differences that arose between them with understanding, compassion, and empathy.

When parents are not communicating and thus not on the same page of the "parenting handout," their children suffer. Therefore, not only does a lack of communication have an impact on the couple, there is a strong trickle-down effect on the kids. Because we also work with many parents in mediation after their divorce, we observe that when parents can't communicate with each other effectively, they have difficulty parenting together. The children ultimately suffer.

In this chapter, we discuss the "dynamic duo" of talking and fighting, which lie at the heart of all relationships. By learning to talk and also to fight well, you increase your likelihood of success in your next committed relationship, in your relationship with your ex-spouse, and in your other personal and professional relationships.

## How to Talk with Each Other

In this section, we suggest some basic rules of communication that, if followed, will dramatically improve any of your relationships.

### Rule 1: Set Aside Time to Talk

A common complaint among couples is, "He just doesn't 'hear' me." What the person is actually saying is, "He just doesn't *understand* me." We all need to be understood by the other people in our lives. And because our intimate relationships seem to offer the greatest opportunity for true understanding by another person, we expect our partners to make an effort to understand us. We want to share all our desires, fears, concerns, needs, intentions, day-to-day happenings, life history, and so on with our partner, and we want him or her to care about these things as much as we do.

During a marriage, the partners often stop sharing themselves with each other. We've all seen couples in restaurants eating their dinner in silence as if their dinner companion wasn't even there. We assume that they are an "old married couple," old not in age but in length of marriage. We've probably also found ourselves in that situation, at least occasionally. What happens to couples who, when they first fell in love, couldn't stop talking together? In fact, that is often one reason the relationship flowers, "because he's so easy to talk to." We feel understood; we feel valued and important. Can we maintain that level of intimacy found in the early stages of romantic love?

Consider Jane and Harold. They had been great college chums. They were friends in a larger group of friends that did everything together, but were not romantically involved. When Harold told a joke, he could count on Jane to be the first to laugh because they had similar senses of humor. Many evenings they stayed up late sharing their latest ideas gleaned from their college courses and the insights about life that burst like fireworks in the heads of university students. When they realized that they were actually interested in each other romantically, they were shocked. As best friends, they had enjoyed the easy camaraderie and intimacy that they thought might be threatened by a romantic relationship. However, Harold convinced Jane that they should try "going out," and if it felt too "weird" they would chalk it up to an interesting experience and go back to being best friends. They were delighted to discover that their friendship had blossomed into a love that was both sensual and secure. They married and settled in to live happily ever after.

But as we are reminded in Chapter Two, there is no absolute happily ever after. Marriage and long-term commitment take work. As Jane and Harold each started careers in academia, the demands of "publish or perish" caused them to spend very little time together. They stopped sharing all their new insights; they became insulated in their own little worlds, much as the students insulated themselves in their carrels in the university library. They had become the "old married couple" who had nothing to say to each other at dinner. And yet both were involved in intellectually exciting research and teaching; they had plenty to say to their colleagues and students.

The routine of their lives and the chores and home maintenance had intruded into their "couple time." Not until they realized that they were drifting apart did they begin to make the effort—and at first it was an effort—to purposefully talk to the other about their happenings, thoughts, and discoveries and to listen to the other. Once they began setting time aside with the intention of communicating even just the mundane happenings of their lives to each other, they began to feel more connected to each other and were able to restimulate their loving feelings.

## Rule 2: Make an Effort to Understand Your Partner's Reality

Intention to communicate with our partner is the key to a vital, intimate relationship. We must share who we are in the here and now and listen and receive that same sharing from our partner. But you might say, "I really wanted to communicate with my ex when we were married, but she just wasn't there for me." Perhaps not, but we'll repeat the mantra of this book: What was your role in the problem? How were *your* communication skills? Could you do better next time to nourish communication between you and a romantic partner?

We look to those closest to us for affirmation about our perceptions of the world and of our experiences. When our mate sees the world differently, we don't feel as secure as we would like and need. In order to regain that interpersonal security, we must connect to our spouse by acknowledging that *he [or she] is not me.* We are separate people who express ourselves differently, perceive the world around us differently, and react differently. Our goal is to understand our mate's reality. If our main goal of talking with our spouse is only *to be understood,* we will miss the opportunity to make a connection with another person. What is essential to our relationship is also that we are able *to understand.* After all, the purpose of communication is a mutual sharing with another person, not just a one-way street. But often the way that we "communicate" gets in the way of being understood, and prevents the other person from comfortably sharing his or her own self with us.

## Rule 3: Stop, Look, and Connect

You've probably said of someone, "He's an excellent communicator," meaning that he speaks well and articulately. He makes his points effectively and in an interesting and perhaps humorous manner. He *talks* well. Ironically, however, the most important communication skill is *listening.* Sitting and talking to someone who is really listening and trying to understand you feels so good; you feel comfortable with that person, at first sharing superficial things, but later moving on to deeper and perhaps more painful or embarrassing feelings. You will only feel understood when someone has truly listened to you.

Listening is more than *hearing,* which is a passive activity. Our ears pick up sound waves, and our brains interpret those waves into noise, music, words, and sentences. *Listening,* in contrast, is a very active process. It is more than merely hearing the words and sentences that someone is uttering. It is also more than looking at the other person, nodding your head from time to time, and saying, "Uh huh" and "Yes." You've probably heard of active listening, which is a model of listening that requires the listener not only to hear what the other person is saying but also to reflect back what the listener heard. Our messages always contain a substance or content component and a feeling component. Only when the listener gets both parts of the message right do we feel heard.

Nate and Sylvia had been married for ten years. One evening at dinner, Sylvia noticed that Nate hadn't eaten much and seemed distracted. She asked him if anything was wrong. He replied with a tinge of anger and sadness that he had found out today that his boss was retiring and that the company was going to do a national search for a replacement. Because the two of them had often discussed Nate's job situation, Sylvia had a clue as to Nate's feelings.

"You've enjoyed working with George [his boss], and you're sad that he's leaving," Sylvia said. "Are you also disappointed that they seem to be overlooking you as a replacement? I know that you had really hoped for a promotion when George retired."

Nate sighed, and said, "Yes, it just doesn't seem fair. I've been a loyal employee, and now they're going outside the company to hire. I've put up with a lot of hassles because I knew that I could do George's job when he retired." Because Nate felt that Sylvia understood not only what was happening at work (the substance) but also his resentment and fear about it (the feeling), the couple was able to continue discussing the situation and Nate's options. Listening with active reflection and empathy, showing that the listener understands how the other could be feeling the way he or she does, creates understanding and a willingness to continue sharing.

Compare that interchange with another between Sylvia and Nate. One day as they were driving into town to do some shopping, Nate said, "I hate these ugly condominiums that are going up on the old Thompson farm. Those developers should be shot!" Sylvia was mentally reviewing her grocery list and said, never looking up, "Uh huh, but what can you do?" Nothing else was said until they got to the market.

Did Nate feel heard? Probably not. Is this one instance of not being heard going to disrupt their marriage? Probably not. But if you add up all the many times that spouses don't respond to the other's seemingly innocuous statement or piece of information, the immensity of the lack of communication becomes staggering.

John Gottman, author of *The Relationship Cure*, calls these attempts to make connection with our partners "bids." Even a simple statement, such as the one Nate made about the condominiums, or a look or a touch, is a request to be connected to the other person. By responding to these bids with mindfulness, we build the trust, caring, and understanding that will be needed when the difficult issues arise. It's what Gottman and Silver call "an emotional bank account" (pp. 83–86). This is an important concept to remember in all our interpersonal relationships with colleagues, friends, and children, and especially with spouses.

A simplistic example of a "bid" is how one of Christie's little dogs, Jo-Jo, periodically comes over to her when Christie is working on her computer. Jo-Jo stands on her hind legs and begins scratching at Christie's lap, asking to be picked up. Christie acknowledges Jo-Jo, picks her up for a moment, and puts her down again. Jo-Jo is satisfied with the attention that she received. Her "bid" was responded to. Of course, a partner's needs for connection are even more important to attend to.

If a spouse continually fails to respond to our bids for connection, we eventually stop offering them. We shut down. We must also respond in a genuine and active way to what our spouse says. Just any old response, however, will not foster communication and understanding. There are ways of responding that can get in the way of effective communication, as we discuss in our description of Rule 4.

## Rule 4: Advise Only When Asked, or Ask First and Advise Second

One common mistake in listening is to try to solve the person's problem (as perceived by the listener) rather than focusing on what the person is saying. What would have happened between Nate and Sylvia if she had responded to Nate's information about his boss by saying, "You need to get your application in as soon as possible so that they'll know you're interested in the job"?

That may be what Nate needs to do, but his feeling about the situation would have been ignored. Jumping into problem solving and offering advice before the speaker is ready leaves the speaker feeling unheard.

There may be a gender difference in the propensity for this behavior. Deborah Tannen, author of *You Just Don't Understand* and other books about gender differences in communication, observes that women talk to be understood and to talk about a problem out loud, whereas men want to take action and solve problems. This difference often results in misunderstanding between couples.

Let's look at another interchange between Nate and Sylvia. At dinner one evening, Sylvia tells Nate about an incident with a coworker that disturbed her. The coworker had taken credit for an idea that Sylvia had actually come up with to increase the productivity of the human resources department in her company. "I couldn't believe it! How could she do that?" she exclaimed. Sylvia continued to describe the coworker and other things that she had been doing recently.

Nate, who had sat silently eating his dinner, finally said, "Well, it's clear what you need to do about this," and went on about the course of action that she should take. Sylvia finally jumped up from the table and exclaimed, "I'm no dummy. I'm tired of you telling me what to do," and then stormed out of the room. Nate was flabbergasted. "What's wrong with her now? I was only trying to help," he thought to himself. They didn't talk to each other for the rest of the evening.

What happened here? Sylvia just wanted to tell Nate what was going on with her and how she felt about it. She wanted her feelings of shock, anger, and surprise to be understood. She wanted empathy about what she was going through. Nate thought that the bad situation needed to be fixed, and he had the solution. The two of them experienced a "failure to communicate": they totally missed each other. Sylvia wasn't asking for a solution or for Nate to fix anything, and Nate wondered why she brought it up if she didn't want his help with the situation. Although this is an example of the classic gender-based difference in communication style, there certainly are women whose style is to try to offer solutions, and men who are very empathic. The point is *to refrain from offering advice unless asked*—or at least to wait to offer advice until after you have actively listened to the other person's story and empathized with the person's feelings.

## Rule 5: Do Not Interrupt—You'll Get Your Chance

Interrupting each other is also a common listening problem. In our work in mediation with divorcing couples, we always suggest the guideline that both spouses will not interrupt each other. Some couples are able to discuss their issues and work on joint decision making with little or no interrupting, but many, especially the very high conflict couples, seem incapable of letting each other finish a statement or a thought without interrupting. They acknowledge that this is the way they have always communicated—and that it hasn't worked.

It's true that in some cultures, talking at the same time, talking over each other, and interrupting are common and the norm. Unless all parties to the conversation have the same style, however, constant interruption is a barrier to effective communication. The person who is interrupted does not feel heard or understood because he or she never gets to finish a sentence or a thought. And the interrupter usually is busy trying to respond to what the other is saying and thus is not letting the speaker know that he or she has been heard.

In formal meetings, only one person "has the floor" at a time, as we can't hear and attend to more than one or two speakers. A chairperson decides who has the floor and can talk at any given time. A common technique in more consensus-oriented groups is to use a "talking stick" or other physical object to denote who has the floor. The parties all agree that only the person with the talking object (a stick, a feather, a small piece of sculpture or rock) gets to talk. That person gets to talk until he or she is done, then passes the object to the next person who wants to talk. As is true of all communication processes, these methods of talking and listening work only if the parties agree to follow the rules.

Almost all couples' groups and classes teach methods of talking and listening to their participants. In one variation of exercises to practice these listening skills, the speaker says something, the listener says what he heard, the speaker speaks again, the listener again reflects back what he heard, and so on, until the speaker is done. The listener continues to ask "Is there more?" until the speaker is done. Then the listener will make some sort of empathic statement, such as, "I can understand that you would feel [insert a feeling word] about [whatever is going on]." Then, if and only if the speaker has nothing else to add, the listener will respond with what she wants to say about the topic, and the new listener will again reflect back. It's harder to do than it sounds, certainly at first, because we are conditioned to try to have an interesting or witty response to what others are saying. However, the goal is to let the other be understood before we respond to his or her statements.

Here's an example of this listening model:

*Sylvia:* I saw Mary today, and she looked like she had gained twenty pounds. I couldn't believe it!

*Nate:* You were surprised to see that she had gained twenty pounds?

*Sylvia:* Yes, she's always been so trim and healthy looking. But she was pale, and her face was puffy.

*Nate:* She's always looked so slim and healthy.

*Sylvia:* Yeah, I'm worried about her. What do you think could be the matter?

*Nate:* Well, I don't know. If her face is puffy, she may be on some sort of medicine that's causing it.

*Sylvia:* You think it could be a medicine?

*Nate:* Yeah, my friend George was on a steroid that caused him to gain weight and very noticeably in his face.

Conversations would certainly be long and stilted if this were the only way we communicated. But it illustrates that listening takes time, is active, and doesn't involve cross-examining the other or solving the problem. Nate really wants to hear the full story that Sylvia wanted to tell him. Compare it with the following:

*Sylvia:* I saw Mary today, and she looked like she had gained twenty pounds. I couldn't believe it!

*Nate:* Where were you—at the market? Did you get the tomatoes?

*Sylvia:* Yeah, I was at the market, and I *did* get the tomatoes, but I'm really worried about Mary. She—

*Nate:* You always worry about everyone. We're all putting on weight. I read in the newspaper that people put on a pound a year after they hit twenty-five. So of course she'd be heavier.

*Sylvia:* Well, of course, but it's not that. She didn't look good, she—

*Nate:* Yeah, I know what you mean. She's always been a damn good-looking woman. Remember that bikini she wore to the club picnic two years ago? Every guy in the place had their eyes on her.

*Sylvia:* I'm so tired of you turning everything into a discussion about sex. That's the only worth a woman has to you—how she looks. Why are you with *me,* anyway?

So now Nate and Sylvia are off and running in a fight. Sylvia's concern about Mary's health is totally forgotten. Unfortunately, this type of conversation is common. We often rush to respond or to give our opinions. When we don't try to listen to all of what our spouse is saying—both the content and his or her feelings about it—we discount their thoughts and feelings.

## Rule 6: Comment on What You Observe to Find Out What Really Lies Behind the Words

We also need to observe our partner's nonverbal behavior as she talks to us. Does what she is saying match her facial expressions, the tension or relaxation in her body, and so on? We all have looked at our partner and, just by the set of her mouth or the way she is moving, known that something is going on with her. We may ask, "What's wrong?" When our spouse says, "Nothing," we disagree and say, "No, you're not telling the truth. I know something's going on—what is it?" We've learned that the question "What's wrong?" is likely to be answered with "Nothing," whether asked of spouses, children, or friends. A clear message that states your observation with a concern is more likely to get an honest answer. For example, a better question than "What's wrong?" might be, "I noticed that you have a frown on your face. Is anything going on?"

## Rule 7: To Get Better Information, Ask Open-Ended Questions

One of the best responses that a listener can give is "Tell me more." It lets the speaker know that the listener is interested and engaged, and cares about what the speaker is saying. These words can also be attached to a statement or concern—for example, "Tell me more about how Mary looked to you." This invites a narrative response rather than a quick factual answer. "Her skin was pale, and her face was really puffy, especially her eyes. She almost couldn't see through them; they were just slits. And her fingers and ankles were really puffy like she was bloated." If Nate had asked, "Was her skin pale?" Sylvia might have answered, "Yes, sort of." The flow of information is more limited with direct questions.

The listener should also try to avoid asking yes-or-no, either-or questions. When we ask our child, "How was school today?" ninety-nine times out of a hundred we hear, "Fine." If we follow up with "Did anything interesting [or exciting or unusual] happen?" the answer is likely to be no. But if we ask instead, "What happened today in English class when you presented your book report?" you may get a little story about your child's presentation.

In legal terms, yes-or-no questions are called leading questions. One of the skills of a trial lawyer is to know when to ask open-ended questions ("Tell me what happened when you saw the car") or leading questions ("Isn't it true that you screamed when you saw the car?"). Leading questions are designed to get the answer that you want. The lawyer skilled in the art of cross-examination depends on knowing the answer to each of the questions before she asks it and gets out only those facts that she wants the judge or jury to hear.

Cross-examination effectively builds a court case, but it is devastating to communication because the questioner doesn't really want to learn any new information, thoughts, or feelings from the person answering. In contrast, an open-ended question is designed to get information and a story told. The artful use of open-ended questions is actually a skill of *listening* rather than of speaking.

Therapists almost always ask open-ended questions in order to get their clients talking. "And when that happened, what were you thinking?" In mediation, we also ask many more questions than we make statements. Questions should open people to creativity and to learning something about themselves and their own situations that they may not have considered previously. Later in this chapter, we'll see how questions can be used effectively in resolving conflicts, but now we are focusing on the use of questions in communication.

Another type of question that is very helpful is the one you ask to determine if you understood correctly what was said to you. For example, asking, "Are you angry because you need . . . ?" lets the speaker know that you were trying to understand not just that he was angry but *why* he was angry. So a skilled listener not only reflects back what was said but also may take it another step to understand the *need* that the speaker is expressing. In our earlier example, Nate could have responded to Sylvia, "I see that you are really worried about Mary and need to know if anything is going on with her health," to let her know that beyond just the facts, he also heard the feeling (worried) and the need (to know).

## Rule 8: Be Sensitive to Your Body Language—It Speaks Volumes

When we listen, ideally we also give the speaker nonverbal cues to let her know that her statements are worth attending to. Nonverbal cues differ by culture and gender, but in general, we look directly at the speaker, usually making some sort of eye contact. We may nod our head occasionally, and even say "umm hmm" or utter little noises that just show that we are listening. When we are giving the speaker our full attention, we are not thinking about what we plan to say next. Although a conversation is sometimes seen as a game of catch—I throw my statements to you, you catch them and then throw statements back to me; I catch, respond, and so on—good listening involves much more than simply responding to the other person. When we are listening with empathy and attention, our "catch" is to let the other know that we heard him, are empathic, and are anxious to hear him say more.

## Rule 9: Be Sensitive to Your Partner's Body Language—It Speaks Volumes

It's hard to talk to someone who doesn't appear to be listening. In relationships, it's important to stop what we're doing when our partner is talking, look at him, and let him know by our responses that we are listening.

After four months of marriage, Laura insisted that she and her husband Mike go to see a counselor because Mike "never listened" to her. Mike said he did, that he heard every word she said. But when they began discussing the issue with the counselor, it became clear that although Mike may have physically heard Laura with his ears, he hadn't been truly *listening* to her, as we have defined listening in this chapter.

For example, when Mike came home from work, he would give Laura a kiss, ask "How was your day?" and then pick up the mail and begin opening and reading it. As Laura would begin to answer him and tell him about her day, he would sort the mail and toss the letters and advertisements that he didn't want, walking back and forth between the credenza where he was sorting the mail and the recycling bin. Without saying anything, he would then go into his study to change his clothes. When he came back into the kitchen to help prepare dinner, he would begin telling Laura about his day, making no comments about what she had told him.

Except at meals sitting at the table, Laura had to follow Mike around and talk to his back because he wouldn't stop and attend to what she was saying. He was the master at multitasking, always doing at least two things at once: reading his e-mail while talking on the phone, brushing his teeth while straightening his study, listening to Laura while he sorted his papers.

The counselor worked with Laura and Mike on the basic listening and communication skills that we've been discussing in this chapter, and the couple was able to make a fresh start in their marriage. It was hard at first for Mike to stop what he was doing to give Laura his full attention, and it was hard at first for Laura to ask gently for Mike's full attention when she wanted to talk. But because they were motivated to stay married and communicate with each other effectively, their new skills helped them create intimacy and closeness between them.

We see many similar divorcing and divorced couples in our practices for whom poor communication skills contributed to the demise of their marriages. Good communication skills would have smoothed the way to self-understanding and understanding their partners.

Lilac and Jonah experienced their first married disagreement when Jonah exclaimed loudly to Lilac one morning when getting ready for work, "Why can't you put the cap back on the !X%^\*#! toothpaste and roll the tube from the bottom? I can't believe you are so self-centered." Lilac was stupefied! Her quiet Jonah had become a raving monster over the toothpaste! But Lilac was also a skilled listener. Instead of defending herself—"How dare you curse at me and tell me I'm self-centered. Who in this relationship has moved halfway across the country for the other partner's job? ME!"—she initiated this conversation:

*Lilac:*  You're really angry that I didn't put the cap back on the toothpaste tube.

*Jonah:*  You bet I am. The top of the toothpaste is always dried out. I can't stand that crust on the top. And you always squeeze it in the middle. What a mess! Don't you care that it's always messy and hard to get out?

*Lilac:*  It really bothers you that the toothpaste is always messy and crusty. You'd like to find a neat toothpaste tube when you go to use it.

*Jonah:*  Yeah. It's gross. And all that hair stuff and makeup all over the counter. I feel like I have no space. At least my toothpaste could be right.

*Lilac:*  You need a neater space when you dress?

*Jonah:*  Yeah. You know, I've never had to share a bathroom before. I really need some sense that this is my bathroom, too.

*Lilac:*  Jonah, I understand you need some bathroom space of your own. I've sort of taken over, haven't I? I'm sorry. Poor baby—sharing your bathroom for the first time with all this girly stuff—and look at those pantyhose hanging on the towel rack. I can see how you must feel like you've been invaded by aliens. Is there anything else about the bathroom that you want to tell me before we talk about what to do about it?

*Jonah:*  No, I think you've got it. Thanks for listening to me. I can't believe I blew up about such a little thing.

Now Lilac and Jonah were on their way to resolving the bathroom issue. Reading Jonah and Lilac's conversation, you may think it sounds stilted. You may be able to invent better dialogue using the principle that you nondefensively reflect back what you have heard. Trust us, it talks better than it reads!

## Rule 10: Empathize with Your Partner

Notice what else Lilac did in her listening. She not only tried to understand what Jonah was saying and why but also empathized with him. Sometimes we confuse empathy and sympathy. Empathy is not sympathy or feeling sorry for someone: "Oh, I'm so sorry that happened to you." Empathy is trying to understand and put yourself in the shoes of the other person—to see through her eyes: "Oh, I know how sad you must be that . . ."

If at the end of listening to your partner, you can empathize with what she is telling you—even if she is attacking you—then you have opened the door to effectively resolving the issue and to being heard yourself. Lilac's statement "Poor baby" could have been seen as patronizing or just giving sympathy, except that she followed it up with statements that showed that she really understood how difficult it was for him. Everyone wants to be understood. If Lilac had brushed off his complaint with "What a petty thing to be so upset about! All couples have to learn to adapt to each other's stuff. I don't like finding your whiskers in the sink every morning either, but tough, I'm not yelling at you about it," Jonah would not have felt understood, and his concern would have been trivialized. Because Lilac was able to contain any frustration or defensiveness she was feeling, she was able to listen to Jonah. This is an extremely difficult part of listening: getting out of the way and focusing on your partner. Stick with the topic that the speaker has raised and go on to something new only when both of you feel that the speaker has been heard and now wants to hear from the listener.

## Rule 11: Use "I" Statements, Not "You" Statements

Once you have listened to and understood the other person, you can respond. It is important to stay with the topic raised by the speaker until it feels reasonable to go on to something new. It also is important always to speak only for yourself. This is called making "I" statements. Instead of saying, "You don't listen to me" (with emphasis on the *you*), an "I" statement would be, "I don't feel understood." Instead of "You don't take me out to dinner anymore," an "I" statement is "I really like to go out to dinner with you and would like to do that more often." It is easier to hear another person and to respond lovingly and nondefensively when the statement comes from the "I" place rather than the "You" space.

Dr. Marshall Rosenberg has developed a process of communication that he calls nonviolent communication or compassionate communication. In his book *Nonviolent Communication,* he combines many of the basic tenets of communication into a four-step model. In his model, we first state our observation about what is happening, without any judgment, using our five senses. Second, we state our feeling about that observation. Third, we say what our need is regarding that feeling. And fourth, we make a request based on our observation, feelings, and needs as stated.

For example, Laura, instead of complaining to Mike that he never listened to her, could use Rosenberg's model, saying the following: "When you ask me 'How was my day?' and I begin to tell you and you continue to sort the mail and not look at me [observation], I feel discounted, unheard, and uncared about [feeling]. When I talk to you, I really need to feel understood and listened to [need]. Would you be willing to stop what you are doing and listen to me when I am telling you about my day?" [request]. Notice that she is not nagging him (which is what Mike had been feeling), nor is she demanding that he pay attention to her. Mike is free to respond to her request. This model of communication (which, of course, has much more depth than this simple example) provides an opportunity to the listener to hear what the speaker is saying without being threatened and to respond to the request.

## Rule 12: Respect Your Listener's Time, Energy, and Skills

When you are talking to someone about a concern or just telling a story, it's important that you don't go on and on. You need to let the listener paraphrase and do active listening. You need to make sure that you are being heard. People tend to tune out long monologues after a while. Have you ever noticed that often people who say, "To make a long story short . . ."—don't? Usually they just make short stories longer and more boring. Especially when talking to your partner, you need to come up for air in your talking and allow your partner to participate in the discussion.

When you have a partner who doesn't seem to have good listening skills, you may have the urge to try to get in as much as possible before she changes the subject or begins tuning you out. However, this technique is counterproductive. You can always stop talking and say, "I'm not sure you've heard what I'm saying. Would you mind telling me what you've heard me say?" to determine if you have been heard.

Obviously, good communication is easier when both partners have learned some of the same techniques. Marriage preparation classes often teach basic communication skills that provide a common vocabulary and model to use. But even one person trying to use good listening and communication skills can have a major impact on the communication in a relationship. Your goal must be to *intend* to understand the other and to connect with him through listening and self-disclosure rather than to prove that you are a paragon of good communication and that he is a dolt.

### Questions to Ask Yourself About Your Communication in Your Marriage

- Did you habitually fail to respond to something that your spouse said, or just nod or say "uh huh"?
- Did your spouse tell you that you didn't understand him?
- Would you become defensive if your spouse expressed a complaint?
- Did you use the words never and always when complaining about your spouse's behavior?
- Have you ever said, "I know just how you feel. That happened to me," and then launch into your story before responding to your spouse's feelings with empathy and caring?
- Have you ever jumped in to give advice to your partner before she asked for it?

**Pitfalls to Avoid in Listening and Talking with Your Partner**

- Not making eye contact
- Making faces (rolling your eyes, for example) that convey a message of boredom, disgust, impatience, and the like
- Not giving your partner your full attention
- Rebutting what your partner is saying before fully exploring the substance of the message or your partner's feelings and needs
- Interrogating—asking too many questions to get "all the facts, Ma'am, just the facts"
- Giving advice
- Interrupting
- Getting defensive

In other words, follow the communication rules!

## How to Resolve Disputes Together

The ability to effectively manage conflict in a marriage is crucial to the survival of the relationship. As we have seen, the skills of listening and empathic responding contribute to building intimacy and safety in a relationship. These skills are also the basis of effective conflict management in a relationship. In fact, some researchers, such as Howard Markman, a professor at the University of Denver and the coauthor of *Fighting* for *Your Marriage* and other books about marriage, state that they can predict which marriages will succeed and which will fail simply by observing how the couple handles conflict. Differences in background, temperament, and education are less important than whether a couple can effectively discuss their issues and handle the inevitable conflicts that arise in marriage.

How each of us views conflict in our relationship varies depending on our family's view, the way that our parents did or did not resolve their differences, our religious upbringing, and our own temperaments. It is important for you to think about how you react to conflict and how you tend to handle disagreements as they arise. Although we are all different, researchers have identified some basic styles of conflict management. Which of these styles is closest to the way you tend to handle conflict?

## Avoiding

Do you tend to deny that conflict exists? When someone disagrees with you or you feel disgruntled, do you ignore the situation or withdraw from it, much like the proverbial ostrich with its head in the sand? Do you postpone dealing with conflict, leaving the issue unresolved? Do you believe that conflict is necessarily harmful and destructive?

Sylvie and Larry had been married for fifteen years when Larry asked Sylvie for a divorce. She was shocked, and tearfully told their mediator, "I had no idea that Larry was unhappy. Everything was fine until two weeks ago when he told me that he wanted a divorce. I don't even know why he wants a divorce."

When Larry heard this he was extremely frustrated. Larry told the mediator, "I have repeatedly asked Sylvie to go into counseling because I was unhappy. Although I love Sylvie and would love to be married to her—she's a wonderful person in so many ways—she refuses to talk with me about some things that are really important to me. I want to travel and see the world, but Sylvie only wants to use our vacations to visit her family who live in another state. We have never had a vacation anywhere except to see her family (I have no family, as I was an only child and my parents died in a car accident before I met Sylvie). I'm willing to work out an arrangement that would allow both types of travel, but Sylvie keeps putting me off. We're not getting any younger, and I want to do some things that I have always wanted to do before I get too old to do them—like traveling." Larry added, "This issue is just indicative of how she deals with any differences of opinion. She denies that they exist and puts them out of her mind. She expects me to do the same."

Sylvie's unwillingness to handle her conflict could be based on fear of losing control or being abandoned or on a belief that conflict is evil. But whatever the reason, the blinders she wore kept her from experiencing the magic of conflict. Conflict can lead to new understanding of another person and an expansion of your limited view of the world and how things "should" be done. If you approach it properly, conflict teaches you about yourself and your needs, and can help you have your needs met. When you avoid conflict, no one wins.

## Accommodating

Do you put aside your own needs and desires and give in to the other person's requests or demands? Do you always think about everyone else's needs and never about your own? Are you concerned about being selfish?

Let's look at Larry and Sylvie again. In their situation, Larry never insisted on getting his needs met. In fact, he gave in to Sylvie on vacations and everything else in their marriage. He went on for fifteen years harboring resentment that he couldn't go on vacation where he wanted. This was also his style in other aspects of the marriage. When they decided to purchase their first home, Larry wanted a low-maintenance town home, because he wasn't thrilled with yard work. Sylvie wanted a single-family residence in the suburbs with an expansive yard, trees, and a garden, as this is what she had grown up with. Larry only once broached the idea of a town home. Sylvie said that she thought that a suburban single-family residence would make more sense. Larry dropped the subject, and Sylvie began working with a realtor to find a property.

Larry didn't complain, telling himself that women need to have homes that they love, so he would let her have it. They found Sylvie's dream home, and although Larry didn't like yard work, he took it on as his obligation as a husband. They didn't discuss an allocation of the household tasks, and Sylvie had no idea that Larry hated gardening until he asked for a divorce and listed that as one of the reasons. Because Sylvie avoided conflict, refusing to see that they might have had a significant difference of opinion, and because Larry accommodated Sylvie's desires, they missed an opportunity to collaborate on finding a home that they both loved and would enjoy owning and maintaining.

Accommodation inevitably breeds resentment in the marriage. Even though the accommodator may give in to avoid a fight or to be the "good guy" or to be unselfish, the result is a lopsided relationship in which one person always gets his or her way. One spouse wins, the other loses.

## Horse Trading

Do you quickly try to resolve a conflict by splitting the difference? Do you try to find an alternative solution that is between what your partner wants and what you want?

Jill told her husband, John, that she wanted to go to Hawaii for their tenth wedding anniversary. They had gone to the Islands on their honeymoon, and she thought that it would be romantic to return to the places where they had spent their first days of married life. John really desired a different type of vacation, and thought that an Alaskan cruise up the Inside Passage would be different and more adventurous. So Jill suggested that instead of going to either place they go to Cape Cod instead, where neither had been. John reluctantly agreed but didn't feel satisfied with the decision. Although the vacation was nice enough, both Jill and John felt a vague dissatisfaction because the compromise failed to meet either of their needs.

A compromiser resolves conflict quickly and efficiently by seeking a fair and equitable split between the partners' positions or what they each are asking for. Splitting the difference, or what some people call horse trading, may work when buying a car, but most people are somewhat dissatisfied with the result. When compromising, each person must be willing to concede some of his or her issues in order to win others. The difficulty with this style of conflict resolution is that you never ask for what you really want or need. You usually start high or low, knowing that the negotiations will result in something in between what each of you is asking. The negotiations tend to feel dishonest. Both spouses win a little, both lose a little.

## Competing

Do you always need to get your way? Are differences of opinion an opportunity to show that you are smarter, faster, more knowledgeable, and more logical than your opponent? Is winning the name of the game for you?

Lester is known for having to get his way, no matter what the cost in his relationships. This style serves him well in his profession as a trial lawyer and on the tennis court, because the goal is winning. However, his competitive nature has been devastating to his marriage. His wife Mary has learned over the years that Lester will never agree with anything that she suggests, so she is never honest with him in her desires. She is a smart, savvy designer who has decorated the homes of the rich and famous in their city. However, in the remodeling of their own home, Lester insisted on having final say on all decisions—carpet, wall colors, fixtures, and so on. For example, Mary would pick out samples of several colors of paint that she liked and felt would work in the space, and Lester would nix all of them. He would insist on something different. Mary's strategy became one of holding some choices back and presenting them only after Lester vetoed her original suggestions, manipulating Lester into thinking that he was making the final decision. Although this allowed Mary to get her needs met regarding the decorating, she felt totally devalued and unacknowledged for her expertise. Whereas she had originally selected decorating features that she thought both of them would like and that would create the home of their dreams, Lester was interested only in being right, getting his way, and winning.

Competitors seek to win their position at the expense of the other person losing theirs. They enjoy the competition, but must come out on top in all areas of disagreement. Winning at all costs becomes the driving force—in small matters, such as whether the catsup should be kept in the refrigerator or in the cabinet, and in large, such as which house to buy. This style always results in a one-upmanship relationship. As seen in the example of Lester and Mary, if only one spouse has a competitive style, the other may resort to manipulation and deceit to get her way. And if both partners use a competitive approach to conflict, the conflict will never be resolved. One spouse wins, the other loses.

Avoiding, accommodating, compromising, and competing are styles of conflict management that may be useful in certain circumstances, but they do not work well in marriages. For the relationship to thrive, both spouses need to use a style that allows both spouses to win.

## Collaboration

Do you seek to find creative solutions to disagreements? Is your goal to meet your needs and the other person's needs, too? Is your relationship important to you, such that you want to preserve it with integrity?

Let's look again at Jill and John's conflict about where to go for their tenth anniversary vacation. If John took a collaborative approach to conflict, he might approach the issue something like this:

*John:* I was thinking that we ought to go somewhere special for our tenth wedding anniversary. I've been thinking about a few places. I want it to be really special—a trip that we'll remember for a lifetime.

*Jill:* Well, I've been hoping that we could go back to Hawaii. I love that old hotel we stayed in on Maui. It was so romantic. I'd love to do that all over again.

*John:* So it's important for you to go somewhere romantic. Does it have to be Hawaii? Our honeymoon was so wonderful and so romantic that I believe we could never recreate it. You know how I like adventure; I'd love to do something that would just blow our socks off in terms of something entirely new.

*Jill:* I want Hawaii. It's the most romantic place I know.

*John:* Well, I was thinking about an Alaskan cruise. I'd love to see the whales and the glaciers up close. I've never been on a cruise. Is there a way that we could meet your need for a romantic vacation and mine for something novel with a sense of adventure?

*Jill:* Well, a cruise does sound romantic. At least it looks that way on TV. But I would really like to walk on the beach, look for shells, and have quiet little dinners at sunset. It looks like cruises have a lot of people on them.

*John:* There are cruises that you can take in small boats with fewer people. But it might not have the romantic factor that you want. Can you think of anything we could do that would combine the romance with a little adventure?

*Jill:* Well, what if we did something like a resort that had little huts right on the beach with hammocks—maybe something all-inclusive. I would also be willing to go on some day trips to snorkel, whale watch, or kayak. Would that be possible?

*John:* That sounds intriguing. Why don't we look into some type of vacation with a beach, isolation, but activities to do if we want? Would that work?

*Jill:* Yes. It might be fun to do something different. After all, we have seen Hawaii.

Jill and John developed a plan of gathering information so that they could decide together on a vacation that met her need for romance and his need for adventure. As Jill and John demonstrate, collaborators cooperate with each other to try to resolve a common problem and achieve a mutually satisfying outcome. Both spouses win.

Although everyone engages in different styles of conflict resolution from time to time, we want to urge you to collaborate most often. When you use this style, your goal is to meet both spouses' needs to the greatest extent possible. Both of you need to be willing to say what you want, but also to talk about why it is important to you. And you both have to listen to the other spouse, using the rules of communication and listening we've described in this chapter so that you can understand each other's needs. Only when both people's needs are on the table can you creatively explore options that meet them.

It's not always easy to articulate your needs. Many of us have been brought up to think that making requests based on our own needs is selfish or rude. Christie and her family laugh about the Coates family method of resolving disputes—nobody says what he or she really wants. When asked, for example, "Where would you like to go for dinner?" each family member involved in the discussion always answers, "I don't care, where would you like to go?" Then a mind-reading game ensues with each family member trying to guess where the other family members would really like to go. Making even this simple decision can take hours; the family does eventually agree on a restaurant, but not necessarily with much enthusiasm for the choice. Painfully aware of this pattern, the younger family members are attempting to be more forthcoming with their opinions and needs.

Other people have been brought up in families in which family members have no trouble advocating for their own desires, sometimes to the exclusion of other people's needs. In some families, the decision of choosing a restaurant becomes a competition. "I want Chinese." "I can't stand Chinese. I want a hamburger." Each person vociferously repeats his wants without listening to the others, and if someone doesn't get his way, he goes out to eat on his own.

Collaborative decision making is done in a manner between these two extremes. In selecting a restaurant, for example, each person states his or her needs (for spice, ethnic food, atmosphere, interesting menu, fast or leisurely pace, and so on), but also listens to the other people to determine their needs. Then everyone engages in a creative process of selecting a restaurant that meets as many of the participants' needs as possible. This can take time, but usually less than processes that involve avoidance, accommodation, or competition. After discussing everyone's needs, sometimes the participants may compromise: "You want Italian, I want Mexican. What if we go to that chain restaurant that has a little bit of everything?" In a collaborative discussion, each party stays open to getting his needs met in a way that perhaps he hadn't considered initially. It is an invigorating and satisfying way to resolve disputes and make decisions.

## Rules of Collaboration

No marriage is without arguments and fighting. Misunderstandings must occur when people live intimately together. But when you are engaging in a disagreement with your spouse, there are some rules you should follow to allow the collaborative process to work, and to preserve the integrity of your relationship.

### Rule 1: Let Go of Your Pride and Your Belief in an Absolute Right Decision

Both Bob and Christie in their work with divorcing couples have seen that rarely is there an absolute right answer to any dispute. Usually there are many good options that could resolve a conflict satisfactorily. The creative work is in uncovering and discovering those options, evaluating them to see how well each meets both spouses' needs, and then selecting one to try.

Only when the issue is one of morality or intrinsic values is it reasonable to hold fast to your own way. Even then, you must evaluate your motives to determine whether the issue is truly one that would offend your most deeply held moral values or those of society, or whether it is simply a matter of "principle." When a person tells Christie that he is holding fast to his lawsuit and refusing to settle because of "principle," she realizes that the conflict may not be resolvable in mediation or negotiation. More often than not, she has discovered that the "principle" is merely stubbornness or a need to be right.

---

### Questions to Ask Yourself If You Are Holding Out for One Right Decision

- What is the principle?
- Is it truly nonnegotiable?
- Could a reasonable person see it otherwise?
- What do I gain by not being willing to negotiate a mutually acceptable solution?
- What do I lose if I don't negotiate a mutually acceptable solution?

---

## Rule 2: Don't Blame the Other Person for the Problem

Conflict is inevitable in a relationship. Even the most congenial, easygoing spouses get into arguments and conflict. However, if you want to resolve your issues with your integrity intact, don't play the blame game. Blaming your spouse only causes the other person to defend himself or herself, and the conflict escalates. Instead, when you want to blame the other person, use your best communication skills and empathy as we discussed earlier in this chapter. Be willing to look honestly at your role in the problem and to acknowledge the part you played. Then ask for your spouse's help in finding some common ground.

## Rule 3: Don't Call Names or Insult Your Spouse

We were told as children to say, "Sticks and stones may break my bones, but names can never hurt me" to someone who called us names. That singsong response was suggested as the alternative to physical retaliation, crying, or hurling names back toward our tormentor. However, we know very well that names do hurt deeply. We remember the one negative remark said to us more clearly than the one hundred compliments we may receive. Even when our self-esteem is fairly well developed, an insult can cut to the quick. When you call your spouse a slob, S.O.B., jerk, or bitch, or tell her that she is arrogant, lazy, controlling, or fat, you hurt your spouse. Even though in that instant you may simply be trying to put words to your own pain or anger or fear, if you are to handle the conflict productively you must take a deep breath and think before you speak. Do you want to hurt your spouse? Or do you want to be understood? This time your mother's admonition to count to ten before responding in anger is absolutely wonderful advice. Focus on your needs rather than on your spouse's failings.

## Rule 4: Don't Use Emotional Blackmail

When you don't get your way, do you withdraw? Do you withhold physical affection until your partner acquiesces to your desires? Do you mope around sadly or stomp around angrily when your partner has not agreed with you? If so, you are using emotional blackmail to get your way. You are behaving like a spoiled three-year-old who has been told no. You may end up with what you want, but the price is very high. You will forgo the opportunity to collaborate with your partner in mature and creative conflict resolution.

## Rule 5: Let the Stuff Go Once the Argument Is Over

Some people are conflict junkies. They like the high that engaging in fighting gives them; the adrenaline rush is intoxicating. They may want to prolong the battle to fuel their own needs because when the fight is resolved, life doesn't look as bright to them. We all know that sometimes making up is the best part of the fight. But the making up must be the end of the argument. To continue to push the replay button over and over again about the nasty stuff your spouse said or did will only distance you from your partner. Carrying around the gunnysack of past grievances toward your spouse will only weigh you down and keep you from enjoying life. If you want to be happy, let it go!

## Rule 6: Look for Your Similarities and Rejoice in Your Differences

As we have seen in earlier chapters, we choose our partners as much for the characteristics they share with us as for those that are different from ours. Remember that when you see a fault in your partner, you probably have it too, and maybe even to a greater degree. Whenever possible during an argument, highlight and point out to your spouse when you see that the two of you agree. And when you have widely divergent views or opinions, remember that the creativity of conflict is in acknowledging the differences and looking for solutions that meet as many of both spouses' needs as possible. In mediation we use what is called the joint problem statement. You would say to your spouse, "If you are needing $x$ and I am needing $y$, what options can we think of that would meet both $x$ and $y$?" In this way you acknowledge that you would both like to resolve the fight but that you have different needs you would like to meet. By combining the similarities and the differences, you both are able to move to a resolution.

## Rule 7: Don't Exaggerate the Negatives in the Situation

Accentuate the positive. Eliminate the words *always* and *never* from your fighting vocabulary. These are polarizing words that beg for a fight. The phrase "You never picked up your socks" is a lie if he did it once in twenty years, because *never* is an absolute word. Similarly, "You always burned the Sunday roast" is a bid for a fight if she cooked the roast just fine even once in the marriage. Hold the hope that no matter how bad the situation feels in the moment, resolution is possible—and you may have to hold that hope for the both of you. This is not a Pollyannaish denial of problems but a resolute belief that good can come from any situation.

## Rule 8: Don't Bully Your Partner to Get Your Way or to Be Heard

There is no room in collaborative decision making for bullying. Threats, such as "The next time you [do *x*], I'm leaving you," or "Like it or leave it" when your partner complains about something, or "I'm divorcing you if I can't have things my way," only create inequality and resentment. Your partner may give in, but there will not be peace in the situation. Use good communication skills instead.

## Rule 9: There Must Be Absolutely No Physical Violence

*Never* punch, pinch, pull, push, or pound your mate in an argument or even in jest. Physical violence is absolutely unacceptable and is against the law. If you are a victim of physical abuse or if you are a perpetrator, please get immediate assistance from domestic violence resources. There is no room for physical abuse in intimate relationships.

The wonder of lasting intimate relationships is that two unique human beings are able to forge a bond that can be sustained and repaired through a lifetime of shared experiences. Effective communication and conflict resolution skills help us bridge the gap between our differences, repair our misunderstandings and hurts, and discover and emphasize our similarities. If you want to have lasting, fulfilling relationships, these skills are imperative. If you already have them, honor them. If you don't, it is never to late to begin developing them.

### Rules of Good Communication

1. Set aside time to talk.
2. Understand your partner's reality.
3. Stop, look, and connect.
4. Advise only when asked, or ask first and advise second.
5. Don't interrupt.
6. Comment on what you observe to find out what really lies behind your partner's words.

7. Ask open-ended questions.
8. Be sensitive to your body language.
9. Be sensitive to your partner's body language.
10. Empathize.
11. Use "I" statements, not "you" statements.
12. Respect your listener. Do not drone on and on and . . .

### Rules of Collaboration

1. Let go of your pride and your belief in an absolute right decision.
2. Don't play the blame game.
3. Don't insult.
4. Don't use emotional blackmail.
5. Clean the slate when the fight is over.
6. Seek similarities and enjoy the differences.
7. Do not exaggerate the negative and polarize.
8. Don't be a bully.
9. Absolutely no physical violence. Like they say in kindergarten, use your words (but mind rules 3, 4, and 7).

# Chapter Six

# The Trajectory of the Divorce Process

Divorce involves at least three different processes for each person in the family. We call these processes the logistical divorce, the legal divorce, and the emotional divorce. Because a family is a system of relationships among its members, when any relationship or any one member of the family is changed, the entire system is affected. So when spouses are going through divorce, every member of the system—the spouses, their children, and any extended family members that are a part of the system—is affected logistically, legally, and emotionally.

## The Three Aspects of Every Divorce

Although the most obvious divorce is the legal divorce, we will examine all three divorce processes and their effects on you and the family. As we examine these processes, keep in mind that *all* family members are being affected. If you are a parent, you will experience special challenges because parenting after divorce involves logistical, legal, and emotional changes for you and your children. We will discuss parenting after divorce later in the chapter.

### Logistical Divorce

When spouses separate, they will usually have two homes, new schedules, and new roles. Everyone in the family suffers disorientation from a separation and divorce. Usually the roles that each spouse has had with regard to children, household duties, financial organization, and so on are changed. For example, no longer does Wife automatically make dinner and Husband take out the trash, or Mom read the bedtime story and Dad play catch with the kids after dinner. There is a period of adjustment, with confusion reigning at first. It's a period of immense challenges and forced coping.

When Christie and her first husband separated many years ago, she stayed in the family home and he left. Her first husband had always handled all of the home repair responsibilities very capably. He could fix almost anything, and if he couldn't, he knew whom to call. In the first weeks of their separation, the sink in the kitchen clogged, and the chemical drain cleaner did not work. Christie had no clue what to do. She cried in frustration for a while, then went to a hardware store and, on the recommendation of the clerk, bought a "snake" to use to clear the drain. When that didn't work, she cried some more, got out the yellow pages, and called a plumber. She remembers the two plumbers who came to her home on a rainy Sunday in Houston, Texas (she now wonders why *two* came), unclogged her drain with some kind of a rotor, and then sat at her kitchen table and had coffee with her.

She laughs now at the naïveté and helplessness she felt, but it was a major turning point in her healing. After this experience she then had confidence that she could handle just about anything around the house, if not by herself then with help from someone other than her husband.

## Legal Divorce

Our legal system determines the rules of marriage and the rules of divorce. Filing for divorce triggers the family's entry into the court system, with its complicated rules, requirements, and paperwork. The legal process of divorce includes restructuring the parenting and financial situations of the family. Many of the logistical details, such as where the children will reside when, how the bills will be paid, and who will transport the children for soccer, will be made a part of the legal divorce and will often become court orders that must be followed. Legally, a marriage is like a business partnership that must be dissolved expeditiously and fairly for the smooth functioning of society.

Many couples are finding that using mediation to resolve issues together is preferable to going to court, and we both support a collaborative approach to divorce. However, because the rules are decided by our legal system, you need to consult with a lawyer who knows those rules and can advise you of your options.

It is important to recognize that the legal system is essentially adversarial. What this means is that the goal of litigation is to win. Thus, a lawyer's job is to present you and your situation in the best possible light and to present your spouse's situation in the worst possible light. In a divorce, this can create wounds that take a very long time to heal. The court is not a good place to make child-rearing decisions. If you can make them yourself with your soon to be ex-spouse, do so. If you cannot and if mediation fails, then the court is your only recourse.

Clearly, the legal aspects of getting a divorce can exacerbate the tension and hostility between you and your spouse and make it harder to move forward in your life. Our clients often say they want the legal divorce to be over so that everything can settle down. However, we have found that even when the legal divorce is final and the logistical arrangements have been settled, the emotional divorce process is usually not complete. Although the final decree or piece of paper dissolving the legal marriage may provide some closure, the court order does not terminate the emotional upheaval. And sometimes the legal battles continue long after the marriage is legally over. If you have children and you cannot let go of your anger or your sense of victimization or the blame game, your divorce will continue your relationship in hate as you once were in love, because you are parents forever.

## Emotional Divorce

Although the legal divorce may be the one that the outside world sees, the internal emotional divorce is the hardest to accomplish. The emotional divorce is a long process of healing, which begins with grieving. Before you do the work suggested in this book, you must grieve. You must mourn the loss of your best friend, your lover and partner, your family, and your dreams. But as you mourn, remember that divorce does not mean the true loss of family, of self, or of dreams. You will just need to reconfigure and rebuild them.

## Grieving

You must work through your grief before you can expect to recover from your divorce. Each of us is different, but there are common ways that we as humans handle our grief. Elisabeth Kübler-Ross, through her work with people who were struggling to accept their impending death, was one of the first people to help us see that grief is a process of healing and growth with stages to go through. She named the stages she observed Denial, Anger, Bargaining, Letting Go, and Acceptance. (These stages are ordinarily sequential but may also jump back and forth in no particular order.) In going through your emotional divorce, you will need to grieve in much the same way that you would if a loved one had died. However, a big, obvious difference from that grief process is that the spouse is still very much alive and in your face. And not only are you grieving the loss of that person, but often that same person has attacked your self-esteem with the reasons for the divorce and may even be continuing to attack you through the legal process.

In this book we call the stages of divorce grief Shock and Denial, Intense Emotional Pain, and Recovery. As you read about these stages, try to determine for yourself where you are in your grief process.

### Shock and Denial

In this initial stage of grief, you are in total disbelief and have a feeling of emotional numbness. You will think, *This can't be happening to me.* You will want to deny that it is happening: *Maybe if I go to bed I'll wake up and find that it was just a bad dream.*

During this stage you may find that keeping busy is a way to cope. The logistical details can fill your time and keep you going— finding a new residence, dividing up your possessions, arranging for child care, and figuring out how to pay the household bills. You will not have time to think a lot about what has happened.

To illustrate this and the other stages of grief, we'll follow one woman through her emotional divorce. Janet married Tom on the day after her high school graduation. Her dreams had come true; all she had wanted to be was a wife and mother. Tom was a sophomore in college, and they settled into a spartan existence in the married student housing of Tom's college while he studied and she worked as a secretary in an insurance company to support the two of them. During the summers Tom was able to work at a local chemical manufacturing plant to earn money for tuition and books for the next year. Although they were living on a shoestring, Janet didn't mind because she enjoyed the challenge of cooking economical meals and furnishing their apartment with garage sale finds.

After Tom graduated and got a well-paying job, they decided that Janet would stop working and that they would start their family. In quick succession, Tom Jr., Mary, and Melinda were born. Being a full-time, stay-at-home mother was everything that Janet had imagined, and she found that she was really good at it. Her friends even jokingly called her Super Mom. Although Tom was proud of her and the children and the home that Janet had created, he felt something was missing.

One weekend, after eight years of marriage, Tom broke down and told Janet that he was having an affair with one of his coworkers and that he wanted a divorce. Janet was stunned! She couldn't believe it. For three weeks after Tom moved out, she still prepared the daily large evening meal with all of Tom's favorite foods, thinking that he would walk in the door any minute. She began a re-upholstery project on her sofa that she had been putting off, selecting a fabric that contained Tom's favorite shade of blue. She threw herself even more intensely into her work as chairwoman of the preschool's Halloween carnival. Her friends didn't even know that Tom had left, as she had told them that he was out of the country on a business trip. Her denial and busy-ness were keeping her from realizing the enormity of what was occurring.

Staying busy at this stage of grief can be helpful, as it keeps you from being swallowed up by what has happened. Getting up every morning to fix breakfast for the children, going to work, picking up the kids, fixing dinner, doing homework, getting ready for bed—all are important activities to maintain and to help you cope with the loss of your spouse. However, at some point, keeping busy becomes a way to avoid feeling the pain and keeps you stuck in denial. To move through the grief process, you will have to feel and experience strong emotions.

## Intense Emotional Pain

Once the immediate logistics of separation have been settled, you have time to think. And the thoughts will make you nuts! Everyone is a little crazy at this stage in his or her grief process. People in this stage do things that they would never have expected themselves to do.

When one woman we know was first separated, she would drive with her three-year-old son in the car past her husband's new apartment crying hysterically. (Not only was this very unsafe, it was traumatic for her child.) She found herself begging her husband to come back. She found herself crying at work and not being able to stop. She had never, ever, behaved like that before, and she was amazed at her reactions. She was at her worst, as most people are when going through a divorce. The pain obscures rationality.

### *Bargaining*

During this period of grief you may find yourself bargaining with God ("Oh, God, just bring her back to me and I'll go to church for the rest of my life") or with your spouse ("I'll change and do whatever you want if you will just come back to me"). This is normal, but until you begin to accept that the divorce is occurring, with or without you, you will not move from this painful stage of grief.

Let's go back to Janet's story. One afternoon Janet answered the door, and a stranger asked her if she was Janet Smith. She nodded assent, and he handed her an envelope and left. In the envelope was a paper called "Petition for Dissolution of Marriage" that had Tom's and her names on it. At first she couldn't figure out what it was, but then she realized that she had been served with divorce papers. At that moment the dam she had built to protect herself from her sadness, fear, and pain burst, and she collapsed into a heap on the dining room floor, crying hysterically. Her four-year-old wandered in. Janet gathered him in her arms, but couldn't stop crying. He squirmed free, but she stayed sitting on the floor. Only when dinnertime had come did she realize that she needed to feed the kids. She had no appetite, but her sense of responsibility to her children forced her to get up and moving.

The next several months were agonizingly painful. Janet lost weight, had no interest in maintaining the house, and asked friends and family members to care for the kids. On the advice of friends she got a lawyer and began responding to the legal divorce. She also began seeing a psychologist, who helped her talk about her feelings of betrayal, anger, and sadness. Although Tom wanted to work everything out quickly, she found that she just couldn't concentrate. They were able to agree to a temporary parenting time schedule, and on the nights that Tom had the kids, she watched old romantic movies by herself. She begged him to go into counseling with her, but he refused. He said that he had outgrown her. She angrily accused him of abandoning the children. They fought over support and time with the kids, both saying and writing ugly, negative things about the other.

Eventually their lawyers negotiated a settlement, but Janet couldn't even be in the same room with Tom. She had no respect for him. She received an award of alimony designed to provide her with several years in which to get a college education and become self-supporting. She was devastated; this was not the life that she had wanted.

### Physical Ailments

It's not unusual to experience mood swings during this period, accompanied by physical ailments. One's immune system is compromised by intense grief, and psychosomatic illnesses occur for which there is no obvious physical cause. You may catch a cold four times in the season when you usually have none. One of our clients developed excruciating headaches that lasted for hours, which no amount of painkillers would stop. People are also more prone to accidents when they are experiencing intense grieving, as they are distracted and not paying attention to what's going on around them. Car accidents and fender benders are not uncommon. Helen, in a hurry to go pick up her kids from school one afternoon, backed her car out of the garage, forgetting to open the garage door. She was not injured (except her pride), but she had to replace her garage door.

### Anger

During this period of intense psychic pain, you will be angry—at your spouse, the situation, perhaps your children, and yourself. Lilly had told Dan that either they go to counseling or she wanted a divorce. He agreed to counseling and found the first two sessions very helpful. He heard what Lilly's concerns were and had just begun getting in touch with his role in their marital problems. Lilly started their third session by announcing that the counseling was not enough and that she wanted a divorce. The therapist tried to focus her on working on the marriage, but Lilly refused, saying that she had come to her senses and had seen that Dan would never be the husband she wanted. She abruptly gathered up her things and left the room. Dan sat nonplussed. He couldn't understand what had just occurred. He had been acknowledging his errors and failings. Why had she done that?

Driving home from the therapist's office, he decided that she had never meant to work in counseling, but had just used the sessions as a way of ending the marriage and justifying her decision. Furious, he rushed home and found her packing up his clothes. He shouted that if she wanted a divorce, she could leave. He wasn't going anywhere. Grabbing an armload of her clothes from the closet, he rushed out the front door and threw them on the lawn. He then had the good sense to leave before he did anything else rash. When he came home, the closet and bedroom were empty of Lilly's clothes, and all of Dan's clothes had been ripped and shredded.

Unfortunately, when one moves from denial and shock into anger, the impulse is to hurt the other person. It's OK to be angry, but you must attempt to channel that anger in positive ways. Use that emotional energy to do something productive or creative, such as cleaning out the basement, painting a picture, or playing kickball with your kids. And absolutely try to avoid using your children to get back at your spouse. Children should never be put in the middle and used as weapons against the other parent. We'll talk more about parenting after divorce later in this chapter.

## Guilt

If you are like most divorcing people, you will feel guilty. You will tell yourself that there must have been something that you could've, should've done. You will worry about your precious children and what the divorce will do to them. It is vitally important at this time to remind yourself that you are fundamentally a good person, that the situation will not be changed by beating yourself up about it, and that what you tell yourself about your loss will make the difference in your outlook and ability to cope with it.

Runaway guilt, anger toward your spouse, and low self-esteem can all lead to depression. It is common to have the feeling that your pain is for eternity. You can lose your perspective. If you find that your sadness hangs on like a dark cloud for a long time, that you feel your life is over, or that you see no way out of the pain, please consult a psychologist or another mental health professional. You may be clinically depressed and need professional help. It is not weakness to seek help, especially during a divorce; it shows strength and determination to get through your divorce.

You owe it to yourself and to your children to be as emotionally and physically healthy as you can possibly be. We believe it is imperative that individuals in this stage of grief have someone to talk to who will listen empathically, nonjudgmentally, and calmly. Mental health professionals are trained to do this; it is harder for friends and relatives who care about you to remain empathically neutral.

## Acceptance and Recovery

Kübler-Ross's last two stages of grief, Letting Go and Acceptance, are what you do to "recover" from the emotional divorce. This book can be useful in your recovery, as we offer suggestions and guides for self-discovery and growth. As you recover, your self will begin to emerge from the devastation of the divorce, and you will begin to move forward with your life. You will be attempting to make some sense of what happened and to understand the how and why of it. When the sadness begins to subside and the pain becomes less acute, you will be ready to examine your own responsibility more clearly and move into recovery. Here are some guidelines for this part of the process.

### Take Your Time

What do *you* need to do to recover? There are many excellent resources available to help you: books on surviving divorce, websites, divorce recovery groups, singles groups, mental health therapists, and friends who have been through it. But, as we have advocated so many times before in this book, you mostly need to take the time to know yourself.

You shouldn't try to rush your grieving, because one essential aspect of knowing yourself is to allow yourself to feel sadness and pain. Grieving only becomes pathological or dysfunctional when you cannot or will not let it go. Grieving cannot be gotten around, but it can be gotten through. Some of the things you will be doing as you grieve and as you get through the legal process will help you understand yourself better.

### Get Out in the Real World as a Person, not as a "Divorced Person"

It is very hard at first to tell people you are getting a divorce. You feel like a flawed human being with a big red *D* on your chest. You feel alone and isolated. However, as you've seen, the realities of daily living do not go away. You have to go to work, whether outside the home or as the primary caregiver for your children; you have to continue to be the best parent you can be; and now you also have to begin to have a social life as a single person. Part of your growth is to expose yourself to other relationships to determine what works and what doesn't and why.

It is normal to want to begin going out socially as your divorce progresses. As an adult, you need adult companionship. Be careful not to overdo your social activities, however. Many people become, as Steve Martin would say, "wild and crazy"—dating three or four people at the same time and sleeping around. There is absolutely nothing wrong with enjoying yourself by dating and meeting people. It feels good to revel in being desired and desirable. But we do urge caution in a couple of areas. In this era of AIDS and other sexually transmitted diseases, unprotected sex is physically dangerous. Unrestricted sexual activity can be emotionally dangerous as well. You can be hurt by companions who do not have your best interests at heart. Every single person has been through the rejection of the suitor who doesn't call back, the broken date, the false statements of affection calculated to get sex. Just remember that you are very vulnerable as you recover. Do not put yourself in emotional danger.

It's also very easy to get caught up in the drama and excitement of new relationships and not to take time to do your internal work. In fact, getting swept up in a new love and sexual relationship is a "wonderful" way of avoiding doing your work. Please realize that you will not find your next love right away. The oft-quoted axiom "You have to kiss a lot of frogs to find your prince" is absolutely true. If you feel that you are in love with one of the very first few people you date, be careful. You must give relationships time to grow and develop.

"Friends first, then lovers" is our motto! Until you have recovered from your divorce and gained an understanding of yourself and your needs, you will not be ready to commit to one person. There are people out there who are professional rescuers. They find those who are suffering the pain of a divorce and become a confidant, a supporter, and a sexual partner. But once you have done your work, their job description has to be rewritten, because you no longer need rescuing. This is why rebound relationships have about a 95 percent failure rate. Depending on when you start dating, you will still be grieving at the same time that you are becoming social again.

Remember, you must do your work first before bringing someone else into your process. The friendships you make and the people you meet will enrich your life immeasurably and will help you know yourself. But don't settle down again too quickly. Give the glow of early infatuation and "falling in love" time to fade. If a friendship only becomes stronger and love deepens, then time spent getting to know each other before making a commitment is time well spent. If you are becoming emotionally involved with someone who is also divorcing or divorced, you need to pay attention to where he or she is in his or her recovery process. Be careful of getting involved too quickly with newly separated or divorced people. They still have their work to do.

At some point, about a year-and-a-half to two years after you have been back in the social scene, you may get tired of it. We have seen that right around two years after divorce, many people who really enjoyed experimenting with new relationships begin to feel the need for a more committed, exclusive relationship. If you have been doing your work, you will be ready when you begin to feel that "urge to merge."

### Spend Time Alone

It is tempting to fill every minute you have during the divorce recovery period with activity—going to the movies with friends, dating, exercising, and so on. Some people get so caught up in the social whirl that they are never alone. If you have children, you may want to fill up the hours and days when they are gone to avoid missing them. But do give yourself the gift of a date with yourself when you have an opportunity. Use your alone time to think, meditate, read, maybe even cry, and do the other things suggested by this and other books.

### Learn to Love in a New Way

One of the questions we often hear is, "How can I go on when I still love him [her] so much?" It is possible to be divorced and still love your ex-spouse. Many couples come into mediation with us to work out the details of their parenting plans and financial settlements and say, "We love each other but just can't live together any more. We've been through counseling . . .," and they will detail the things they have done to keep the marriage together. However, for whatever reasons, the marriage between them is over. But they still care about each other, want the best for each other, and want to create a situation post-divorce that is not destructive to either spouse or to the children.

The love and caring you may feel for your spouse has to shift from "me-centered" love—he makes me feel good, sexy, cared about, and so on—to a more generalized feeling of wishing your ex well. Spiritual traditions call this a divine love, and psychology calls it unconditional love; that is, it is love that is offered from the highest part of our consciousness and is not attached to being with the person or having the person meet our needs. The goal is to detach—to realize that what you may perceive as love may be need, insecurity, or fear. It takes courage to let go of your spouse, wish him or her well (either actually or to yourself), and release that attachment.

If you try to stop loving your spouse by telling yourself how awful he or she is—how unloving, selfish, and the like—and then spew this same line of negativity to your friends, relatives, and children, you will not attain your goal of release, but instead will actually bind yourself more painfully to that person. Psychologists call this attachment *negative intimacy* in that the relationship is prolonged and the intensity is retained by negative behaviors and thoughts. We've seen many couples who cannot give up fighting even many years following their divorce because they just can't let go of each other. They are now as married in hate and anger as they once were married in love.

Instead of trying to distance yourself by judging your spouse, use your self-talk to tell yourself positive things about yourself. "I am a person who is capable of learning, loving, and changing." "I am loveable." "I am strong and can meet the challenges in my life." Your self-talk will define your progress. Instead of lamenting loudly and often, "Ain't it awful? He done me wrong," positively affirm that your divorce is an opportunity for growth, learning, and personal development. Your experience of your divorce will change based on how you talk about it. Many people reconnect with their childhood religion or find a new spiritual path that offers support and understanding of the human dilemma during their divorce recovery period. It can be a beautiful opportunity for renewal and connection to your deepest values.

### Forgive

Before you can forgive others, you must first forgive yourself. Part of the reason for this book is to encourage you to look at yourself—your upbringing, your needs, your weaknesses, and your strengths—in order to understand your motives and behaviors. Instead of berating yourself for your mistakes during the marriage, tell yourself that it's OK. You did the best you could at that time, and now you have learned better ways to behave, think, listen, and so on. You are involved in one of life's lessons that you may have wanted to avoid but from which you now must learn. You are becoming a person you would like to spend time with. Remember that mistakes are only op-portunities to learn! Our point is that you are not a bad person be-cause you made a mistake. The job is to learn from the mistake and move on. It is not helpful to wallow in self-pity for the rest of your life. Seize the day and move forward in self-wisdom.

Peace of mind and lightness of heart and soul will only come from forgiving yourself and then from forgiving others. You actually forgive for your own well-being so that you will not be held captive by fear, anger, and resentment. It takes a lot of psychic energy to be angry, to hold a grudge, and to dislike another person. Although your former life is gone, your new life can be even better when you release the energy that is bound up in negative thoughts and actions. Thank your partner mentally for providing you with the opportunity to move on to something better. You may be asking yourself, Are they crazy or what? My life is ruined and they want me to *thank* that slimy ex of mine? Yes, that's exactly what we want you to do—because it is what will help you recover.

Forgiveness does not mean turning your back on your own needs and the needs of your children or accepting any unjust ac-tion from another. But a major step in your recovery is to release the past, have faith that the future will be good, and simply use the present moments of your life to their fullest. It will take time to get to this place of acceptance and willingness to release the hurt you have felt because of your marriage and divorce.

Everett Worthington, the author of *Five Steps to Forgiveness,* sug-gests that unforgiveness has a negative physiological effect on the body—and says that forgiveness can actually make us healthier. His five-step formula for forgiveness involves recalling the hurt objec-tively, empathizing with the person who harmed you (authors' note: this usually takes the longest and is the hardest step), altru-istically choosing to forgive, committing publicly to forgiveness, and holding on to forgiveness even when you backslide.

As difficult as it may seem to do, shedding the victim mental-ity and assuming responsibility for your present situation and the future will make your life go more smoothly. You will be empow-ered to do whatever is necessary to recover from your divorce. If you cling to victimization, at some level you are saying, "I do not want to look at myself. I will not grow. I do not wish to change. Play-ing the blame game is so much more comfortable because I never have to look at myself and my responsibility." Forgiveness often takes time, but it is a choice that you can make for your own sake and for that of your children.

What happened to Janet? After she was legally divorced, she enrolled in college and pursued a career as an interior designer. She had to give up a lot of her volunteer work with the children's activities, but she realized that she couldn't do it all. She and Tom settled into a routine of coparenting that basically went well—as long as he deferred to her decisions regarding the children. They disputed a few decisions, but they worked through them in mediation. When Tom married the coworker with whom he had had the affair, Janet thought she would die! However, instead of moping, she invited a girlfriend from school out to dinner. She made many new friends at school, several of whom were single parents as well, and they commiserated about their situations. When a guy in her lit class invited her to the movies, she almost didn't go, but she went out with him, had a good time, and her social life as a single woman began. She began to see that she had neglected herself and her intellectual and emotional growth when she had thrown herself totally into being the best wife and mother in the world. Her recovery had begun.

### Where Are You in the Grief Process?

#### Shock and Denial

"I feel numb. This can't be happening to me. Divorce happens to other people."

"I'm really not worried about divorce. She'll change her mind."

"I don't have time to think about divorce—my kids need me, and there's so much to do."

#### Extreme Emotional Pain

"I would give anything or do anything if my spouse would cancel the divorce."

"I can't sleep at night—every time I think about my spouse I cry."

"I feel totally unloveable and undesirable."

"If I wasn't taking this antidepressant medication, I couldn't function."

"My life is ruined forever."

"My poor children; I destroyed them by leaving my spouse."

### Recovery

"You know, if he hadn't left, I never would have learned how to be independent."

"That woman smiled at me. It might be nice to go out."

"We were both so young when we married; we didn't give ourselves a chance to grow up before we started playing house."

"I love my kids, but it is really nice to have every other weekend to myself so that I can catch up with friends."

"He's still nasty to me, but I know that I am a good person doing the best I can."

## Parenting After Divorce

If you have children, one of the biggest challenges in your divorce is learning how to parent in two homes, or to coparent, as parenting after divorce is commonly called. Because a major part of your life is spent in parenting your children, we want to offer some basic suggestions for effective coparenting based on our combined experience of forty years working with divorced and separating families.

Although you shed a partner in a divorce, you don't shed your children. You will always be their parent. Further, you don't shed the fact that the children do have another parent—no longer your spouse, yet still their parent. One of the hardest shifts for a couple to make is that from being spouses to being simply coparents.

The harm to children in a divorce comes from the level of conflict between the parents and how the parents act out that conflict. The more the children are caught in the middle, the more psychological harm befalls them. Research indicates that it is the unresolved conflict between parents, be they together in a bad marriage or apart in a nasty divorce, that is the psychological killer for children. If the conflict between the parents stops, be they married or divorced, the children improve in their functioning.

A family provides three functions for children: nurturing, socializing, and providing a sense of personal identity. When we nurture our children, we feed them, clothe them, house them, love them, make them feel safe, and support them as they venture out into the world. When we socialize our children, we teach them to use words and not to hit, to wait their turn, to not be rude to people yet still express their feelings and stand up for their beliefs, and to have a sense of personal boundaries about where it is safe to tread or not in relationships. We provide our children with a sense of personal identity by teaching them about our family and what it stands for, about what we take pride in as a family, and that they belong to something greater than themselves.

Bob's family is very proud of the fact that his ancestors were New England whaling captains. As a boy he probably couldn't have cared less and as a teen felt he always had three hundred ghosts staring over his shoulder as he broke the rules, but knowledge of his heritage did instill in him a sense of the past having meaning in the present. You will be sending your children the same kinds of messages. The important point is that even though a family may break up through divorce, the *functions* of the family are continued, now in two different households. In that sense we never stop being parents because we must not stop being parents. Our children need us to continue to perform the functions of nurturance, socialization, and identity building even if now there is a division of labor.

## When Children Are at Risk

Separation and divorce can increase the possibility of adjustment problems in children and adolescents. The situation isn't always grim, however. For many children, living in a home without the parental fights and with a general reduction in the level of conflict is a welcome change. At the same time, though, there being two households to move between puts the child at risk of being caught in the middle. Risk of emotional damage to the child increases under certain circumstances, which we discuss here.

### Less Effective Parenting

Children are at risk when parents are preoccupied with licking their own wounds, getting their lives together as single parents, and perhaps finding and adjusting to new jobs. In other words, the more self-absorbed and preoccupied a parent is, the greater the difficulties for the child. Parental input diminishes, and the child is essentially psychologically abandoned. The functions of the family as redistributed by the divorce are weakened.

### Hostility Between Parents

Research findings are sturdy and resounding when it comes to the harmful effects of parental conflict. Bob teaches a Parenting After Divorce class that is required of all divorcing couples with children in the five-county metropolitan Denver area. One of his favorite questions to ask the class is, "When you were a child, what did you do when your parents fought?" The single answer he receives is some variation of "I would leave." Parents taking the class talk about running out of the house, going to their room and turning on their stereo, or going to a friend's house. The basic message is that they fled.

Imagine that you could not flee. Imagine that every time your parents exchanged you, it was World War III and you could not escape because you were in the parking lot of some fast-food restaurant because the judge felt exchanges in a public place would be safer for you. Essentially there was no escape, and you just had to stand there and take it.

Think what the impact would be if it simply were not safe to love the parent you were away from when with the other parent. You would be in a situation where it was not safe to follow your natural instincts and love both parents. It would be like being Poland between Germany and Russia in World War II—a very uncomfortable and dangerous place to be.

### Decline in Economic Resources

Some research has found that keeping two separate households after a separation and divorce increases expenditures by about 30 percent, while, of course, you still have the same level of income from both parents. These costs adjust over time, but immediately upon separation both parties take a large economic hit. This can translate into something as simple as not being able to buy the important designer-label clothes for an adolescent or as drastic as having to move and change schools. Children are totally dependent on their parents for the structure of their lives; for them a sharp economic downturn can be devastating.

### Disruptive Life Changes

This effect is often tied to an economic decline, but there are additional issues. The separated or divorced parent who moves in with a new significant other places a heavy burden of adjustment on the child, especially considering that such transitional relationships have about a 5 percent chance of lasting. When the child is in a situation where he has a "new parent" about whom he has risked caring and then that relationship breaks up, he suffers yet another loss. Bob worked with an adolescent boy a number of years ago whose mother, the primary residential custodian, had been married four times. By the age of sixteen the boy had a biological father and three stepfathers. One day in therapy, he was asked how he coped with the quick succession of fathers in his life. With a cynical laugh that covered his pain, he replied, "I just don't get involved with them. I call them the drones and just don't get involved."

### Use of the Child to Hurt the Other Parent

Children are to be loved as people, not used as instruments of destruction of the other parent. It is never appropriate to get at the other parent by withholding parenting time or making false accusations of physical or sexual abuse. The child becomes the pawn in a deadly war and is the ultimate victim. Children are entitled to a relationship with both of their parents unless their physical or emotional safety is truly threatened. False accusations and the resulting investigation and possible legal action traumatize children and have devastating, long-lasting effects.

### Making the Child Responsible for a Parent's Happiness

A parent's goal is to take care of his or her children. However, some parents going through a divorce reverse that role and depend on their children to make them happy. For example, the parent who begins allowing her child to sleep with her and telling the child repeatedly how she would be lost and wouldn't know what she would do without her little angel now that Daddy has left, is expecting the child to be her caretaker. Children should not have to assume this responsibility for their parents, as it keeps them from doing their own grieving and is an unbearable burden for a child to bear.

## How Parents Contribute to Good Adjustment

Parents can help their children adjust well to separation and divorce. If both parents can function as we describe here, the child is at far less risk for a poor post-divorce adjustment.

### *Parents Are Warm and Nurturing*

As we said elsewhere in this chapter, by nurturing we mean giving a child a strong sense that he is special, loved, and important to his parents. We are not talking about indulging the child in response to paroxysms of guilt, but rather doing the little day-to-day things that tell any human being that she is valued and loved. It is often the little stuff that makes the difference. Here are what some divorced families have shared about how they have sent the "you are loved" message:

- A cartoon placed in the lunch pail. The parent who did this learned later that the child would unpack his lunch, take out the cartoon on the morning school bus, and pass it around. The whole bus looked forward to it, and the boy was very popular on the morning ride. Although the parent had not anticipated this positive side effect, the "I love you" message delivered a double whammy.
- Friday snuggle movies. Here Dad would let his two under-ten children pick out a movie, and they would watch it on the floor in front of the sofa with quilts, blankets, and popcorn. His children looked forward to it every Friday they saw him.
- You get to name the meal. A mom chose a night each week when one of her three children in rotation could choose the meal. They loved it. She laughingly said that they never go much beyond homemade pizza, spaghetti, or macaroni and cheese, but she noticed how excited the children got when it was their day to choose, and major negotiations would take place between the chooser and sibs as to what they were going to have.

- Guaranteed undivided attention. A father negotiated that he would have a Wednesday night dinner visit with his three children, but he arranged it so that on week one of a four-week rotation he saw all three for dinner, on week two he saw only the oldest, on week three the middle child, and on week four the youngest. He commented that it was the best thing he had ever done with his parenting time choices because he could devote a whole evening to just one child with no competition from the other two. He got to know his children much better in these private moments with them, and they were very proud when it was their night alone with Dad.

### Parents Continue to Monitor Their Children and Maintain Appropriate Expectations

A second "lower-the-risk" factor is for parents to continue to oversee their children and what is going on in their lives and hold on to their standards of expected behavior. Research shows that children whose parents are involved in their school do much better than children whose parents are not involved. If you have adolescents, you have probably heard the wail, "But Dad [Mom], all the other kids' parents let them do it!" Although kids may screech and whine in protest from time to time, they like and need you to set limits, hold to standards, and stay involved. A task of childhood and adolescence is to learn self-control and to make good judgments. Parents encourage this by setting firm and fair limits and being involved in their children's lives. Believe it or not, children take comfort in knowing there is someone there to set and enforce limits, because if they get out of control, who is going to help them get back in control?

Falling prey to guilt is a common failure in parenting. If you are feeling bad as a parent about having put your children through a divorce, guilt may prompt you to lighten your standards. You may say to yourself, Since I've inflicted this on my child, maybe I should let him take life a little easier—let him stay up really late on the weekends, or not impose consequences when he doesn't do his chores. Succumbing to this impulse will be doing your child a great disservice. Life does not offer a lifting of the rules just because you and your child are hurting. You have to continue to do your job. Children need to be socialized in preparation for dealing with the real world. Do not let guilt be your guide!

### *Parents Coach, Not Control, Their Children*

The goal of parenting is to help your children grow away from you. We do not mean to stop loving you, but to be able to function independently and to make their own wise decisions. What skills does a person need to be able to make good decisions, and how can parents teach these skills? Research indicates that there is a parenting style that ultimately is best for instilling independence and good decision making in children. It has been given a number of descriptive names in the literature; we prefer the term *authoritative parenting.*

An authoritative parent has expectations of his or her child, one of which is that the child will do the right thing. Because of this expectation, the parent creates a climate that says the child is innocent until proven guilty. When a child does make a mistake, the parental approach is more in the line of, "What would you do differently next time?" or "What have you learned from this?" (which is the message of this book as well). The message is not that the child is a bad person, but rather that he has made an error in judgment and needs to learn from the error. With this approach, the child is not demeaned or put down. He is a "learner" rather than a "failure." When a parent's goal is control, when in effect the parent is saying, "I will prevent you from doing wrong because I will watch you every minute," the child will be obedient when authority is present but become a wild person when authority is not there. If you are interested in learning more about authoritative parenting, Haim Ginott captures this style in his book *Between Parent and Child.* It is an oldie but a goodie.

## The Normal Emotional Responses of Children to Divorce

For children, the divorce actually begins when the parents separate, and it is at the time of the separation that you can expect to see an emotional response to the breakup of the family. Research indicates that the emotional responses listed here are normal. You should expect them to diminish within six months to a year. If they are intense and overwhelming to you or the child after a year, you then may wish to seek therapeutic help.

Anger

Sadness

Fear

Confusion

Self-blame, guilt

Abandonment fears

Regression

None of these is what you might call an "exotic" response for any human being whose life has been suddenly wrenched apart. As an adult you will probably experience these feelings yourself. A couple of these responses merit further comment, however.

It is very common for children to blame themselves for the divorce, and it is important to reassure them that they are not at fault. "You did not break it. You cannot fix it. This is an adult decision." These are phrases that children may need to hear again and again in the early period of separation.

Fear of abandonment can cause children to become very clingy. One mother said, "For about three months I had a Velcro child. She was attached to me at the hip. She had a lot of questions about who would take care of her if I died and was I going to die. It took a long time to reassure her I was going no place."

When we say a child regresses, we mean that she retreats to an earlier level of functioning where she felt more comfortable. For example, "losing" toilet training or wanting a bottle or pacifier again are signs of regression. In our opinion, it is best to indulge the whim; the child is regressing as a self-comforting exercise and will stop when he feels life is back under control again. As Bob has said in his classes, "I guarantee you your son will be toilet trained by the time he is nineteen!"

## Children Caught in the Middle

As we stated earlier, the greatest psychological damage occurs to the child when parents are in conflict in front of the child or include the child in the conflict. Most damaging (although it is all damaging) is when parents place the child in the middle. The "dos and don'ts" we discuss in this section are ways to avoid placing your child in the middle.

*Do not discuss issues having to do with the children in front of them.* Here's a classic example: when a child is being exchanged, the parent says, "I have tickets for the circus in two weeks. I know it is your weekend, but could we change things? I know she would love to go." This kind of request blindsides the parent on the receiving end and puts him in a bind: if he says no in front of the child, he becomes the bad guy, and he may have plans he hasn't yet discussed with the child. The child is placed in the middle because she is pressured to take sides. Does she take parent A's side and go to the circus, thus abandoning parent B, or does she say no to the circus, thereby disappointing parent A? For the child it is a lose-lose situation because she is forced to choose between two people she loves.

- *Do discuss child issues with the other parent directly when the children are not present or in a place where they can't overhear.*

*Do not ask children to carry messages.* An innocent "Please tell your father I will pick you up half an hour late on Sunday night. I will be having dinner with Grandma and Grandpa" might be just fine. Dad can say, "Sure, I want all the time with you I can get, so this is great!" But Dad could also say, "That mother of yours! She will be late to her own funeral! She is so tied up with her Mommy and Daddy that she can't make time for you! Now you see why I divorced her!" The child bears the brunt of a tirade during which the parent vents his or her anger at the other partner on him. This is destructive.

- *Do relay messages directly—by phone, voice mail, e-mail, or fax— not through the child.*

*Do not ask children to play detective and use them as a source of information about the other household.* Children can be put in the middle and placed under great pressure if they are asked to be a spy in the other household. In this situation, the parent is essentially asking the child to rat on the other parent; for the child there will be an underlying fear that she will be an active agent in getting that parent into trouble. She is placed in a position where she will have to either lie or share information. For instance, a child comes home from a visit and is asked how the visit went and what she did, all fair and valid questions for the receiving parent to ask. But the conversation can take a harmful turn. Assume it is Mother talking, and Carol is Dad's new girlfriend:

"You went to the zoo. That must have been fun . . . Did Carol go with you? . . . She did? . . . Did she come home from the zoo with you? . . . Oh, she did. Did she spend the night? . . . You don't know? Well, who cooked breakfast?"

Here Mother is using Junior as a spy—little Junior, the eight-year-old detective. If the child is aware that Mother does not like Carol or does not approve of the relationship or does not approve of overnights for Carol while the child is there, the child is placed in the middle. By answering Mom's questions he may be getting Dad in trouble, so his visits ultimately become harmful to his father because of his mother's wrath.

- *Do obtain necessary information about your ex by asking him or her directly or by asking someone other than the children.*

*Do not ask children to keep secrets from the other household.* Secrets are either too minor or too good to keep. Asking children to keep secrets puts them in collusion with one parent against the other. Or, if they are young, a secret is such a treasure that they will want to share it but know they should not, so they set it up for you to pry it out of them. We are not talking about secrets like, "Don't tell your mom about the present I helped you buy for her birthday next week." We are talking about secrets like, "Don't tell your mother I am going with Betty to Hawaii next week for a vacation" or "Don't tell your dad I just got this beautiful bedroom suite this week." The child will pick up the message that a parent could get into trouble if the other parent knew the secret. This places the child in the difficult position of lying either by commission or omission and, as with our other examples, puts him into a stressful loyalty bind.

- *Do encourage your children to speak freely to both parents.*

*Do not respond to reports of disparaging remarks made about you by the other parent.* This caveat includes other family members as well. When Johnny comes back home and says something like, "Mommy says you never were able to hold a job and that is why I could not have my dirt bike" or "Daddy called you money-hungry. What did he mean?" your natural tendency will be to say something along the lines of, "Why, that is not true; let me tell you how it really happened."

*Don't!* By defending yourself you place the child in the middle and perhaps unwittingly set up game playing on the part of the child. If you tell her how it "really happened," you are guaranteeing that the child will go back to the other parent and say, "But Dad, Mom said it was like this." If Dad defends himself, then we are off and running on some variation of the game *Let's You and Him Fight (While I Watch)!* In the future, if the child wishes to stir the pot and yank your chain, he just has to come bearing another tale. You keep your child out of the middle by keeping your mouth shut and not playing the game. An appropriate response would be "That is a grown-up issue, and I am not going to talk with you about it" or "Your Dad and I disagree about a lot of things; that is why we got divorced, but that is adult stuff between your Dad and me, and I do not want you in the middle of it." You can also say, "I am sorry he feels that way, but that is between him and me, and I want to keep you out of it. That stuff is not for kids, and I am sorry it got shared with you." Tell the child that it is an adult matter and will be discussed by adults. Don't play the game!

• *Do avoid rising to the bait offered by the other parent's badmouthing of you.*

We spoke at length in Chapter Five about how to communicate with your ex and will not repeat that information here. Needless to say, raising a child in separate households is greatly aided if the parents can talk with each other. You might wish to review those guidelines.

### Things to Do to Help Your Kids

- Be warm and nurturing but not out of guilt. A little specialness now and then will not spoil them but will support them.
- Continue to parent. Hold on to your expectations of them, set appropriate limits, and don't let your children take care of you. You are the parent, and it is your job to take care of them.
- Coach your children; do not control them unless they are out of control.
- Keep your children out of the middle of the adult conflict. Make it safe for them to love the other parent when they are with you.

As you can surmise, a divorce calls on you to reframe many of your roles. In addition, you need to do your personal work to examine the kind of person you are and what it is about you that gets you into problems in your intimate relationships. Few people can do both these activities simultaneously. You must get your life back on an even, functional keel first. When you have mastered the role changes, then it may be time to look at yourself. But don't rush it! Chapter Seven outlines how to go about doing your personal work—when you're ready.

*Chapter Seven*

# Doing Your Work

The time has come to get down to work. Up to now, this book has offered information and advice on learning from your divorce, and we have included questions in previous chapters to help you understand yourself. Perhaps you have had glimpses of self-knowledge or at least have said to yourself, That's interesting; I wonder how it applies to me? However, until you become honest with yourself in looking closely at who you really are, you will not experience true learning.

When we were in secondary school, many of the exams we took were really tests of memory. By repeating back what our teachers had told us, as accurately and with language as close to our teachers' as possible, we were able to make good grades. But were we really learning anything that would change our behavior or the way we approached life? If your education was like ours, most of the time the A was earned by meeting the teacher's expectations of "right" answers. We learned to play the game well. But simply memorizing the concepts and ideas in this book will not help you at all. You must apply them to your life, to your thoughts, and to your actions for you to truly learn from your divorce and move forward as a stronger and more confident person.

We suggest that you use this chapter and the next as the focus of your activity over the next several months after you finish reading this book. Answer the questions in this chapter and in all the previous chapters and try the activities we suggest. You must make a commitment to growth—it will not spontaneously occur without willingness and intention. And remember: self-examination is a lifelong process.

# Who Are You?

We have consistently asked you to get to know the real you. The real you, the *authentic* self, as psychologists call it, is the person you are when you are not trying to meet someone else's expectations. The real you is the you who wears no masks. The word *personality,* by the way, comes from the Latin word for mask. Although you may think that your personality is who you are, it really is who you are when you are interacting with others. It's how others see you and how you want to be seen. We want you to delve even deeper than the level of personality to the level of Being.

"Yeah, right," you may say. "I don't have a clue anymore who I really am." Divorce has a way of shaking us up—of destroying the beliefs we have held about ourselves. You couldn't ask for a better opportunity to engage in introspection. As your life settles back down, you are in an excellent place to investigate and connect with your authenticity.

## Connecting with Your Authenticity

One way to get to the feeling of authenticity is to think of the happiest moment in your life. What were you doing? At the time of your greatest happiness, you were probably doing something that you truly loved and that provided great joy. You may have felt excited or even peaceful and calm. You may have lost all sense of time as you were totally in the flow—in the Now. These moments of great joy and peace, when you feel that you are truly in the most perfect place you could be, are when you are the most in touch with yourself in the moment. You are not asking yourself, What will they think of me? There is no judging or comparing—only Being.

Most of us have a hard time achieving this authentic state. From the earliest age, we learn the behaviors that we can do to get approval, hugs, and smiles or the ones that garner anger, rejection, and frowns. We begin to adopt ways of acting that will get us the good things that people can give us. We begin to define ourselves in others' terms so as to be acceptable and loved. This is how we are socialized, as we saw in Chapter One, and it is a normal part of human development. But sometimes the processes of socialization send us the message that if we don't do things the desired way, we are bad people or morally bereft.

Imagine a child in a mothers' Thursday playgroup. He gets into a fight over a sand bucket and pail with a little girl. Mother jumps up shrieking, "No! No! Bad boy! Be a nice boy and share. Only bad boys don't share! Be nice to the little girl!" Then she gives his bottom a whack. Mother behaves consistently whenever her little boy refuses to share. He is told he is a bad person.

Actually, he is not a bad person; he is undersocialized and needs to understand the give-and-take of living in a group. His mother's actions instill a moral statement in his mind: "I'm bad when I don't share." As an adult he begins to realize that he is terribly taken advantage of by people. When they want something from him, he cannot say no. He has several friends who owe him pretty hefty sums of money; he fears he won't get it back, and he also fears asking for it because he feels he is being rude and demanding. In an effort to avoid displeasing others or being thought of as bad, he has unknowingly given up a reasonable part of himself: the part that allows him to establish boundaries between himself and others—to set appropriate limits.

We all need to learn the cultural norms of our society to fit in. But when we totally forget who we are, what we want, and what brings us joy, we are living to meet others' expectations. We lose the true source of our power, our life force. It takes a lot of energy to deny and repress who we truly are. But many of us are the walking wounded, with no idea of our true selves or what brings us joy.

The discovery of your Self with a capital *S* is an exciting process in which you reveal layer by layer, as though peeling an onion, who you are and maybe even why you are the way you are. Doing so takes courage, but you have nothing to lose. You have lost your marriage, which for most people is one of the worst experiences in their lives. If you are very afraid, you may need a guide—a psychotherapist or coach—who can figuratively hold your hand while you explore this unknown terrain. In any case, take baby steps at first and go slowly. You don't need "brutal" honesty—we want you to give yourself "loving and compassionate" honesty. Know that you are a very special person (we all are!) with unique talents, gifts, and qualities. Your goal is to understand yourself so you can be the best

You that you can be. Only *you* can be You—no one else can do that job as well as you.

We suggest that you keep a journal, whether a spiral notebook, a beautiful journal from the stationery store, or a file on your computer. Keep a daily log of what is going on in your life and what you are learning. You can describe your fears, resentments, and anger—what we often deny to ourselves or tell ourselves is "bad" to say. As you work through the questions in this book, write down your answers with statements of their meaning to you. Don't censor yourself; the journal is for your eyes alone.

We also suggest that you find some time each day to sit with yourself and your journal. You may want to meditate during your quiet time and then write. Meditation is an excellent way of accessing your true Self. There are many ways and methods of meditating. If you are interested, check out books on meditation or resources in your community for instruction. You may already have a ritual of meditation, prayer, journal writing, or a combination of these that you use to clear the jumble of self-talk from your mind and to center yourself. Whatever works for you is what you should do. But commit to some time alone with yourself each day. If you are not already doing this, you will be amazed at the results in your process of learning and growing.

### Personal Growth Questions

- How do I see myself?
- What do I value?
- What do I fear?
- How do others see me?
- What roles do I play in life?

## How Do You See Yourself?

To begin your exploration into You, here's the first exercise. Get your journal or a piece of paper and answer the following question: How do you describe yourself? Make a list all of the adjectives that describe you: honest, dishonest, loving, cold, intuitive, angry, happy, caring, sad, witty, distant, sexy, and so on. Keep writing until you can think of nothing else to say.

Next, cross out any adjectives that describe your physical appearance or physical qualities. Although how you look and how you describe your appearance is important to your self-esteem, we want you to look at your internal qualities—those that represent your true self.

## How Do Others See You?

Now make a list of the ways that other people would describe you or have described you. Think of what you look like in the eyes of your friends, coworkers, ex-spouse, family, and so on.

Compare your two lists. Do people see you the same way that you see yourself? If not, where is the discrepancy? Write a paragraph about what you notice.

Very few people have mastered the art of being themselves. Don't you love to watch small children? They are so free to be who they are, living in the moment. They don't hold back their feelings. If a child gets a smaller piece of cake than his playmate, he will complain. As children grow and are socialized, they learn to hide their true feelings. When those feelings and desires are given negative labels—for example, *selfish*—children take those labels to heart and begin to tell themselves these same things. However, the goal of knowing yourself is to look behind the labels, both negative and positive, that you and others have given you, and to find your authentic self.

## What Do You Value?

Next, make a list of ten things or qualities that describe what you value or consider most important in this world: honesty, family, shopping, literacy, having fun, books, music, art, and so on. Think about the activities that you enjoy. Why do you enjoy them? If you like to camp, do you value the feeling of freedom in being away from home, the closeness to nature, the self-sufficiency? Those are some of your values. If you like to sing, what gives you happiness in singing? Is it being able to express yourself, to bring pleasure to others, or to be one with the music? The reason for the joy is the value.

Victor Frankl, author of *Man's Search for Meaning,* said that we are "pulled" by our values. That is, our values do not motivate our actions, but rather offer us choices in how we conduct our lives.

Do your values reflect how you see yourself and how others see you? Compare your lists to see if anything incongruous jumps out at you. Be honest: Does your behavior reflect your values? If family is on your list of top values, does your family get your attention and care, or does your job come first? If you say that you value honesty but you often tell little white lies to save face ("the check is in the mail"), do you really think that honesty is important? Write your answers down. In our interactions with others, our values should help us set priorities and goals.

Be aware, however, that if you have been in an abusive relationship, with either a parent or spouse, the descriptions that others have given you and that you might have accepted will not be accurate. The little child who is constantly told she is ugly, selfish, and stupid will begin to believe that. The spouse who is criticized for every attempt at humor will begin to believe that she is not funny and will be afraid to express herself.

But now is the time to examine all these labels to determine which fit, which don't fit, and which we may want to change. We suggest that each day you take quiet time for yourself and reflect on one of the descriptors that you or someone else has given you. Think about when the term has been applied to you, in what circumstances, who used it, and when it was first used. Is it true? If not, why not? Describe examples of how you behave and think and what you tell yourself that show why the label is wrong. You will begin to get a feeling of whether the descriptors are accurate or not. And if a description is accurate but you don't like it because it doesn't match your values, you can choose to change your behavior. We all behave in ways that we don't like—the key is to recognize those behaviors, own them, and change them.

## What Are You Afraid Of?

Often a fear is blocking you from acting in ways that are consistent with who you really are and with your values. To find out, ask yourself, What am I afraid of? Write down everything that comes to mind. Your fears are likely to have a common thread, one that reflects your needs. Bob calls this a metaphor for your life. For example, if you identified many situations in which you are afraid that someone won't like you or will leave you, you have a fear of rejection. Your metaphor or need is for acceptance or perhaps security. Are your interactions with others or reactions to them driven by a need for safety, excitement, or peace, for example? If you can identify a primary metaphor or need, you will begin to understand your self-defeating behavior. Your analysis will bring results and understanding over time; don't rush it. Remember, it takes the removal of layer after layer of your conditioning to reveal your authentic self. You may gain understanding that feels uncomfortable, or uncover some painful memories (it hurts to realize that, yes, you were hypercritical of your ex), but as you forgive yourself and release the pain, you will be lighter and happier. If you begin to uncover terrifying or traumatic information, you may want to work with a psychotherapist. This book is not meant to take the place of psychotherapy, but is designed to give you a jump start to understanding and learning.

## What Are Your Roles in Life?

Next, make a list of your roles—who you are in interaction with others: mother, homemaker, aunt, supervisor, teacher, coach, son, big brother, and so on. Are you the same person in all these roles? Would all the descriptors that you listed apply to you in a particular role? Do you behave the same way in each? Do the people with whom you interact in each of these roles see you in the same way? If not, why not? We all tend to behave somewhat differently when acting in different roles; for instance, we're not the same in the office as we are at home. But to the extent that you have to put on a mask and be someone you are not—to the extent that you are *inauthentic*—you are depriving yourself of the opportunity to be who you were meant to be in this world.

Of course we behave in certain situations because of social expectations. You don't spit in the piano, nor do you interview for a job at IBM in a tank top, cutoffs, and flip-flops if you really want it. We are not talking about conforming to the expectations of a functioning society. We are talking about what society expects that makes you fearful enough to put on a mask.

Now look at your roles and compare them with your values—those qualities, relationships, and activities that you hold most important in your life. Are the things you are doing in your life promoting or reflecting your values? Be tough here. You may see that your service on a neighborhood political committee, although valuable work, really doesn't promote your core values of education and beauty. You joined the political committee because your neighbor asked you and it was hard to say no. But are you enjoying it? Maybe you are having fun learning about political activism. But maybe you find yourself dreading the work and making up excuses to miss meetings. If so, you can do something else. Perhaps helping in the school library once a week or designing bulletin boards for the central hallway at school would give you more pleasure. The goal is to examine each of your roles and determine if you are being the authentic you or simply doing something to meet another person's expectations.

Although doing our chores may seem to take lots of time, we can actually learn about ourselves when engaging in our daily activities—cleaning house, dumping the trash, making copies at work, for example—that may seem to be mundane and not particularly pleasurable. We do these tasks because we have to in order to maintain the household or keep our jobs. Perhaps they are associated with a role that we truly value—wife, mother, boss. Even these routine activities, however, can help you focus on what's good in your life and on who you really are, if you pay attention to your self-talk. Mystics would say that the goal in life is to be totally present in each moment. If you are present, you will be content; it's only what we tell ourselves about the past and the future in any moment that keeps us from appreciating the present. For example, one evening while performing the common chore of washing dishes after dinner, Christie paid attention to her thoughts. (She had been reading *The Power of Now,* by Eckhart Tolle, which suggests watching your thoughts to see that most of the time we are not in the present moment.) Christie realized that rather than observing the warmth of the water on her hands, the rainbow in the soapsuds, and the smell of the dish detergent, she was thinking that she had to get this chore done quickly because she had to prepare for her law school class. And then she began criticizing her husband to herself. *Why isn't he helping? After all, I cooked dinner, and the least he could do is help with the dishes. That happens all the time; he just doesn't care about me. He knows I'm stressed out . . .* On and on the self-talk went. The dishes didn't get done any faster, but Christie was irritated and more stressed out when she finished. She was thinking about the past and the future and not paying any attention to the present moment. She could have chosen to enjoy doing the dishes because her role as wife is important to her and she strongly values her time at home having dinner with her husband. Instead she chose to make herself unhappy, and missed out on the pleasure of the Now.

We spend much of our time on autopilot, not really paying attention to the present. Haven't you gone into a room and, once there, not known what you were going in for? Or when driving, have you ever arrived at your destination with no memory of what transpired to get there? "The more you are focused on time—past and future—the more you miss the Now, the most precious thing there is . . . because it is the *only* thing," states Tolle (pp. 40–41) about the need to be in the Now to find your Self. Listen to your self-talk as you go about your day, and you will learn a lot about yourself.

---

### Discover Your True Self

1. Describe your happiest moment.
2. Describe yourself as you see yourself.
3. Describe yourself as others see you.
4. Compare the two preceding descriptions; look for consistencies and inconsistencies.
5. List your ten most important values.
6. Compare your values with how you and others see you; is your behavior consistent with your values?
7. List your roles. Are your roles in keeping with your values?
8. Make a plan for change.

---

## Working the Exercise

Jonathan, a newly divorced father, decided to get to know himself and did the Discover Your True Self exercises. Let's see what he said.

First, he thought about the happiest time in his life and wrote in his journal, "When I was about 10 years old Dad used to take me fishing with him. We would fish, side by side, not speaking much, just sharing the experience. I loved the beauty of the water, the sunshine and the trees. The quiet was so wonderful—being miles away from other people, me and my dad together. I remember thinking that when I had a son, I wanted to be just like my dad. I couldn't put words to it then, but I felt so cared for and loved, not just by Dad, but by nature, sort of."

He then wrote down how he would describe himself. (His responses appear in the left column, "All of Me," in the list that follows.) Then he went back and crossed out all the adjectives that described him physically, and was left with the descriptors in the middle column ("Inside Me"). Finally he wrote down how others might describe him or have described him; these he put in the right column ("Others"). He underlined the characteristics that appeared in all three columns.

| *All of Me* | *Inside Me* | *Others* |
|---|---|---|
| Sad | Sad | Self-contained |
| Athletic | | High achieving |
| Loving | Loving | Workaholic |
| Compassionate | Compassionate | Honest |
| Helpful | Helpful | Fair |
| Quiet | Quiet | <u>Quiet</u> |
| Funny | Funny | Caring |
| Thin | | Polite |
| Short | | Dutiful |
| Middle-aged | | Respectful |
| Graceful | Graceful | Demanding |
| Artistic | Artistic | Sarcastic |
| Dark | | Patronizing |
| Italian | | |
| Angry | Angry | |
| Impatient | Impatient | |
| Passive | Passive | |
| Energetic | Energetic | |
| Thoughtful | Thoughtful | <u>Thoughtful</u> |

| Intelligent | Intelligent | <u>Intelligent</u> |
|---|---|---|
| Loving | Loving | |
| Paternal | Paternal | |
| Skeptical | Skeptical | |
| Creative | Creative | |
| Critical | Critical | <u>Critical</u> |
| Cold | Cold | |

Are you beginning to get a feeling about who Jonathan is, or at least how he and others see him? When Jonathan looked at the lists and compared them, he saw a few traits in common, but others that were very different. Here is what he wrote after he had thought about the consistencies and differences:

It seems like my belief about myself that I am a loving, caring person is consistent with how others see me. They have told me those things, at least that I am a caring teacher. Also, that I am quiet, thoughtful, and intelligent. However, while I feel that I am a fairly easy-going guy, I know that my ex found me demanding at times and somewhat driven. I never thought of myself as a workaholic until my ex-wife complained that I worked all the time. I love my teaching job, but all the preparation I need to do can't be accomplished during the school day. I have to work nights and weekends to do a good job. I am respectful to people, but I guess that my way of saying what's on my mind is a bit indirect as I use sarcasm or humor. I know that I don't share my feelings with other people— I've heard the words "self-contained" from my sisters—my wife said shut down. She said that although I may have a lot of love inside, I didn't show it easily. I know that I have deep feelings—I'm really angry at my ex-wife for breaking up our family and sad, too—but I don't show these feelings to other people. My parents always said that I didn't give them any trouble and their friends always commented on how respectful and polite I was. I try not to burden others with my problems. However, myself, sometimes I felt like Eddie Haskell—nice on the outside, but mean-spirited inside. I love taking care of my kids and consider myself a good father. However, my ex said that I was patronizing of her when all I was trying to do was be helpful and give her advice. I am somewhat of a perfectionist and I know that I can be critical of how others do things if they are doing them different from me.

After rereading his answers to the previous questions, Jonathan listed his values:

Family

Education

Nature

Art

Compassion

Peace

Home

Solitude

Love

Spirituality

But when he compared his values—those things he considered most important to exemplify in his life—he was struck by a couple of things. He saw that his list of values included peace and compassion, yet he is very angry and sad. Although he valued peace, he realized that he didn't feel peaceful. Although he valued compassion, he was not being compassionate with himself. He began exploring whether he had always been angry; if he was, Why? Who or what was the target of his anger? He asked himself if he had always been sad. As he thought about his anger and sadness, he wrote in his journal: "I realize that I have felt sad and angry for a long time, ever since childhood, and I have rarely felt totally happy. For some reason, I seem to have a well of sadness that seeps out into my relationships with others and with myself. I become critical of others when I really want to be helpful. I'm thinking that I'm afraid of being happy. Why? I can't think of anything right now. I'll have to continue to explore this."

He used this moment of insight as the first step to learning more about himself. Then he listed his roles:

| | |
|---|---|
| Teacher | Employee |
| Father | Ex-spouse |
| Son | Brother |
| Painter | Volunteer |

| | |
|---|---|
| Single parent | Lover |
| Learner | Congregant |
| Seeker | Sunday school teacher |
| Nephew | Coach |

Comparing his values with his roles, he decided that the things that he was doing in life really did match his values. He valued being a father more than anything because he got to love, teach, and help his boys. All of his other roles also reflected his values. He decided that he wanted to continue doing what he was doing, but to be more joyful. This would be his work: to experience joy and receive pleasure from the things he did. But he also wanted to be more connected with people around him. He decided to spend more time talking to his coworkers and also to find an outdoor activity through which he could make new friends. He joined the Colorado Mountain Club and started going on weekly hikes when his kids were with their mom. He continued to write in his journal every day, and slowly began to reclaim his Self.

As part of his self-reclamation, being an energetic person, Jonathan deliberately made a plan for change. He asked himself the following questions:

1. What do I want to change?
2. Why do I want to change?
3. Am I willing to change?
4. What will I do differently?

Here are his answers:

1. I want to change how much I criticize people.
2. I want to change because I hurt people and they react defensively to me. I am not being helpful. My marriage was affected, my children's self-esteem is suffering, and my coworkers don't like me.
3. I am willing to stop criticizing other people.
4. I can do the following things:
   Tell myself I am OK. I do not have to point out other people's faults and mistakes to feel better about myself in comparison.

I will keep my mouth shut when I am tempted to be critical.
Instead I will count to ten and say something neutral or
positive. I will tell myself to ask myself mentally, what is
going on with me? Why do I feel angry or frustrated or
whatever? I will ask myself if this comment is necessary,
helpful or kind.

I will ask people to forgive me when I have been critical.
I will let them know I am sorry and am changing this
behavior.

I will learn and practice better ways to communicate.

## How Has Your Past Affected Your Divorce?

You will find it useful to look at your past and see how it affected
your current situation and your self-perceptions. The first chapters
of this book discussed our early conditioning, the factors that influence our choice of mates, and other developmental issues. Now
we want you to examine your past for themes, patterns of behavior, and relationship issues. However, we advise you to use your insights about the past for understanding and to avoid blame, guilt,
and victimization. Sometimes when an individual has an insight
about how a person or situation in the past has affected his life neg-
atively, rather than assuming responsibility for changing the negative self-talk or current situation, he will wallow in blaming the
person who harmed him. He becomes a victim who wants revenge,
rather than a survivor who seeks healing.

So please be careful how you use your recognition of the
sources of emotional difficulty; use the knowledge to make
changes in your behavior. The blame game stunts growth because
you cannot change the past nor can you control the behavior of
other people. You *can* control your reactions to the past and
to what people have done. In order to get the most out of this
section, carefully consider these questions and write your answers
in your journal. Take your time. As mediators like to say, slower
is actually faster. The more time that you take carefully considering, writing, and thinking about your answers, the more help
you will receive in uncovering your past influences. This is doing your work!

> **Questions to Help You Understand the Impact of the Past**
>
> - How did you function with your parents?
> - What was your role in the family?
> - What were your teens and early twenties like?
> - If you could redo your life, what would you be doing now?
> - What are you like in relationships now?
> - What did you like in your marriage? What didn't you like?

## How Did You Function with Your Parents?

1. Who were your parental figures (mother and father, grand-parent or other relative, guardian, foster parent, and so on)?
2. List at least ten words that describe your father (or male parental figure). Which qualities do you like, and which do you dislike? How are you like your father?
3. List at least ten words that describe your mother (or female parental figure). Which qualities do you like, and which do you dislike? How are you like your mother?
4. Who were you closer to, your mother or your father?
5. How were you treated? Did you feel special and loved? Did you feel unloved or overlooked? What five words best describe your feelings about your parents?
6. How was affection shown in your family?
7. How did your parents discipline you? Were you emotionally or physically abused? If so, what did your parents do, and how did you react?

As we saw in earlier chapters, sometimes we choose the mates we do because they are like one of our parents or seem to be very different from one of our parents. Our parents are the first people from whom we learn about ourselves. If our parents are unconditionally loving to us—that is, if they love us wholeheartedly just because we are their children, with no expectations of particular behavior—we will be more able to love ourselves and others. However, if our parents labeled and judged us and withheld love to exact particular behavior from us, we internalize those labels in our self-concept. So although you may tell yourself you are stupid when you make a mistake, because that is what you were always told, you are not stupid. You simply made a mistake, which, as we have emphasized several times in this book, is an opportunity to learn.

People tend to parent the same way that their parents did. Most new parents say that they want to do things differently from their parents, even if their parents were pretty good parents. Each generation has new ideas about raising children, and we all want to do the best we can. But every parent has also been surprised to hear their mother's or father's words coming out of their mouths when talking to their children: "Don't run with that stick—you'll poke your eye out!" or "Because I said so, young man!" Where on earth did that come from? From our early conditioning and training. Children's minds are sponges that soak up everything that's happening and convert unconscious learning into behavior. If our mother was not demonstrative with her affection, never holding us or kissing us in public, we will probably not be comfortable with demonstrating affection publicly either. We can change that behavior, however, which is the theme of this book. Learn about yourself: acknowledge what you like and decide to change what you dislike.

## What Was Your Role in the Family?

1. Did you have siblings? What was your place in the birth order?
2. Which of your siblings was your favorite? Why?
3. Did you feel that you had a particular role to play in the family in relation to your siblings? For example, were you the "trouble-maker" and your sister the "good girl"?
4. Did you feel that either of your parents or both had a favorite child? Were you that child? How did it feel to be (or not be) the favorite? How did any favoritism affect your relationships with your siblings?

We learn about being in relationship with others from our siblings and parents. When we have had a particular role in the family, we will replay that role in our intimate relationships. If I was the "scapegoat" on whom all the family's frustrations and dysfunction were focused, it will not be surprising that with my husband I will become the focus of our marital dysfunction and may believe that all the problems are my fault.

If you felt that you weren't the favorite (think of the classic Tommy Smothers' line, "Mother loved you best"), this inferiority will continue to play out in all your relationships. You will feel not quite good enough until you come to grips with the fact that Mother's preference (or your perception of it) has nothing to do with who you really are. Those feelings of inadequacy can have far-reaching consequences later in life, affecting relationships with romantic partners, peers, and siblings. If you were the favorite, then you may feel guilt that you were treated differently from your siblings, or you may go through life with a sense of entitlement. It is critical that you find a balance between reality and your past conditioning.

## What Were Your Teens and Early Twenties Like?

1. What kind of person were you attracted to?
2. Did you feel attractive to members of the opposite sex?
3. Did you have a boyfriend or girlfriend?
4. How did those relationships unravel? (Think beyond the obvious answer, "too young and immature to maintain a relationship.")

## If Your Experiences Had Been Different Growing Up, What Would You Be Doing Now?

Do you have dreams that were never fulfilled or that you were afraid to have? Looking back, would you have made different choices if you knew then what you know now? (Well, "duh"—of course.) Do you believe that your background and past have kept you from fulfilling your heart's desires? Well, guess what, it's never too late to change direction in your life! But it's also not too late to think about what you have accomplished and who you are now and to be happy with your present circumstances, even "in spite of" your past. This is another choice you get to make.

## What Are You Like in Relationships Now?

1. Are you dominant or submissive?
2. In what ways do you like or not like being taken care of? Do you consider yourself more dependent or independent? Are you the "caretaker" in a relationship?
3. How do you handle anger?
4. How do you handle criticism?
5. What about control? Do you have to be right?
6. How do you express affection? How do you like to have affection expressed to you?
7. Do you usually work to please others or work to please yourself?

Throughout this book you have read stories about people who have divorced for many reasons. Your answers to the questions here can help you think clearly about your role in the breakup of your marriage. What did you bring to the relationship dysfunction? Why did you choose a person with whom it was so difficult to be the best You?

Alice had a temper. She blew up at every little slight from friends or family. In the car, her road rage was off the chart. Her parents had called her feisty and laughed about her "red-haired temper." They tried to set limits for her, but often gave in to her temper tantrums. An only child, Alice was able to get almost anything she wanted from her parents. As she got older, she lost friends because she would blow up at them if they did anything that she didn't like.

Obviously, she wasn't popular in school. She was an average student, but she excelled in one class: drama. Her flair for exaggeration and lack of inhibitions helped her escape into other characters very easily. She majored in theater in college, and everyone said that she would be a big star some day. She began dating Lincoln, an intense theater major who wanted to direct.

The two made quite a dramatic couple—they swooped across the campus dressed in black capes with long red scarves. They began living together and pronounced themselves married. Unfortunately for them, they were both used to being in control in a relationship and to being the dominant mate. Their fights became legendary, with neighbors calling the police when they heard the loud screaming and dishes breaking. They broke up within a year.

But headstrong Alice was miserable because Lincoln was her first big love. After a dramatic attempt at suicide, she went into therapy.

There she learned rudimentary lessons, such as that the best relationships have give-and-take and that differences must be negotiated. She worked with her therapist to express her needs in a less strident manner and to learn to replace anger with other more positive behaviors. Alice's examination of her role in the relationship helped spur her to make major changes in her behavior. Her next relationship was much less stormy and intense and more satisfying to her.

## What Did You Like in Your Marriage? What Didn't You Like?

No marriage is perfect. Married couples learn to make adjustments for things that they don't like in their partner's behavior. However, you may have encountered behavior or situations that were very difficult for you to cope with. What were those things that really drove you up a wall? Until you have identified them you won't know if these qualities, behaviors, or situations are ones that you could learn new skills to handle, or if they are totally outside your value system, making the relationship unworkable.

For instance, Luanne hated the way that her husband Johnny cut corners on their family budget. He counted every penny they spent, and saved almost 45 percent of their net income "for a rainy day." She knew that he had been raised by his single mother and had had to work since he was eleven just to help buy groceries. There had been no extras in his family. Now Johnny worked two jobs because he said that he needed to "build up their nest egg."

Luanne was also working, and her income went to pay for groceries, utilities, and clothes for herself and her two boys. She understood Johnny's fear of not having enough to get by, and made allowances for his working so much. Her main concern, however, was that as the boys went into school, Johnny was unwilling for them to participate in any extracurricular activities because of the cost, and he begrudged every dime she spent on them. He interrogated her if she bought a pair of shoes for a child from the discount store. He wouldn't allow them to be in soccer or Cub Scouts like all their friends.

Luanne tried to negotiate with Johnny, and when that didn't work, she began badgering and whining. But he refused to budge.

She finally had enough and demanded that Johnny go into counseling with her. When he refused because "it cost too much," she found a lawyer and filed for divorce. She was willing to be frugal for herself because she also believed in saving, but she was not willing to deny her children reasonable amenities that they could afford. She valued her family and children and decided that the only way they would have a happy childhood free from want was to divorce Johnny.

Ironically, Johnny today pays more in child support and alimony than he would have paid for activities for the children, and he curses Luanne every time he writes his monthly checks to her. He rarely sees his kids because he is working. His economic security, which had a higher value to him than his family, became his metaphor for living and his driving motivation in all that he did. Luanne knew that in future relationships she would want to find a mate who was not a spendthrift but who was generous and saw money as a means to an end, not an end itself.

## Add Action to Your Understanding

Understanding without action will not help you learn from your divorce. Once you have taken a close look at yourself and how your past contributed to the way you behave today, you must use that insight in creating your life after divorce. We hope that as you read the many stories of other people in this book, you identified similarities and differences between them and you. We want you now to focus on who you are in a relationship and what that may mean as your enter into future relationships.

---

### Tasks You Need to Accomplish to
### Create a Life After Divorce

- Teach people how to treat you.
- Find your strength(s).
- Put fun in your life.
- Pay attention to your self-talk.
- Define your purpose in any relationship.
- Practice an attitude of gratitude.

## Teach People How to Treat You

If you were treated badly by your ex-spouse, you are probably still recovering from the dishonor and betrayal that you experienced. Each of us enters into relationships with vulnerability and fragility. It hurts to be rejected, ignored, abused emotionally or physically, or lied to. The pain seeps into our souls sometimes and creates fear of future relationships. Will I be hurt again—will I choose another abuser? These are valid questions.

For many divorcing individuals, the danger signs indicating that the marriage will be difficult are often present before the wedding. Our intuition, our gut, says something is not right, but we ignore it because we are in love. We have fallen for the old adage that love conquers all. Certainly two committed people in a marriage who are both willing to do their work and grow and learn can conquer many of the challenges that life presents them. However, simply loving another person will not change abusive or dysfunctional behavior. Women in particular enter into relationships truly believing that once they are married their husband will change. Disillusionment is sure to follow such irrational thinking. If you are treated badly before the marriage, you can be almost 100 percent sure that you will be treated even worse after you've said your vows.

Dr. Phil McGraw, author of *Self Matters,* has repeatedly told his television audiences, "We teach people how to treat us." This doesn't mean that we are responsible for the abusive behavior of other people, but that we can and should tell others when their behavior is unacceptable. If the bad treatment does not stop, we end the relationship. Insecurity and fear of failure keep us in damaging relationships. When you are secure in your view of your own value and goodness—that is, when you have high self-esteem—you won't allow people to treat you disrespectfully or abusively.

## Find Your Strength(s)

One of the goals of doing your work will be to become strong. During your period of divorce recovery, you may feel weak and unable to cope with the world around you. For most people, divorce is one of the worst things that they can imagine happening to them. However, please realize that if your divorce has been one of the most traumatic experiences of your life, you will gain strength and self-confidence by surviving it. Believe it or not, people who do their work actually say that their divorce is one of the best things that ever happened to them. Not that they would have chosen this route toward self-discovery, but by doing their work, they have come into their power, independence, and selfhood. You have capabilities and reserves of strength that you probably had no idea existed.

In the period after your divorce and before you enter into other relationships, the time you spend to assess your capabilities and learn new skills is time well spent. If you depended on your mate to take care of you, this is the time to learn new skills. What would you like to learn to do to be an independent person?

Remember Christie's story in Chapter Six about the plumbers? After she and her husband separated, she was also terrified about something going wrong with her car. (Do you see the theme here? She had totally depended on the men in her life to take care of anything mechanical.) She knew that she had to conquer that fear, so she took action. She enrolled in a community college auto mechanics class designed to teach basic automobile maintenance. Every Tuesday night for eight weeks, she showed up in her jeans and old T-shirts and practiced changing the oil, checking the battery, changing tires, and performing the other sundry tasks associated with car ownership. Her ex had left her a toolbox of basic tools and a socket wrench set that fit her car. She learned enough to know how to talk to her mechanic when something was wrong with the car and to do basic maintenance if she desired.

Christie also joined an automobile club that provided service calls when her car was disabled. She found that a godsend! The first time she tried to change a tire by herself, she could not get the lug nuts off. She began telling herself how weak and stupid she was, and finally called the automobile club for emergency service. When the auto club guy began changing the tire, he told her, "Of course you can't take them off. They were installed at the factory. I wouldn't be able to get them off either!" Instead of muscle, he used a power tool, and off the nuts came. Whether or not he was telling her the truth, Christie felt better knowing that she was not totally incompetent. She will admit that she has regressed during her second marriage because her current husband takes care of her car—but she still belongs to the automobile club and calls it instead of her husband.

Shortly after her divorce, Christie also wanted to learn more home repair skills, so she took a part-time job as a painter's helper. She learned to do interior painting and even helped with hanging wallpaper and laying linoleum. Although she'd be the first to admit that she did not fully master these skills, she felt stronger for having done the work.

So if you had let your spouse handle any of the household duties, whether it be cooking, child care, or home maintenance, now is the time to discover hidden talents and abilities. As a single person, you are now forced to fend for yourself. Instead of feeling overwhelmed, decide what you need to know how to do, and go learn. You will bring this sense of independence to your next relationship.

You will also find your strength in the emotional and spiritual work that you are doing. Lao-tzu, the Chinese philosopher, said in the *Tao Te Ching*, "He who overcomes others has force; he who overcomes himself is strong." Your abilities to resolve conflicts in a collaborative rather than adversarial way, to communicate effectively, and to know your needs and be able to express them directly and respectfully will be a gift to future partners. You honor yourself and your partner when you are operating from strength and empowerment rather than from fear and insecurity.

## Put Fun in Your Life

As you get to know yourself, you will begin to reconnect with the activities that give you the most joy. Taking time for fun is important to your health and well-being. All work and no play not only makes you dull but also can make you sick. Make a list of what you enjoy doing that you may not have done for some time. Do you love going to concerts, dancing, hiking, building radio-controlled models, knitting, baking bread, or sculpting? When you were single, what did you do for fun? Is there anything you have always wanted to try, but for whatever reason haven't? Do it now! Engaging in activities that bring you joy allows you to experience your Self in the present moment. Think of the last time you did something that was purely fun for you. Didn't you lose track of time because you were so in the Now? Put this joy back into your life. You may feel that you have absolutely no extra time now, but you must find it. Join a class or a group that meets to engage in this activity; you may also make new friends, which is a secondary benefit.

Once you've connected with this source of joy and fun, do not give it up when you begin a new relationship. Many people think that they can't do fun things unless their partner joins in. However, each person in a relationship must be able to connect with his or her own sense of joy. One spouse may like to ski; the other may not, and may even hate skiing. Insisting that your spouse accompany you in activities that he hates will not increase your fun; doing so will only bring resentment and hostility. It is important for spouses to find activities that they both enjoy and can do together for fun, but it is also vital that each spouse continue engaging in his or her own fun activities. Balance is important: some fun time together, some fun time individually. To deny ourselves the opportunity to experience joy just because our spouses don't like our favorite activities is to dishonor our authentic selves.

## Pay Attention to Your Self-Talk

What you tell yourself determines how your life will unfold. If you constantly berate yourself when you make a mistake or when something doesn't go as planned, you will be unhappy. You will not feel worthy in a relationship, and your self-esteem will suffer. Furthermore, others will react to you in the same way that you react to yourself. Listen to the labels and the mental scoldings you give yourself. Change the labels. Use *challenge* instead of *problem, opportunities to learn* instead of *failure.* Rather than tell yourself that you are stupid or a klutz or selfish, talk to yourself about what you are really feeling. Be as nice and compassionate to yourself as you would be to your best friend. This sounds simple, but it's not. It takes vigilance to listen for those negative messages, and many repetitions to change them. You may want to use affirmations to help you focus on your positive qualities. You may not be able to change your situation, but you can change what you say to yourself about it.

Mary's marriage ended abruptly. Her husband, Leroy, left her suddenly with no explanation. She had known there were problems in their marriage, but had never imagined that things were this bad for Leroy. Over the next several months of the legal divorce, Mary told herself she was stupid for not recognizing Leroy's unhappiness and that she was a horrible person for not being able to be a good wife. She felt totally unloveable; Leroy had been her high school sweetheart and her first love. If he didn't love her, if she had failed him so miserably, how could anybody ever love her?

A friend gave Mary a book about creating the life you want through the use of affirmations. Affirmations are positive statements of truth that when repeated again and again begin to sink in and take hold in our consciousness. Even though Mary didn't believe that it would help, she created an affirmation that she repeated again and again like a mantra every day: "I am loveable and a good person."

At first she consciously rejected these ideas. Eventually, however, she began to believe that she was worthy of love and that the problems in her marriage were not all her fault. She began to talk to herself differently as she explored her role in the divorce, her needs that had not been met in the marriage, and how she had given up her own sense of self. Whenever she began to beat herself up because of Leroy's leaving, she would gently tell herself that although she may have made mistakes in the marriage, she was now learning how to do things differently. She then repeated her affirmation and slowly began to realize that she could go forward and create a new life. She joined a quilting group, made many new friends in a singles group at church, and found a source of joy and happiness that she hadn't felt in her marriage. She combined positive self-talk (for Mary in the form of affirmations) with doing her work. She was ready for whatever life brought her, and she had faith that it would ultimately be for her good.

As we discussed in Chapter One, your self-concept—that is, the sum of your beliefs about who you are—is created by what people tell you, what you have been taught is true, your past experiences, and what you tell yourself. Change your life by changing your story.

## Define Your Purpose in Any Relationship

A chapter on doing your work would be incomplete without a discussion of finding your purpose, and because this book is about learning from divorce, you need to look at why you were or are now in a relationship. You find your personal purpose for being on this planet from the values you hold. The starting place for discovering your purpose is to honor and recognize your authentic self. From that knowing will come guidance about career, fun activities, friends, and the other ways that you make your life better. Having a simple mission statement that guides you through each day can help you prioritize your activities when things get crazy. You can ask yourself, for example, Does joining this group promote my purpose?

But you also need to think about your reasons or purpose for being in a relationship. Why did you get married? You've seen that feeling romantic love is not a good reason to marry if that is the only reason. Marriage should provide an opportunity for both partners to experience their authentic selves together and to join their individual purposes into a partnership of purpose. We've also seen that marriage requires a level of maturity and character that can sustain enlightened self-interest (as opposed to selfish ego-gratification), that can refine such characteristics as loyalty, devotion, and commitment. The partners don't have to be engaged in the same profession, but they do need to have shared values and goals that make the partnership work well. You wouldn't go into business with a dishonest person if an important value to you were honesty. You wouldn't go into business with a partner who wants to build windows when you want to provide mental health therapy. By identifying your personal values and purpose for your life, you will be open to joining in a relationship in which you and your partner are heading in the same direction. Marriage is tough enough without a constant struggle over values and goals.

## Practice an Attitude of Gratitude

Every religious and philosophical tradition admonishes us to be grateful for what we have in order to experience serenity and more abundance. When we live our lives from a place of lack, all we will see is lack and "not enough." Divorce sure feels like not enough! By being thankful for what we have rather than railing against the gods for what we lack, we will be much more in touch with Being rather than having. It places us in the present, in the *Now*.

In her book *Simple Abundance,* Sarah Ban Breathnach suggests that you keep a gratitude journal in which each day you list five things for which you are grateful. Once you start noticing the good in your life, such as the beautiful sunrise, your healthy child, or your safe return from a trip on an airplane, you begin to realize that things aren't all that bad. The "attitude of gratitude" will carry you through the tough times in life and help you appreciate when things are going well. We all would much rather spend time with a person who sees the good in us and the beauty of life rather than with the critical sourpuss who can never be pleased. Developing that sense of gratitude during your divorce recovery will allow you to be in relationship with yourself and with others in a way that benefits everyone.

Doing your work can be hard, painful, and slow, but it is essential to your growth and learning. In the next chapter you will learn how to put all the self-understanding together to move forward to a stronger, happier, and more satisfied you.

# Chapter Eight

# Rebuilding a Life

Once you have an understanding of your contribution to the breakup of your relationship and you are living the life of a single person or parent, the next issue to face is what to do with all this knowledge. Where do you want to go with it? There is an old joke about a man talking to a friend who says, "I have been in psychotherapy for ten years and I'm still afraid to get on elevators, but I really, really understand why!"

Understanding is an important first step, but translating all you know into action is the equally important second step. Rebuilding your life in the direction you want to go is hard work because often you have to confront your demons and try to do things differently. There will be a strong pull to go back to your old ways. Don't! If you have followed the advice in Chapter Seven on doing your work, you will be ready to begin rebuilding. Learn from your divorce and move forward.

To rebuild your life you must start with your insights, set goals, and determine a pathway to those goals.

For example, Athena, a client of Bob's, discovered from doing her work that one of her contributions to the failure of her marriage was that she was conflict avoidant. Rather than standing up for what she wanted, she would just shut down, back off, and silently lick her wounds. Her husband, meanwhile, went on his merry way, blissfully unaware that something was wrong and that he was walking all over her. His cluelessness was greatly enhanced by a self-centeredness that made it very hard for him to see anybody's point of view but his own. As is so often the case, out of all the people in the United States, they found each other: she unable to be normally self-assertive, he unable to recognize another person's need if it hit him in the face. Learning how to be self-assertive became a major goal for Athena in her divorce support group. Recognizing your weaknesses and attempting to correct them is our goal for you.

How do you integrate all that you have learned? As we have consistently stated in the previous chapters, you have control only over yourself and over no one else. Any changes will have to start with you. Your behavior gives others and the world an opportunity to respond to what you are doing. If you don't like how others respond to you, then it is up to you either to "take it" if you feel very strongly about what you are doing, or to change your behavior to elicit another response from those around you.

## Starting to Rebuild

The rules for rebuilding your life after divorce are simple to state.

- Identify the kind of life you want. (Determine your goals.)
- Know your strengths and weaknesses.
- Order your goals as priorities.
- Define and implement a pathway to your goals.

What Athena did can serve as our guide in terms of rules and steps to rebuilding a life. Athena, now thirty-two, had been married to Nick for eight years. They had two children, a boy nearly eight-and-a-half and a boy just six. Athena's husband had asked for a divorce because he said he found her boring and a stick-in-the-mud. Athena, as she looked back on it, was tired of being terrified by her husband's choices. He was a man who loved risk and taking chances.

They met when Athena was an assistant to her father, who was an international judge at a snowboarding half-pipe championship competition in Breckenridge, Colorado. Nick was a top competitor—athletic, graceful on a board, and a high-energy type of guy. Athena found Nick enormously attractive because he was so different from the fellows she had gone out with during her days in an all-girl Catholic high school. She became pregnant within about four months of meeting him. Abortion was not a choice either of them could make, so Nick married her in what he later referred to as a "good old-fashioned shotgun wedding."

As Athena looked back on the marriage, she saw herself as doing with Nick what she had innocently done with her father: being an assistant and a gofer. As Athena put it, "Nick was a constant boy, a Peter Pan." Athena was there to raise "his" children and to do his bidding. Nick was not mean spirited, but he was extremely self-centered. He was a taker. At first Athena enjoyed being the giver, but as the marriage went on she became exhausted with the giving and with getting little in return from Nick. She knew she was a good mom and kept the home fires burning in a competent way, but she also began to feel alone in the marriage. When she spoke to Nick about this, he encouraged her to get a hobby or to do some volunteer work. Athena continued to feel lonely, as Nick's suggestions had no involvement from him. His answer was that she should go off, get busy, and get a life. She did, but ultimately her new life did not include Nick. He could not be reciprocal; he could not *transact*, only act. She finally figured, Why bother with him?

Six months after her divorce and after an exhausting day on her job as a salesclerk at a large department store, Athena sat down after the boys had gone to bed and did an inventory of where she was and where she wanted to go. She felt as though life were running her, instead of the other way around. Life was filled with work, but little pleasure. She knew she was not ready for another relationship, but she was ready for more than life was offering her at the moment. It hit her that she was expecting life to offer her something. She thought, *Maybe I should demand or at least work for something I want in life. I have to build a new life. It is not going to come to me on a silver platter.* Note that it took Athena six months to get to the point where she could ask this question. Prior to that time she was getting a job, grieving over her divorce, and, as she put it, "Running just two feet ahead of the avalanche to stay alive!" There was so much to do related to the change in lifestyle brought on by the divorce that there was little time to think about what she wanted from life. But she finally stumbled on the first rule of getting a life.

## IDENTIFY THE KIND OF LIFE YOU WANT

For the next several nights, after the kids were in bed, Athena sat down with a pad of paper on which she drew a line down the middle, dividing the pad into two columns. The left column she labeled "Goals," and the right column she labeled "Pathways." Under Goals, Athena began to list what it was she wanted to have in her life. When she first started to fill the column, she became pretty playful and listed things like "A castle on the Rhine," "a Rolls Royce," and "a personal body slave." Once that was out of her system, she began to list things that were realistic; some were within her reach, others a stretch. After a few evenings, her Goals column looked like this:

*Goals*

Financial security.

Keep the house so the boys' lives won't get jerked around.

A job that gives me hours that let me be home when the boys get home from school.

Something that helps me feel that I am not living on the poverty level.

Something to do when the boys are with their dad for four days every other weekend.

Make friends who know me as a single parent (not a divorced woman!)

Get some exercise!

Cut out the junk food.

Do something regularly with the kids that we enjoy.

Be done with the divorce scramble and have my life together in three years.

Get over my anger at Nick for eight wasted years!

Athena decided to stop the list because she knew she was the type of person who could create lists that went on ad infinitum, with the result that she would never be able to complete the list.

First she looked at her goals and asked herself what they boiled down to. She went through her list and grouped her goals into what seemed like same-topic clusters and then thought up a name for each cluster. This helped her make the list manageable. She came up with the following:

Cluster A—Financial: financial security, keep the house, job with school-friendly hours

Cluster B—Me: no feeling of poverty, do something when boys are with Dad, make new friends, get exercise, cut out junk food

Cluster C—Kids: fun with kids

Cluster D—Divorce: get over anger at ex, get over divorce in three years

She then started a new sheet on which all the goals that fell within each cluster were listed as a cluster, and brainstormed possible pathways to the goals. That is, she wrote down anything that came into her head without being critical of its practicality. Here is what she wrote for Cluster D—Divorce:

*Pathways*

Hire a hit-man to kill Nick!

Wait for time to heal me.

Therapy.

Read books on how to let go of anger.

Date.

Get busy so I don't brood.

Find out at what points I get maddest at Nick.

See if part of eight years was not wasted. It wasn't all bad all the time.

Try to be civil when I am around Nick, but limit my time around him.

Figure out what I did wrong, and don't do it again.

After she had written down what she could think of as pathways without censoring her thoughts, she went back and looked at her list to determine which were good ideas and possible to accomplish. Right off the bat she dropped, admittedly with a smile, the idea of hiring a hit-man to kill Nick. It was a fun fantasy, but it had no place in the real world. She then evaluated each of the other pathways she had brainstormed.

*"Wait for time to heal me."* Here she had no choice. If the passage of time would help the healing, then it was going to happen. This was a no-brainer, but Athena had a glimmer in the back of her mind that if she nursed her hurts over the years and felt victimized by Nick, time would probably make her angrier and more sour. So she saw that it was not just the simple passage of time that would heal her, but what she did within that time to heal herself.

*"Psychotherapy."* Athena knew several friends who had been in therapy after their divorce, and they spoke well of it. She also knew that her health plan at work had very limited psychotherapy benefits. She really did not want to spend a whole lot of money right now because she did not have a whole lot of money to spend. She was aware of the free Wednesday-night divorce support group at her church. Nick had the kids for a Wednesday evening dinner visit from after school until eight. The support group ran from seven to nine. If she were to ask Nick to keep the boys an hour or so later, she knew he would. That would give her the time she needed for the group, but she would have to be out of there like a shot. Maybe Nick would agree to bathe the boys and have them ready for bed in their PJs if she asked.

*"Read books on how to let go of anger."* Athena liked to read and had enjoyed self-help books in the past, so this one would be easy and might well be helpful.

*"Date."* No! She was not ready for this yet. She did not want to be one of those dates who could talk only about her divorce. More important, she was not at a place yet where she was willing to be open and vulnerable to another man. Dating was not a choice for now.

*"Get busy so I don't brood."* This was a given. She was going to make a new life for herself, so if getting busy would be helpful, she was already on her way. She recognized that when she was focused on doing for herself, she did not have the time or the inclination to lie around and wallow in self-pity. There were moments when she felt sorry for herself, and she was aware that those moments could become hours if she really let herself go. Having something

to do alone that satisfied her was a good antidote to playing what she called "archeologist"—going back over the past and ruminating about its hurts.

*"Find out at what points I get maddest at Nick."* She asked herself, When did he get to me the most? She was not sure of her answer to this, so she decided she would do two things to try to get a sense of how he got to her. She was going to make this a focus of her use of the church divorce group, and she decided she would start to keep a journal of when Nick made her mad. Maybe if she wrote things down, a pattern would begin to emerge. She also knew that when she wrote things down it helped her cleanse her system of anger and petty thoughts. So keeping a journal might accomplish two things: letting her see if there was a pattern to what made her mad and helping her let go of her anger by writing it down, which took it outside herself and onto paper.

*"Try to be civil when I am around Nick, but limit my time around him."* Athena thought that one way to handle this issue would be to cut down on the number of times she had to see Nick. Having fewer contacts related to the children would probably go a long way toward increasing her civility. After giving the idea careful thought, she decided that she would ask Nick to pick up the boys from school on Thursday when his four-day weekend began and deliver them back to school on Monday morning when school was in session. She struggled with this. There was part of her that out of sheer anger wanted him to have as little access to the boys as possible. But she also knew that the boys loved their father, and he them, and that even though she had divorced Nick, the boys had not. She thought of making Wednesday night an overnight as well to cut down the contact between her and Nick and to give the boys a little more time with their dad. After going back and forth in her mind, she decided that what was most important was the boys' adjustment and stability. Because she could offer Nick a Wednesday overnight later, she decided to hold off on the offer of an extra overnight until she was sure that the boys were doing well in school and adjusted to the current parenting time schedule.

*"Figure out what I did wrong, and don't do it again."* Here was the hard part. It was so easy to see Nick's fatal flaws, but it was much harder for her to see her own. She got herself a new piece of paper with two columns, and she began to list what she had learned

about herself over the last months: how she saw herself, how others saw her, and what was important to her, so that she could look objectively at her strengths and weaknesses. With that beginning, she was observing the second rule of building a life:

## KNOW YOUR STRENGTHS AND WEAKNESSES

After several nights of pondering and writing, Athena's page looked like this:

*Strengths*

I am honest. I tell little white lies but no whoppers.

I pay attention to detail, so my work is thorough.

I have a good sense of humor and enjoy a good laugh.

I am loyal to my friends.

I am slow to anger.

I do not hold grudges.

I do not lose it with my children (very often, anyway).

I am reliable and steady. I like routine.

*Weaknesses*

I avoid conflict. I pull back and stuff my feelings just so as not to cause a fight.

I can sometimes obsess over detail that nobody cares about. I make them angry.

When I am angry, I sulk and punish others by making them feel guilty.

When I am really mad I do not confront. I sabotage by forgetting or refusing to do something. I never tell the person I am mad at that I am mad. I just let them figure it out for themselves.

I did not enjoy sex with Nick.

I am not brave. I do not like to deal with things that stress me, be it my crying child's skinned knee or my checkbook that refuses to balance.

I can be a procrastinator. If I don't do it, maybe it will go away.

I don't like to take risks.

Athena looked at what she had written and with some relief decided she wasn't really such a bad person. As we mentioned earlier, what she had come to realize was that she was conflict avoidant. If there was a problem, she tended to run away from it. In her marriage, Nick was essentially able to do what he wanted to do because Athena never raised her voice to say, "Stop, let's do it differently, even my way for a change!" This is why, she realized, she spent a lot of her marriage being scared. Nick liked skydiving, bungee jumping, and fast motorcycles. Although Athena agreed to do these things with him, for a while at least, she was scared to death and soon stopped joining Nick in such undertakings, which made him come to think of her as a stick-in-the-mud. Athena saw that she had built a trap for herself. By nature she was not a risk taker, but she also avoided saying how she felt when it was counter to what someone else wanted. She began to see that she was also laying a trap for herself in her relationships with her young sons, who already knew that badgering her could often get them what they wanted.

After making her list of strengths and weaknesses, Athena told herself, The next man I get involved with is going to be an accountant whose main hobby is bird watching! She laughed at herself for saying such a thing, but it did signal to her that in general the type of people with whom she would be most comfortable hanging out were gentle souls who were not into taking huge risks. She wanted a relationship with somebody steady instead of somebody flashy. This was hard for her because she thought maybe Nick was right. *Compared to him, I am a bit of a stick-in-the-mud.* She consoled herself that compared to him she might be, but compared to someone else she might be seen as steady, thorough, and reliable—not bad character traits to have! It suddenly struck her that because she was so conflict-avoidant she had let Nick set the context within which she would be judged. She could have called him selfish, reckless, and a man with a death wish, but she did not. Nor would she have even if she had had the courage. What she did realize was that by not standing up for herself and her view of the world, Nick's worldview became the standard against which she was compared, and, of course, she was found wanting. By Nick's standard she was a stick-in-the-mud, but that was a distortion of who she really was.

Now that Athena had established all her clusters of issues and ways she might deal with them and had gained a sense of what she was and was not capable of doing, she wondered how she was going to make sense of it all. How could she decide what to do first, second, and third? This challenge brought her squarely into the face of the third rule for rebuilding your life:

## ORDER YOUR GOALS AS PRIORITIES

She wanted to attack all her goals at once, but realized that some things would take longer than others and that some things would also need a much longer lead time before something started to happen. Where to begin? She remembered a concept she had been taught in an introductory psychology class called a forced-choice questionnaire. Such a questionnaire is constructed by pairing two things and then asking the question, If I could have only one of these choices, which one would I choose? An easy choice would be, "Would I rather win $100,000 or suffer from an incurable disease?" This is a no-brainer. The process gets interesting when you have to choose between fairly equal positive or negative pairs. By forcing yourself to choose between two close-to-equals, you learn a lot about what you hold dear.

Athena took another piece of paper and made three columns. She labeled the first column "Possibility 1," the second column "Possibility 2," and the third column "My Choice." She then took one goal and compared it to all the other goals she had listed across all the clusters. She made a forced choice between items in different clusters in an attempt to see what she really thought was important. A partial listing of her three columns looked like this:

| Possibility 1 | Possibility 2 | My Choice |
|---|---|---|
| Keep the house | Fun with kids | Keep the house |
| Keep the house | Financial security | Financial security |
| Keep the house | School-friendly work hours | Keep the house |
| Keep the house | Make new friends | Keep the house |
| Keep the house | Cut out junk food | Keep the house |
| Keep the house | Weekends for me when the kids are with their Dad | Keep the house |
| Keep the house | Get some exercise | Keep the house |

Athena went through all the goals she had identified and compared them to "Keep the house." The only one that won out over "Keep the house" was the financial security goal. So Athena knew at the end of this little exercise that keeping the house was a paramount issue in her life. Although she noted that "Financial security" beat out keeping the house, she knew that the two were pretty similar: by her definition, if she had financial security, she would be able to keep the house, because being able to live where she wanted to live symbolized financial security. So the exercise told her that financial security was her number one priority. She knew that she would have achieved that goal when she could rest secure in keeping the house that the boys had lived in since birth. She also knew that if push came to shove, her need for financial security outweighed finding a job that gave her school-friendly hours, and it certainly outweighed any issue of fun with the kids, making new friends, or getting over her anger at Nick about the divorce.

Athena then took another goal that had more to do with feelings and tried the same forced-choice listing, but she left off financial stability and keeping the house because she had already identified them as her most important issues. She noted that those issues were the ones that made up the majority of Cluster A. That cluster was her top priority.

Her second list looked like this:

| Possibility 1 | Possibility 2 | My Choice |
|---|---|---|
| Make new friends | Get exercise | Make new friends |
| Make new friends | Cut out junk food | Make new friends |
| Make new friends | Do something fun with kids | Do something fun with kids |
| Make new friends | Get over the divorce | Get over the divorce |
| Make new friends | School-friendly work hours | School-friendly work hours |
| Make new friends | Get over anger at Nick | Get over anger at Nick |

Athena came away from this forced-choice exercise with the strong feeling that making new friends was important but that her kids and their lives and her relationship to them were more important. Also in the more personal sphere, getting over the divorce and feeling psychologically whole again were much more important than losing weight and feeling physically fit. In fact, Athena questioned whether it was necessary to do much more of the forced-choice selections. It seemed obvious to her that Cluster A (Financial) was top priority, Clusters C (Kids) and D (Divorce) were about tied, and Cluster B (Me) was last on the list of goals to be reached.

The process she went through really helped her see how she wanted to prioritize things in her life. She needed to work on finances first. Fortunately, though, Athena was blessed with common sense, so she did not think life would stop on all fronts while she worked on finances. She did not believe for a minute that her sons would sit and patiently wait while she got her finances together before they started putting demands on her as a mother, nor did she think she could totally ignore nurturing herself as she tried to restructure her life. What the process did give her was some sense of where she should start. It also clarified her priorities in the event that life put her in a forced-choice situation. In other words, if an interview for a plum job conflicted with attending one of her son's ball games, then the job interview had to have priority. Further, it probably would be wise to fill the kids in on what her priorities were so that if there were forced-choice situations, the boys would better understand why she was making the decisions she was. Athena had reached the point of implementing the fourth rule:

## DEFINE AND IMPLEMENT
## A PATHWAY TO YOUR GOALS

Now that Athena had a sense of what her goals and priorities were in the context of her strengths and weaknesses, what then was her pathway to her goals? She had already done some of this work in the first exercise when she listed the pathways she might take to meet her goals. Now it was a question of going back and looking at the pathways she had identified and deciding which to take.

For Cluster A (Financial), Athena had written the following pathways:

### Cluster A—Finances: Pathways

- Check with the bank about refinancing the mortgage to reduce house payment burden.
- Explore jobs that pay better than mine as a department store clerk and that have flexible hours, as in:

  Pharmaceutical sales?

  School teaching (revive teaching certificate)?

  Book editing?

  What jobs will let me work from home on Internet with minimal at-the-company time requirements?

  Part-time office manager to professionals who don't need full time?

  Medical record transcription?
- Take in a roommate to help cover monthly mortgage payments and upkeep.
- Ask parents for financial help (last resort!)

Athena then looked over her list of pathways for what she had identified as her top goals and decided that talking with the bank about refinancing the house was a quick and easy first step. She decided that she would put together some timelines for herself as to what to do for the next month to begin to implement her goals. Her list looked like this:

| Week | To Do |
|---|---|
| Week I | Call Universal Bank mortgage department and find out procedure for refinancing. |
| | Ask my dad about where best mortgage rates are to be found and what pitfalls are. |
| | Start to look at want ads seriously. |

Send out word to friends that I am searching.

Check the Internet for possibilities.

Week II   Follow up mortgage possibilities from Week I.

Keep up with want ads.

Follow up on any nibbles.

Update and revise résumé.

Week III   Check with county school employment office re openings.

Check with state employment office for state job possibilities.

Follow up on any nibbles.

Check with friends who have had roommates as to pitfalls, legal contracts, horror stories.

As you can see from Athena's list, she was very careful not to overdo it and give herself too many things to do within the first month. She had a plan, however, that she could follow in a reasonable way, one that was simple enough that it did not set her up for failure.

Athena had developed a plan to restructure her life without a partner. She did not feel ready for a new relationship because she felt she needed time to heal and to determine her contribution to the failure of her marriage. She felt that if she had a better understanding of herself before she got into a new relationship, she would be less likely to repeat the same mistakes. Further, she knew she had to work on her avoidant personality so that she could be in a reciprocal rather than one-way relationship. She certainly was not swearing off relationships for the rest of her life, but was just trying to get a better sense of herself before she started a new one.

Naturally we strongly recommend that you follow Athena's example and come up with a plan for restructuring your life with or without a partner. The steps Athena took are instructive and helpful. So here are the rules we first mentioned at the beginning of this chapter, but this time we've included the steps that Athena went through and that we strongly recommend. We deliberately left the steps out before because we wanted you to think of Athena's behavior as spontaneous. The steps work!

Rule 1: Identify the kind of life you want.

  Step 1: List your goals for your life.

  Step 2: Cluster your goals under related, manageable headings.

Rule 2: Know your strengths and weaknesses.

  Step 1: Lead with your strengths as you develop your priorities.

  Step 2: Understand your weaknesses and make a plan to correct them.

Rule 3: Order your goals as priorities.

  Step 1: Use a forced-choice method in each cluster of goals to shake out your most important goals.

Rule 4: Define and implement a pathway to your goals.

  Step 1: Generate possible solutions to reach your goal.

  Step 2: Choose one solution as your pathway to achieving that goal.

  Step 3: Implement that solution.

  Step 4: Review and modify your plan as necessary.

The steps to rebuilding a life are not many, nor are they rocket science. Actually they are even harder than rocket science because they require you to have a sense of serious purpose and honesty. There is life after divorce if you make a plan and follow through with it. Life is so much less complicated if you know where you want to go and why you are doing some things and not others to get there. With a plan, you know what to say yes to and what to say no to, so decisions become easier.

In our next chapter we offer some success stories. In many of them, success took a great deal of hard work, but each person had a plan and stuck to it through thick and thin, with some on-the-spot modifications as life threw new curves.

# Chapter Nine

# | **There Is Life After Divorce!**

At the beginning of a divorce you feel as if the pain will never end. You feel that this is the way it is going to be for the rest of your life. You lose all sense of perspective, and that just adds to the over-whelmed feeling and the feeling of sadness. But life does go on. If you see the failure of your marriage as an important learning point in your life, as we have urged you to do, you can use what you've learned (if you follow the advice in this book) and, with a recon-structed perspective, continue on your life's path.

## Success Stories

In this chapter, we want to introduce you to some people who di-vorced, did their work, and successfully rebuilt their lives.

### Noreen

Noreen and her husband, Bill, were married right out of college. He went on to get his Ph.D. in psychology at a major university in the South, a place where neither of them had been before. They lived in graduate student housing, which was essentially Quonset huts that had been put up as temporary housing for the influx of married graduate students right after World War II. Somehow "tem-porary" became permanent. The complex, officially called Victory Village, was laughingly referred to by its residents as the Graduate Student Ghetto. The walls were thin, the heating and plumbing marginal, but there was an esprit among the residents that made it a happy place to live.

Noreen and Bill had two children in quick succession. Allie was born at the end of Bill's first year of graduate school, and Martin was born a short eleven months later. Noreen was happy. She loved children, felt herself lucky to be a stay-at-home mother, and lost herself in domestic bliss.

Bill got his Ph.D. in five years and obtained his first faculty job as an assistant professor in a medium-size school on the West Coast. They packed their bags, loaded up the station wagon with children and possessions, and drove to California, where Bill started his teaching duties immediately. Noreen was left at home with the kids and a house to be made inhabitable. She threw herself into the task and found day care for the children three times a week so that she could have time for herself and to nest-build.

Life went on in a very ordinary way, but Noreen wanted nothing more than to be a housewife and mother. They moved again, this time to Washington state, after about five years. Bill had published, not perished; in fact, he became visible as a research psychologist who was known for his research and his understanding of the criminal mind. Noreen was again happy. The kids were in school by now, and she had time for gardening, volunteer work at her children's school, PTA leadership, and working for the Democratic Party as a precinct coordinator.

With Bill's increasing academic research success came several grants for more research on the criminal mind. He traveled often to present papers at conferences around the country and occasionally around the world. Noreen remained at home as a homemaker and entertainer of her friends and Bill's academic colleagues. Life marched on; the children grew up and went to college. Bill became increasingly visible in his field and began to get honors for his outstanding research. He was fortunate in gathering a highly competent research staff around him made up largely of twenty- and thirty-something graduate students. Bill began an affair with one of his research assistants, who was in her late twenties and quite different from Noreen. She wanted an academic career and was intellectual, career-minded, and very bright and athletic.

One night Noreen came home to Bill's empty closet and a note propped on the dining room table that read:

Noreen,

I am leaving you. Over the course of our marriage
you have become fat and boring. I need a woman who
can stimulate me intellectually and talk about things
at my level rather than about whether the pansies
are blooming earlier this year because of the warm
weather. My lawyer, Al Mainer, will contact you later
this week to get the process going. I am out of here.
I have a guest lectureship in England for three
months. When I come back we can deal with the
issues. Good luck.

        Bill

P.S. You tell the kids, please.

Noreen was stunned and deeply hurt. *Fat and boring? Why hadn't I seen this coming? How dare he! How completely cruel! Damn him! Why does he dump telling the children onto my lap? The coward!* She sat at the dining room table for over an hour, weeping silently and staring into space. She was numb with shock. She crawled into bed that night after a stiff drink (which was very unlike her) and slept for twelve hours. That was *very* unlike her. Today, she says that she cannot remember anything about the month following Bill's leaving. She barely functioned, but was able to keep herself fed and out of bed some of the time. She had many of the classic signs of depression. She did not eat well and lost about fifteen pounds in a month. Food simply didn't interest her. She felt hopeless and would find herself bursting into tears almost without provocation. Particularly deadly was the country music station she listened to. Its songs about unrequited love and failed relationships just set her off into paroxysms of sobbing. Several times when she was in the car she had to pull off to the side of the road and let her crying run its course before she could drive again.

After about two months of weight loss, crying jags, and a general sense of helplessness, Noreen snapped out of her depression. The turning point was when she came across their wedding album. As she thumbed through it, she began to cry. But then something else took over: anger. "I went from tears into a rage, something I had not felt until then," recalls Noreen. "I took the scrapbook and threw it halfway across the room and then I went over to it and stomped on it like a two-year-old having a tantrum. I could not pick it up and put it to rights for about two days. It just lay there. I was so-o-o angry. That was so unlike me because I am usually a happy and content person. It was the 'fat and boring' comment that screamed constantly in my brain. That really hurt!"

Noreen continued with her story. "Once my anger came roaring out I went into a time that I am not proud of. I started hitting hotel bars. I had never been a big drinker, but I wanted a place where I could flirt, where the clientele were a bit upscale, and where, as I look back on it, I could prove to myself that I was not fat and boring by having men fall for me. I wound up sleeping with a number of men in one-night stands. I suppose the nice thing about doing hotel bars was that the men were not going to be around the next day, so I did not have to face my partner in any other context. I am glad my kids were not around during this part of my divorce recovery because I am pretty ashamed of what I did. But I was so hungry for affection, for being affirmed and told I was still desirable. I think that part of it was anger at Bill, too. By sleeping around I was thumbing my nose at him. Of course, he never knew, so it was kind of pointless.

"After about six months of this, it was not OK. I felt like the village whore even though I had managed to avoid being seen by my friends during my escapades. I felt dirty and bad and guilty. The thought came to me that Bill was winning because I was turning into a person that even I was beginning to despise."

Noreen asked her family doctor for a psychotherapy referral. She realized that she was not only beginning to loathe herself but also placing herself in danger in terms of sexually transmitted diseases and violence. Fortunately, nothing had "caught her," but she began to fear that the day would come.

"With my first meeting with Susan, my therapist of two years, I was terrified. There were so many things I felt I had to say about how I hated myself as did my husband. My children had withdrawn from me because it was too painful for them to be around my grief and craziness for very long. They were concerned, but they distanced themselves. It was hard to begin. I sat and wept for about fifteen minutes. Susan just sat there and let me cry, but with a very compassionate look on her face. That helped.

"As I talked over the months with Susan, I realized that through my upbringing I had been 'trained' to be a housewife and a mother. My focus was my home and my children. That was great for my children and my home, but it was not great for the adult relationship with my husband. I saw him as a provider for the structure I was erecting called a family. He probably saw it as my saying, 'Send money and don't bother me.' He complained that I spent more time focusing on the children and their needs than on his. To some extent he was right. This was really brought home to me when Susan gently pointed out that with my children and husband gone, I was adrift. It seemed like I had nothing to do but be angry and forlorn."

Noreen laughingly went on, "So I went and got a life. My new life, as I built it, was an interactional life rather than a cloistered life. I decided to leave home every day and get out into the world and into other people's lives. Since I value home and hearth so much, and in the past probably too much, I decided I would volunteer at a soup kitchen downtown. It took all my courage to go to that part of town the first time. I had always been protected from the 'rough side of life.' At the kitchen, I could play to my strengths [laughs]. I could feed people, I could be nice and caring and maternal, and I could see a slice of life that I never had seen before from my 'cloister,' namely, the homeless and the poor.

"The best part of it was the staff people I met. They were caring, had great senses of humor, and some had life stories that made me feel that I had been raised and lived as an adult in a box filled with cotton batting. As I worked in the kitchen I began to see how lucky I was and how insulated from life I had been. Lucky in that I had a reasonably comfortable life, children who loved me, and skills that I could share and make a difference to lonely people. I was particularly taken by the children. I started to feel good about myself. I am not ready for any kind of love relationship yet. I need to feel emotionally sturdier first."

Noreen is admired by the people of the kitchen for her warmth, her reliability, and her spirit. She started a Christmas gift giveaway for the children who came to the kitchen during Christmas week; that project brought the kitchen newspaper coverage and a rise in donations. Noreen feels very much on the mend and believes that she has her life in much better balance than ever in her life. She is growing and enjoying the trip.

## Martin

Martin had a rather different experience from Noreen, but like hers it was both painful and wonderful when he reached the point of resolution.

Martin and Estelle were married when both were in their late twenties. Both were very career-minded people. Martin was an outdoorsy guy who loved fly fishing. He belonged to Trout Unlimited, had the requisite "I'd rather be fishing" bumper sticker, and generally tried to get in some fishing every other week. Estelle was an accountant in private practice. Her work life between November and April was intense. She was good at what she did, had a loyal customer base, and enjoyed her work. She and Martin met at a backyard party at a mutual friend's house.

Martin began to talk with her about his dream of opening a fly-fishing store with some money his grandmother had left him when she died. He was worried about the financial aspects of running a business. He had much better people skills and fishing know-how than he had financial skills. Estelle laughingly said that he should stop by and do a consult with her, and maybe she could help him set up a business plan if she knew more about his dream. She actually was flirting with him; she doubted he would show. Much to her surprise, he did. One of the first things she learned about Martin was that he was a man of great passions. When he latched onto something, he went after it, "the torpedoes be damned!"

They worked together over plans for Martin's fly-fishing shop and in the process fell in love. Martin was impressed with Estelle's level of organization and her clear thinking. She fell in love with his warmth and his ability to be passionate about things, unlike most men she knew.

They married and had two children over the course of six years. Martin opened his fly-fishing shop. Estelle kept the books and advised Martin on the budget, but otherwise left the running of the store to him. Initially he spent a great deal of time at the store, but after their second child was born, Martin was able to begin to delegate work to others, such as opening and closing the store and balancing the cash register. He started wanting to be home more to enjoy his children and to spend more time with Estelle. Estelle was still busy in her practice that had grown so that now she had three accountants working under her. Her work provided a good income—better, in fact, than what Martin could pull in from the store. She loved her work. The two children were in day care and then in before- and after-school care as they grew.

Martin began to press for her either to cut back or to delegate so that he and the children could see more of her during tax "high season" from November through April or May. It became an issue and an impasse for them. Estelle felt she was being asked to give up what she had spent her life building and began to think of Martin as a nag and a pest. Martin kept up the pressure while spending more time with his children than ever.

One morning at breakfast in March, Estelle's high season, Martin began to press her to take off more time and to do more delegating at work when this tax season was over. Estelle had been under great pressure that week because one of her biggest clients was urging her to do some borderline-unethical tax accounting about which Estelle was having doubts. She heard Martin's comments as highly insensitive to the pressure she was under, lost it at the breakfast table, and impulsively threw a muffin at him. It hit Martin square in the face and exploded into a multitude of crumbs that flew all over the kitchen. The toddler started to cry, and their eight-year-old went white and ducked his head down so no one could see his eyes.

Estelle then began to unload all her frustrations on Martin. He did not earn enough money; he would not be where he was without her; she resented his cutting back at the shop when he did not begin to make it as productive as it could be; and finally she felt very unsupported for what she wanted. Martin went numb. He felt he had been hit by an atomic bomb. Estelle stormed out of the house to work and yelled at him, "Since you want to be such a house husband, you take the kids to school and day care today. I won't be home until late, very late!" She did not come home until 2 A.M.

Something changed in Estelle after her outburst. She realized that she was working hard and that Martin seemed to have hit a ceiling—money did not mean anything more to him. She made more money than he and, therefore, supported their lifestyle. In fact, she began to believe that he was riding on her coattails.

About two months after her outburst, Estelle asked Martin for a divorce. She told him that he could be the primary parent, seeing as how he had so much time to spare and did not seem to care about living well. She hit Martin with this right after the tax season was over and his high season at the store was starting.

Martin did not want to be divorced. His first response was, *Nobody in my family has ever been divorced. She'll calm down. She'll get a grip! This is simply not going to happen.* When Estelle was still in the house, Martin had hope. He begged and pleaded and offered a compromise. "Let us stay together as a family, and I won't bug you about at-home time. I'll try to raise the profit margin at the store. Please stay." His pleas were to no avail. Estelle moved out to her own rented house, and they agreed that they would have a parenting plan in which the children would be with Estelle five contiguous days out of fourteen, except during tax high season when it would be weekends only. She would have them a bit more in the summer to make up for her surrendering time in the late spring at tax time.

Suddenly Martin was the single father of two young children with a business to run and bills to pay. Estelle did send a child support check faithfully, but it was very different from having her there. Martin said, "I became an emotional porcupine. I was angry at the world. I lost one employee at work because I was so unsympathetic when his mother died, and he asked for a week off to go to her funeral. I gave him three days with some tart remarks. He quit instead." Martin continued, "I was curt around my kids, which makes me feel so guilty when I look back on it. I was too tired to do stuff with them. They spent a lot of time being raised by other people while I worked my butt off at the store. The quality of life at home became pretty grim. My oldest son's grades began to drop, and rather than help him, I just yelled at him. When my younger son became more whiney and clingy, I tried to put as much distance between us as possible. I even used expensive weekend day care to give me peace. I had turned into a man I did not like, but felt I could do nothing about it because so many things were taking bites out of me."

Martin did have an epiphany, as he now laughingly puts it, in the parking lot of the grocery store. He was loading his car with groceries with both boys in their seats when he saw, across the parking aisle, a father trying to get his resisting four-year-old into the car. The boy started to cry. The father grabbed him by the arm, picked him up, and shoved him into the back seat. The boy began to scream and clambered across the back seat to the other side of the car, opened the door, and started to scramble out. The father ran around to the other side of the car, grabbed the boy by the belt, slammed the car door, turned him around and slapped him hard across the face, shoving him into the front seat. He then sped off with screeching tires and a sobbing little boy.

Martin said, "I stood there dumbfounded and full of compassion for that poor child. What kind of a father would do that? I looked at my boys and saw them both as white as a sheet. My youngest said, 'The garbage man should take that mean daddy away.' My oldest son just looked at me with teary eyes. It hit me: *there but for the grace of God go I*. I got in the car and just sat there stunned and full of self-loathing. I had placed my hand on the floor stick shift, and as I sat there staring into space and feeling awful, I felt the light touch of my older son's hand on the top of mine. It just lay there and patted me softly. I lost it then. I just started to cry, not sobs, but just tears coming from somewhere deep inside and spilling down my face.

"My eldest looked at me with concern all over his face and asked, 'Daddy, what made that man so mean to his son?' With a quivering voice I said to him, 'That Daddy forgot how much he loved his boy. Daddies forget that sometimes.' We silently drove home, and I vowed then and there that I was going to get back in a relationship with my boys. That parking lot incident really opened my eyes. I could have become that man. He represented everything I did not want to be as a father . . . *there but for the Grace of God go I*."

Martin also said that he had to get rid of some of his anger over a divorce he did not want. "I was firmly ensconced on the pity pot and gaining weight to prove it. I had to stop the self-pity and my anger at Estelle and get on with my life. To flush the system, I—don't laugh—took up tap dancing! It was great exercise and was something I had always wanted to do all my life. My dad had been a tap dancer on a cruise ship as a young man. That is where he and my mom met. I think, as I look back on my choice, I was also bonding with Dad, who had been long dead. It was kind of like 'We dads need to stick together.' Another piece of my agenda was that the classes were made up mostly of women, so it was a good date pool. I have gone out slowly on that front, but I have my eye on this one gal, and she seems to be eyeing me, so who knows."

Martin's life is coming back together, helped by his willingness to set goals, to get off the "pity pot," and to have as the unifying force in his life being a father to his boys. He commented: "It may seem weird, but I am so beholden to that father in the grocery store parking lot. It was like a bucket of ice water had been dumped over my whole body. The killer for me was my son silently patting my hand in comfort. I wonder whatever happened to that father and little boy. I hope they mended like my boys and I did."

## Pearl

Pearl's experience was very different from that of Martin or Noreen. As she rather ruefully puts it, "I had to do it twice before I got it right. I don't recommend it to anybody, but maybe people can learn from my mistakes."

Pearl was the only girl and the youngest child in a family of five children. As the baby of the family, she created havoc with her brothers because all she had to do was turn on the tears and they would get into trouble. As a result, they became her protectors and she their mascot or "toy-sister." They protected her when she first went to school and generally put her on a pedestal. They were particularly protective when boys started coming around. They became gatekeepers to her adolescent love life.

One boy who found favor with her brothers was her next older brother's best friend. Hart was a football player like her brother and had been out of high school about a year-and-a-half when Pearl was a senior. Hart was fairly ordinary looking, but he was charming. He had social skills to spare. He could talk to anyone, could tell a good story, and really liked to be in charge of what the group was going to do. Pearl was introduced to him in her junior year when he began hanging out with her brother and was occasionally at her house.

By her senior year, Pearl and Hart were an "item." They decided to marry in the summer after Pearl graduated from high school. Hart worked for his father, who owned a carpet and flooring store. Hart could both sell and install, so his father valued him as an employee. Certainly the work was steady, and since he was an only child, Hart would probably own the store someday. His financial prospects seemed secure. Pearl's family, and especially her brothers, approved, so an August wedding was planned. When Pearl graduated, she decided not to work but just to kick back, enjoy the summer, and plan the "best wedding ever."

She is now able to say, "There were little signs I should have noticed, but I was so in love and so excited about the wedding that I just shrugged them off or thought I could fix them later with my love for Hart." When asked to give examples she said, "Oh, there were lots. Once Hart and I were in a Chinese restaurant shortly after graduation. I saw a guy that I had been really good friends with between my junior and senior years. We were lifeguards at one of the city pools together. He was a hunk, but we were just friends, never boyfriend and girlfriend. I got up from our table without thinking much about it and said to Hart, 'Oh, there's Roy, let me go say hello. I'll just be a minute.' When he saw me, Roy stood up and grabbed me in a bear hug. We talked for a few minutes, exchanged phone numbers, and promised each other to call to play catch-up. When I got back to the table, Hart was livid. 'Who was that guy? Why did he give me a hug?' and—can you believe it—'Had you slept with him?' Hart was so intense and red faced that I thought he was going to throw something. I got him calmed down and told him about where Roy and I had met, that I hadn't seen him since my junior summer, and, no, I had not slept with him. Hart forbade me to call Roy, but I did later anyway, but didn't mention it. I just thought Hart was being jealous."

Pearl recalled another time when close to the wedding they had gone to a country and western dance club to do some line dancing on a no-liquor night because Pearl was still too young to drink. Hart went off to the bathroom, and a young fellow came over and asked her to dance. She hesitated, then accepted. She figured Hart would see her on the dance floor and know what was up. Besides, it was just one dance. The dance ended, and as Pearl said thank-you and walked to the edge of the dance floor, Hart suddenly appeared, grabbed her by the upper arm, and pulled her back to the table. He held her so hard that he bruised her upper arm. He was angry and spit at her, "Don't you ever do that again. When you are with me I own you!" Pearl felt contrite, as she could see that by accepting the dance with the stranger she could have made Hart jealous.

This is the thought that she comforted herself with when Hart followed her to the ladies room and stood outside the door waiting for her. He said, "I just want to keep you out of any more mischief." Pearl now says, "I should have taken these signs more seriously, but I was too in love to even think of them as 'signs.' When he said he owned me when I was with him, all sorts of alarm bells should have gone off. Alas, they didn't."

Hart and Pearl married in late August. Hart got so drunk at the wedding reception that he slept away their first night together as a wedded couple. Pearl said, "I just thought it was a 'boys will be boys' sort of thing and forgave him, although I was disappointed."

Pearl received her first beating from Hart about three months into the marriage. He had invited a friend he worked with at his dad's store over for dinner. Pearl had made a penuche cake for dessert from a recipe in a cookbook she had gotten as a wedding present and had not used before. Pearl said the cake was like eating brown sugar–flavored tar. It was very thick and sticky, and everybody had to stop talking as they tried to peel the cake off the roof of their mouth with their tongue. Pearl was mortified because she had wanted to make a good impression for Hart's friend. The friend just laughed it off and told a story about how his mom had watched in horror as the Thanksgiving turkey slid off the platter when he was carrying it to the table about four years ago.

After the friend left, Pearl was in the kitchen clearing up when Hart came in. He was in a rage and started screaming at her that if she couldn't cook any better than that they would just not have people over anymore. He grabbed her by the hair and slammed her head into the kitchen cabinet doors—she doesn't remember how many times.

Pearl cried, and apologized profusely because she felt she had embarrassed Hart and that it was her fault. Her face had a bruise on it for about two weeks. She told her family when they asked that she had fallen and hit her head against a cabinet door in the kitchen. "At least I was telling a little bit of the truth," she says as she talks about it now. She also noted how contrite Hart was after the incident. He cried, brought her flowers, and said that it would never happen again. But it did.

Pearl continued, "It just got worse. We tried to have children and could not. We didn't have the money for fertility clinics, so we had no children. Maybe God was protecting a child by not letting it be born to us. I couldn't have children, I couldn't cook, and then Hart began to get critical about the way I kept house. He really beat me down because there was always a kernel of truth in what he complained about. Yes, the house was clean, but there were dust bunnies under the refrigerator and lime deposits on the showerhead. He would not let me work and would not let me see my family. I was a prisoner in my house. He got so jealous that I couldn't have the refrigerator repairman come by when Hart was not there. The beatings increased in frequency. I spent my life trying to do things perfectly so I would not get hit. It was never perfect enough for Hart. I kept getting hit.

"One day I was cleaning the oven, and my best high school friend stopped by unannounced. I was in a tank top and had bruises on my chest and shoulders where Hart had kicked me when I fell in the kitchen after he hit me. I opened the door a crack and there stood Kara, my best friend. I had not seen her for about eight months. She had donuts and insisted on being let in. I thought I would do it and just not tell Hart. She saw me and came unglued. She pressed me for what had happened. I started to cry and told her of the hell I had been living in for the past three years. She said that I needed to get help, that nobody deserved to live and be treated like this. I was very afraid and said that I would think about it.

"Kara coaxed me into letting her come by again. I was so hungry for a friend and human contact that I agreed. I scrubbed that kitchen table and washed and dried that extra cup real hard so that Hart would not suspect I had broken my isolation and let Kara in. She visited me several times in secret from Hart. One day, to my terror she brought along a woman she said was from a safe house. That lady talked to me about how no one deserves to be hit and how there were places I could go where I would be safe. We talked, they left, and Hart came home that night and beat me because I let the water boil away from cooking the rice and burned both the rice and the pan bottom. This time I tried to fight back rather than just taking it, and that made it worse. Hart really became enraged and hit hard. He broke my jaw. He had to take me to the hospital.

I told the doctor in the emergency room that this was the result of a beating by my husband and that I wanted to go home to my parents. I don't know where I found the courage to do that, but I guess it was from that safe house lady. They would not let Hart see me and called my parents, who were angry and appalled. I went home with them with my jaw all wired up. I found out that two of my brothers told Hart that they would kill him if he came near me. Apparently he did try to contact me, but my family kept him at bay. We were divorced quite quickly after that. Hart was compliant because he did not want everybody to know he was a wife beater.

"I should have gone into some kind of therapy for abused wives, but I did not because I was too embarrassed to admit what had happened to me and what a wuss I had been about handling it."

After her jaw mended and her face was back to normal, Pearl got a job as a server in a fairly upscale chain steak house. She is a very attractive and wholesome-looking woman. She had waited tables in her senior year to earn spending money, and the manager of the steak house was her boss at her old restaurant. He had moved up in the restaurant business during the time Pearl was married to Hart. The job was a good one, and tips were great. Pearl was so happy to be out in the world again. She thought all would be well now. In essence, she avoided doing her inner work and just moved on through life while trying to forget the hell with Hart. While she was happy to be out in the world again, she was sad about her life with Hart and felt she needed someone to lean on while she got her life back together.

Not long after she started work at the steak house she met Christian, one of the guys behind the bar. Christian was from another state and starting to make a life in Colorado, a place he had come vacationing with his family when he was a boy. He liked to ski but was not a ski bum; he wanted to make his way in the restaurant business because of the flexibility in working hours it offered. As the evenings at the restaurant ran to the end, and there would be just a few patrons left before closing time, Christian and Pearl would stand by the pickup station at the bar and talk about their hopes, dreams, and past lives. Christian had been divorced, too, and spoke of a wife who had an affair early in their marriage and just dumped him and moved out without so much as a good-bye. He did not know where she was and didn't care.

Christian seemed to know a lot about the world and had been many more places than Pearl. She saw him as worldly-wise, sophisticated, and kind. Since he had been divorced, too, he really seemed sensitive to the pain of feeling like a failure. She noticed that Christian would drink toward the end of the night, but he never seemed drunk, just happy.

Christian asked her out for a Sunday morning brunch at a restaurant on a small pond. In this beautiful setting, Christian asked Pearl if she would be willing to consider moving in with him. It would get her out of her parents' home and in with a guy so she could have a life; and besides, they both worked at the same place, so they could be together a lot more than many couples.

Pearl accepted, and things went well at first. They worked together nights at the steak house, and since tips were good, money was not a problem. What *was* a problem, however, was that Christian continued to drink after they got home about midnight each working night. Pearl knew that he drank slowly and evenly each night as a bartender, but she really had not been aware that he drank when he got home and much more heavily than at work. They could only have sex when they woke up in the late morning because Christian tended to drink himself into nonfunctional oblivion at night.

Christian also had a temper when he drank. It seemed to be directly correlated to the amount he drank. The more he drank, the angrier he became. She had not seen this at work because there he gave himself only a happy buzz. Out of deference to her parents, she had never spent the night with him until she moved in.

About six months into the live-in arrangement, Christian became very upset at work. Someone had taken two days' worth of bar tip money out of a jar he kept at the bar. It was the first time he had ever had money stolen. He came home with Pearl and, as usual, drank. He kept getting angrier and angrier. He ranted and raved. At first Pearl tried to comfort him and be sympathetic. He would not calm down. Feeling very tired, she finally said to him, "Christian, it's only money. Get over it!"

Pearl said, "He came after me with a wild scream. He threw me on the floor, sat on my stomach, and slapped me back and forth across the face. I started screaming. It was like life with Hart, and all the terror and anger I had stored up over the years came pouring out of me. I screamed and screamed." A neighbor, awakened by the uproar at about 1:30 in the morning, called the police. They arrived, interviewed both of them, and took Christian off to jail. Their city required that one person be arrested and taken to jail in the case of a domestic violence incident.

"I looked in the mirror and saw my 'Hart face' again. My eyes were all puffy. One was black and blue. My cheeks were bright red and puffy. I was a mess. This time I left because I had vowed when I left Hart that I would never, never let this happen to me again." She went back to her parents' house and quit her job at the steak house the next day. She needed Christian out of her life.

Pearl was referred to a therapist who was skilled in understanding the dynamics of domestic violence. She helped Pearl first develop a plan of what to do if Christian showed up on her doorstep or otherwise tried to contact her. They then plunged into talking about Pearl's life and why abusive men chose her. In time, Pearl began to understand that she chose abusive men as much as they chose her. Pearl began to see that because of her life as a princess in a household of protective brothers, she was drawn to men who were charming and protective. Further, she tended to idealize them and not see their faults. She agreed that there had been signs in the courtship that might have raised an alarm with a person more guarded than she. She wanted a man who would be a protector, but she could not differentiate between a protector and a controller. In her childhood home, her parents intervened if her brothers tried to control her. Her parents could not intervene in her adult relationships.

Pearl worked hard to understand that she did not need protection and that she could be quite whole without having a man in her life. This led to a brief bout with depression as she grappled with the thought of being alone. She recognized that she needed to learn to be independent and not rely on her parents or a man to make her life work. She could be safe all on her own.

Now she laughs about this period in her therapy. "This was my 'aha!' moment when I realized I was alone and could be alone. I also realized that for my life to have meaning I had to decide what I wanted and go for it. Nobody was going to hand my life to me, and those who promised me a life were into control. No more was I going to be controlled!"

Pearl is now the manager of the women's intimate apparel department at a major store in her city. She has a boyfriend. His career at the moment takes him out of town fairly frequently. Pearl is happy with this arrangement because it gives her space and helps buffer her from sinking into an overly dependent relationship. She has made it very clear to him that she has a life separate from his, and he respects this need. Pearl feels she is now on the road to independence but knows she still must be vigilant because her skills are new. The urge to go back to her old ways is still crouching in the background, ready to pounce should she falter.

## Keith

Our final story is about Keith and his extremely messy divorce. Keith and Paula married right after Keith graduated from architecture school. The two of them lived together for his last year-and-a-half of architecture school and decided to tie the knot when he graduated and got his first job.

Keith set out to become a senior partner in the prestigious architectural firm he joined right out of graduate school. He vowed he would make it in seven years, which for an architect would be an extremely fast rise to the top. He worked about one hundred hours a week, which meant that he worked evenings, weekends, and holidays. He and Paula had three children in close succession, but Keith was not around them very much. He felt that he and Paula had an unwritten marital agreement that he would build a career and make good money and she would protect hearth and home and raise the three children. The kids loved Daddy dearly and were always excited to see him, but they were on a lean diet of fathering as he pursued his career.

Around his third year as an associate in his firm, Keith began to work with a new fellow, Adam, who introduced him to cocaine. Cocaine awoke a sagging body at the end of the day and gave Keith that extra boost to keep him working. He began to use it fairly regularly—not so much that one would call him an addict, but regularly nonetheless. He would come home from the office wired and manic sometimes. Paula did not pay too much attention because she was often in bed and asleep when he came home.

Keith did indeed make full partner in seven years. He threw a big celebration party at his home for the office and its staff. It was at this party that Paula was confronted with the fact that Keith used cocaine. She walked into the bedroom unannounced, only to find Keith, Adam, and another friend snorting lines of cocaine on her glass-topped bureau. They were as startled as she was. She turned and walked out.

When the guests had gone, she went after Keith about how long he had been using cocaine; she told him that she wanted him to stop and that she did not want the substance in the house for fear the children might find it. Keith promised he would give it up and not keep it in the house. He did not keep his promise; Paula discovered four packets of cocaine in his bottom bureau drawer when she was putting away some clean hiking socks.

When Keith came home that night, Paula told him that she wanted a divorce and wanted Keith out of the house within four days. She would not tolerate drugs, and she had given him ample warning. She also pointed out that he was already almost an absentee parent anyway, so the children probably would not miss him that much. She gave him the name of her lawyer, who was one of the best divorce attorneys in town. She told him that she would tell the children he was leaving and that the reason was that he had a problem with drugs. He was so stunned that he did not protest, although later he felt he should have insisted that they all sit down together to talk about it. It was pretty clear from the behavior of the children that Paula played the blame game when she told the kids.

Keith took a suite with a kitchenette at a local motel. Fortunately it had a swimming pool, although Keith had not thought of that one way or the other when he rented it. The children were happy to see him because they knew they could go swimming, which they loved to do.

As soon as he left the house, several things happened. Paula began to withhold the children when he was scheduled to see them, saying "they had other commitments" or that "they did not want to come and should be able to choose." Her attorney began to paint Keith as a danger to the children because he was a "heavy" cocaine user, which added further justification to reducing his visiting time with his children. Keith began to feel like a medieval castle being stormed.

Paula was fairly successful in keeping the children from him. Keith was suddenly aware of what he was losing. He had taken his children for granted because he knew they would always be there when he wanted to dip into their lives. Now he couldn't. He began to feel very sad because he no longer had casual access to them, and he began to realize how much he had missed while he built his career. Although that had been the "deal" between Paula and him, it did not seem like such a good deal now that he was out of the house. He was reminded of the truism that you never know how much you value something until you lose it.

His divorce lawyer said he did not have a chance in court unless he could show that cocaine was no longer a part of his life. Keith entered an outpatient drug treatment program that required a week's stay in a treatment facility and weekly individual and group therapy sessions. Treatment focused on the drug abuse more than it did on his divorce. He asked the court to appoint a mental health professional to investigate and report to the judge regarding the best interests of the children. The court-appointed professional was to monitor and facilitate the temporary parenting plan and report to the court about the efficacy of Keith's drug treatment program.

Keith and Paula's children were assigned a psychologist, who set to work immediately monitoring the parenting time plan. She gently pointed out to Paula that Paula could not eliminate parenting time for Keith just because she wanted to. Keith's time with the children increased and improved, although there were still problems with the kids' not being where they were supposed to be at pickup time or not being home when he was scheduled to make his evening good-night call.

Keith struggled with the direction his life had taken. He had achieved partner in record time and was making huge amounts of money as an architect in a popular and busy firm. He drove a BMW and had purchased a house in a fashionable part of town with enough bedrooms so that each child had his or her own bedroom plus one for overnight guests. Unlike many people who divorce, Keith felt minimal impact on his pockets because they were so deep to begin with. He had forsaken intimacy for career success and prestige, which now seemed like empty achievements.

Keith began to feel that he had used his wife and kids as part of the props necessary to advance in the firm. He had not set it up that way intentionally, but he did wonder if at some level marriage and children were part of the Full-Partner-in-Seven-Years Syndrome. He did not like that possibility. He was besieged by his wife and her attorney. If ever he failed to take a child to a piano lesson or a soccer practice, she was on him like a lioness on an antelope. He felt as though he were picking his way through a minefield, not knowing when he was next going to be blasted for something he unknowingly did or failed to do. The more he pressed for time with the children, the more outraged his wife seemed to become. She saw the children as her property, and she was unwilling now to share what she had spent her entire life raising. To her, he was an interloper, moving in to take advantage of all her hard work and to share credit for great kids when they were her handiwork, not his. She was very angry.

Keith saw his life as being in a shambles. He was in a drug treatment program, he was divorcing, he had lost contact with his children, and his soon to be ex-wife was vilifying him to all their friends. It was a low time for him. Keith was not a believer in psychotherapy, although he would begrudgingly admit that the drug treatment program was helping him.

One night he sat down after a lonely dinner alone and wrote across the top of a pad of paper "Where I Want My Life to Go in the Next 5 Years." Without fanfare, he was in fact beginning the process of setting goals for himself and then charting a pathway to reach those goals. He decided that he wanted to have a much more involved relationship with his three children. He spent some time beating himself up for not having taken advantage of the easy access to them he could have had during his marriage, but emerged from that bout of self-pity with a determination to be involved. He decided that if they could not come to him as much as he would like, he would go to them. As senior partner in his architectural firm, he had a great deal of control over his schedule. He also could work weekends when the children were not with him. He felt that it was very important that he be involved in their schooling.

Keith knew his wife would never agree to a 50-50 split of time with the kids, so he decided to go for a plan that allowed a five-day visit every other weekend with him, with overnights during the off week. He believed that even if the court cut it to four out of fourteen days, he would still have some days that overlapped with school rather than just weekends. He wanted to forge meaningful connections with his children and not to be just a "Disneyland Dad." He decided that as a step on the pathway he would volunteer at his children's school and try to coach at least one sports team a season. This meant he would have to go to the office early so that he could get out early. In the past when he had gone to the office early he had rather liked it because it was quiet, and there were no interruptions until the "thundering herd" arrived at around 8:30. Coming to the office early did not seem a hardship on those days he did not have the children.

Keith's divorce is yet to be finalized; it has been over a year-and-a-half since he left the marital residence. Keith is well into doing his work. He stopped drug treatment at the end of his first year, with the blessings of the clinic staff. He has gotten his wife to agree to weekly dinner visits during which he sees only one child at a time so that he can really get to know them and they him without the interference of another sibling. He has signed up to be an assistant coach for his oldest son's soccer team. His wife put up a fuss because she said she did not feel safe being at the game with the child's father. The psychologist set up rules of conduct for them that the court ordered. They cannot be on the same side of the field, and Paula must arrive no earlier than game starting time. Keith gets to pick up the boy from school so that there is no risk of meltdown before the game.

Essentially Keith is in process. He says that what is most helpful is having goals and pathways to the goals. When in doubt as to what choice to make, he simply has to ask, Which choice will get me (and my children) closer to the goal?

## You Can Be a Success Story

Keith, Noreen, Martin, and Pearl all have different stories. Each of them dealt with different issues and had different struggles, but the process was approximately the same. If you read each story carefully, you will see that at some point there was shock and denial, followed by anger, depression, or both. Some clinicians feel that a depression is made up of two components, anger and sadness. Although it is the sadness that is often visible on the surface, overcoming the anger is what will help reduce the depression. In these success stories, all the individuals did their work, in their own way. That is, they sat down and examined themselves and tried to figure out what they contributed to the problem. They learned from their divorce.

Keith did not spend too much time on this because he was not very psychologically minded, but the rest did, and even he did some variation on what we strongly recommend in this book. Doing your work means trying to identify what *you* contributed to the failure of the relationship. Only you can control you. Nobody else can, and you cannot control what anyone else does.

Divorce can often lead you to feel as though you have totally lost control of your life. To get back in control, you need a plan. You must set goals and come up with pathways to those goals. It is also helpful to know what drives you to seek certain qualities and circumstances in a relationship, so that you know what questions to ask yourself or your partner. The questions should be aimed at preventing yourself from making the same mistake twice. Don't worry; new mistakes are always lurking around the corner.

The old words of wisdom about how those who do not understand history are doomed to repeat it certainly hold in divorce and in your establishing a new and better life. By learning how you may have been self-centered or insensitive or immature, or otherwise may have contributed to dysfunction in your marriage, you can begin to develop your character and avoid making the same mistakes again. In Chapter Ten we offer succinct guidelines and a place to begin building your own success story.

# | **Let Go and Grow**

Here you are at the last chapter of the book. We congratulate you for caring enough about yourself to examine your marriage and divorce and your responsibilities and roles in each. Each chapter has included the information that we think will be helpful in understanding and learning from your divorce. We know that incorporating all our recommendations for personal work and self-reflection will take some time. But we ask that you now focus on some themes that are absolutely necessary to your success in learning from your divorce.

## **Do Your Personal Work**

We can't say this too often: for you to use your divorce as a stepping-stone to a new life, you first must work at knowing yourself. To guide your quest, we have examined different aspects of self-knowledge. You have seen that you are the person you are because of your early parenting and conditioning, family relationships, friends, education, and religious upbringing, and, in fact, because of every action and interaction that has occurred in your life.

### Know Thyself

You developed your personality from your inherited traits and predispositions as well as from learning how to be a member of your culture. You adopted values and moral codes from your family, religious teachings, and cultural norms. You have also made choices about what you believe is right action and have discarded values and moral codes that do not fit anymore with who you are as an adult.

The resulting personality and being that you are right now is unique. You are the only You in this world. Don't you want to know this special person so that you can guide and direct his or her behavior in ways that produce happiness and peace rather than sadness and internal unrest? Only when you begin peeling away those layers of conditioning and upbringing to determine who you really are will you be truly able to take each situation you encounter and use it to create a more wonderful life. Our sincere belief is that if you can put labels on your style and your actions, those labels will give you power to change. Self-knowledge gives you the power to recognize what you are about to do and to ask yourself, Do I really want to do this, or do I want to do it a different way? That question opens the floodgates to change.

## Figure Out What Caused Your Divorce

We hope you took the time to analyze your divorce to determine which of the seven types of breakup apply to you. If you haven't done that yet, go back to Chapter Four and look over our descriptions of the types. The following list of questions can serve as a sort of capsule review:

Did you expect your spouse to satisfy all your emotional needs and resolve all your psychological conflicts?

Were you selfish in the pursuit of your own happiness or professional career?

Were you selfish, self-centered, and immature?

Did you and your spouse gradually drift apart?

Did you or your spouse (or both of you) have affairs during the marriage?

Did you experience a trauma during the marriage, such as a child's death or long-term unemployment, that prompted the downward spiral of your marriage?

Were either you or your spouse dysfunctional and unable to fully participate in the marriage in a healthy way?

Did one of you "come out" as gay or lesbian in your sexual orientation?

Did one of you grow away from the other while you or your spouse
   remained the same?

Were one of you the victim of a relationship predator who manipulated you into a divorce?


The most important question to answer is, What was *your* role
in your divorce, and what can you learn from this?

We urge you look at your marriage on a time line. What were
the significant events in your relationship during your courtship?
What happened in each of the years of your marriage? What events
or behaviors (of each spouse—this is no time for the blame game!)
would you identify as undermining your marriage, even slightly?
By creating this time line you can see more clearly what happened,
when it occurred, how you both responded to it, and what effect it
had on your relationship. This is important information to use in
solving the puzzle of your divorce. If you can analyze your marriage
and divorce this way, you will be prepared to respond differently
in the future.

In this book, we explored the prevalence of the myth of romantic love in our culture. Did you buy into the myth that romantic
love is a strong enough base on which to build a committed relationship? People's acceptance of the myth of romantic love as a
sign that they should dive into a committed relationship head-first
has resulted in many marriages hitting the rocks.

In future relationships, you need to look beyond your physical
and romantic attraction to the practical aspects of this person. Although you may wish, as many others do, to look for the one "soul
mate" who will complete you and bring you the perfect relationship, we believe that this search is futile and perhaps even dangerous. We have worked with countless individuals and couples who
relied on that feeling of familiarity and the feeling that "we belong
together" as justification to marry. Unfortunately, the marriages
often failed when the glow of the romantic fire faded and the practical aspects of living with someone stood out in stark relief.

Marrying for romantic love *alone* is a surefire way to have immense problems in the marriage. Yes, you want to retain the romantic feelings as much as possible in a long-term relationship, but
you must get to know yourself first and then really know the other

person before entering into another committed relationship. Remember: "*friends first,* lovers second, spouses third" works best.

Your goal is to love, not to be loved. If your focus is on getting love, you will miss the deeper, more satisfying, and more enduring gift of giving love. You will be more concerned about lack—why doesn't he love me more, what's wrong with him or with me? You will not find the abundance that results from being a loving person to your spouse and others. When your goal in any situation is to give love, compassion, and understanding to others, you are much more likely to receive it.

## Grieve for Your Lost Marriage

Until you have worked through the full process of grief, you will not be able to move forward into your bright new life. You will remain stuck in the past. So be sure that you allow yourself to feel the pain, the anger, and the emotional upset of the divorce, but don't get stuck. Rage if you need to, alone in the privacy of your home, or describe all of your anger and hatred (yes, you are entitled to feel hate) toward your departed spouse.

But then consciously make a decision to let it go. Release the negativity. You may want to perform a symbolic act, such as writing down your most negative feelings toward your spouse and then burning the paper to symbolize release, or you may just want to consciously give yourself permission to let it go. We have worked with countless people who remain angry and vengeful years after their divorce. Anger and hatred are unattractive at best, and at worst destructive to the person who holds them and to his or her children. Get a legal divorce, but above all be sure to get an emotional divorce. Do not stay married in hate and anger as you once were in love. Let go; move on.

Allow yourself to get support during your recovery process. Join a divorce recovery group whose members will let you know that you are not "crazy" and will support you through your recovery. Get into mental health therapy if you need individual professional support. There is no shame in getting the help you need; it's actually a badge of honor that you care enough about yourself (and your children) to seek assistance during this stage of your recovery. You may even find that continued therapy throughout your learning process will help you move ahead faster.

Take care of your physical needs during this time of grieving. Eat nutritiously, exercise, get enough sleep, and do something fun as often as you can. At this time in your life, you need more than ever to nurture and support yourself. Be grateful for the good that you do have, even if it is only that you have a roof over your head and food to eat. Remind yourself that you are a special person who deserves to be happy. Treat yourself as you would want to treat a good friend.

## Change the Way You Talk to Yourself

Your marriage may have failed, but that is very different from you as a person being a failure. Please work on accepting our mantra that mistakes are simply opportunities for learning and growth. We all make mistakes, but it is what we tell ourselves when we goof up and what we do next that determine our ultimate path. We can blame ourselves, or, even easier, we can blame the other person. Don't blame. Examine your actions to determine what you can do differently next time.

As you have seen in this book, most of us have old critical messages from our past that we replay when we make mistakes. We tell ourselves that we are not good enough, smart enough, handsome enough, loveable enough, organized enough, and so on. There are an infinite number of negative things that we can feel bad about. These old messages have controlled our behavior in the past because we have believed them to be true. But we do not have to accept them.

Listen to what you are saying to yourself and then tell yourself, That's not true! Erase the message and tell yourself something positive instead. For example, instead of labeling yourself a klutz when you drop a dish and break it, simply observe to yourself that you dropped a dish. Ask, What can I do differently next time to avoid breaking my china? Do I need to pay more attention to what I am doing? Do I need to dry my hands before I pick up the plate? Then consciously determine to remember this good advice you are giving yourself. Let your self-talk become your personal wise mentor who loves and understands you and gently teaches you how to do better next time. Begin applying this method of dealing with mistakes in the small things in life; eventually you will be able to apply the same formula for dismissing your old messages in the area of relationships and marriage. Treat yourself with compassion and without judgment. There does not need to be a polarizing right and wrong in every situation.

## Give Up Blaming

To heal and to move on in your life, you have to give up blaming yourself and your ex-spouse for the problems in your marriage that resulted in divorce and for the actions taken in the divorce. Many of the legal aspects of divorce and the actions taken by the lawyer and the parties can be extremely adversarial and painful. Statements are made in the pleadings and in court that cut to the core of a person's being. Feelings of betrayal and of being attacked are not uncommon.

The legal divorce can leave painful scars and can have long-term effects on your sense of security. However, if you beat yourself up about your role in the destruction or continue to attack and blame your ex-spouse, you will find yourself stuck in the very emotions that you are attempting to relieve. You are not permitting yourself to be divorced. Sometimes we falsely think that blaming others will make us feel better about ourselves and will build us up as the "good guy." Blame only serves to keep you from resolving the underlying issues and from finding calm and peace inside yourself. If you blame, you will need the other person in your life forever—you need someone to blame. Let go of blame, and you let go of the other person and are free!

Another shift in your internal self-talk is to forgive the other person and yourself for the divorce and the resulting trauma that may have occurred. Remember, *you forgive for yourself,* not for the other. Let go of blame and move on with your life. You are learning to see things differently and to respond to your self-talk and to others' actions in a new way. It is in your enlightened self-interest to move forward with your life, releasing the blame and anger.

## Be Willing to Work at Relationships

If you have identified that you and your spouse did not talk or listen to each other, you truly need to learn some new skills. All of us need acknowledgment and recognition. In relationships we receive these things by talking to each other, listening to each other, and responding in a manner that allows the other to feel understood. If you felt misunderstood in your marriage, or if your spouse included your inability to understand as a reason for the divorce, your work is clear. In the Resources section of this book, we have listed some wonderful self-help books for individuals and couples on communication skills in relationships. You may want to take a class or work with an individual therapist or coach to boost your ability to talk and listen.

Every couple has differences and conflicts. It is important that you identify your conflict style and the style of your spouse so as to learn how to handle conflict in a way that does not undermine or even destroy your relationship. Beware of seeing only your exspouse's conflict style and ignoring your own by blaming him or her for the unraveling of the marriage. The only conflict style you can control is yours. Understanding it is the beginning of being able to control it. For instance, do you avoid dealing with conflict directly, eliminating the possibility of effective problem solving? Do you fight loudly and vociferously, resorting to sarcasm, blaming, or demeaning and belittling the other? Do you use bickering and jabbing to undermine the other spouse?

As we saw in Chapter Five, approaching disputes with an intention to collaborate is the most effective method of conflict management. To create solutions together that meet both spouses' needs, you must use good communication skills to state your needs clearly and to listen attentively to the other person's needs. Creative problem solving affirms the value that both spouses put on the relationship and strengthens the bonds of love and support.

## Parent Consciously

Your children will inevitably be affected by your divorce; however, your responses and actions can make the difference in both their short-term and long-term adjustment. Chapter Six includes some tips and admonitions for parenting after divorce that we urge you to follow. You may also want to take a parenting class for divorcing or divorced parents (many jurisdictions around the country require such classes) or read books on this subject. But don't blame yourself when you slip up and don't follow the guidelines you have learned. There are no perfect parents! No, not even one. So don't expect to parent perfectly. You will occasionally do things that could hurt your children, such as saying something snide about your ex or fighting in front of your children.

But again, you need to avoid playing the blame game, against yourself and your ex. You are doing the best job you can possibly do. Remain conscious of what you say around your children, how you say it, and of the unspoken messages you are sending your children about the other parent. When you criticize your ex-spouse, your children will feel criticized too, because they are a part of the other parent. When you hold on to anger and hostility toward your ex, you put your children in a loyalty bind that is a crazy-making and destructive place for kids to be. Conscious parenting without blame and guilt is your goal.

## New Beginnings

All life is naturally cyclical, with beginnings and endings. In our beautiful physical world, we experience the progression of the seasons, the turning of night into day into night, the waxing and waning of the moon. As we grow older, we become increasingly conscious of the cycle of birth to childhood to adulthood to aging to death. In our lives, we begin school, and we graduate. (Some of us do this over and over.) We begin and leave careers. We raise children, then see them leave. And although divorce does not inevitably follow marriage, changes in a marriage and in a relationship are inevitable. No one has yet invented the magic button that will stop time and preserve the relationship as it existed during your courtship or on your wedding day or on the day your first child was born. Change is the only constant, for we are not static and are constantly evolving.

Divorce is an ending of one phase of your life and a beginning of another. Trust that the old maxim, "This too shall pass," also applies to the pain of divorce. Even in the midst of your sadness, begin to see your divorce as a golden opportunity to create a better life for yourself than you had in the past. The success stories we describe in Chapter Nine, based on real people we have actually known, show you that it can be done. All life is one big classroom in which you have opportunities to learn and grow and be happy.

You will experience growing pains. If you choose to dwell on the past or if you decide not to do your work, you are destined to run like a hamster in a wheel—around and around, but not moving forward. Hating and continuing the fight stagnate you. Getting stuck in your own self-pity stagnates you. Using your children to hurt the other parent stagnates you. To get the hamster off the wheel, you must open the door of your cage and let yourself out to explore. We have urged you to explore yourself in infinite detail, to set goals for yourself and chart pathways toward those goals. In divorce, the unexamined life is not worth living. Let Go and Grow should be your motto. How long do you have to continue to do your work? As long as you are alive and conscious, you must keep learning.

As the poet Browning said so eloquently almost two hundred years ago, "The best is yet to be"—but you must create it. We wish you well on your journey!

# Resources

Ahrons, C. *The Good Divorce*. New York: Harper Perennial, 1994.

Breathnach, S. B. *Simple Abundance*. New York: Warner Books, 1995.

Buscaglia, L. *Love*. New York: Ballantine, 1972.

Clapp, G. *Divorce and New Beginnings: A Complete Guide to Recovery, Solo Parenting, Co-Parenting and Stepfamilies*. New York: Wiley, 2000.

Fisher, B., and Alberti, R. *Rebuilding When Your Relationship Ends*. (3rd ed.) Atascadero, Calif.: Impact Publishers, 2000.

Fisher, R., and Ury, W. *Getting to Yes: Negotiating Agreement Without Giving In*. Boston: Houghton Mifflin, 1983.

Ford, D. *Spiritual Divorce*. San Francisco: Harper San Francisco, 2001.

Fowers, B. J. *Beyond the Myth of Marital Happiness: How Embracing the Virtues of Loyalty, Generosity, Justice, and Courage Can Strengthen Your Relationship*. San Francisco: Jossey-Bass, 2000.

Frankl, V. *Man's Search for Meaning: An Introduction to Logotherapy*. New York: Simon and Schuster, 1959.

Fromm, E. *The Art of Loving*. New York: HarperCollins, 1956.

Frydenger, T., and Frydenger, A. *Resolving Conflict in the Blended Family*. Grand Rapids, Mich.: Revell, 1991.

Garrity, C., and Baris, M. *Caught in the Middle: Protecting the Children of High Conflict Divorce*. San Francisco: New Lexington Books, 1994.

Ginott, H. *Between Parent and Child*. New York: Avon, 1969.

Gold, L. *Between Love and Hate: A Guide to Civilized Divorce*. New York: Plenum, 1992.

Gottman, J. *The Relationship Cure*. New York: Crown, 2001.

Gottman, J., and Silver, N. *The Seven Principles for Making Marriage Work*. New York: Three Rivers Press, 1999.

Grever, C. *My Husband Is Gay*. Freedom, Calif.: Crossing Press, 2001.

Hendrix, H. *Getting the Love You Want: A Guide for Couples*. New York: Harper Perennial, 1988.

Hetherington, E. M., and Kelly, J. *For Better or For Worse*. New York: Norton, 2002.

Jones, R. *Negotiating Love: How Women and Men Can Resolve Their Differences*. New York: Ballantine, 1995.

Kline, K., and Pew, S. *For the Sake of the Children: How to Share Your Children with Your Ex-Spouse in Spite of Your Anger.* Rocklin, Calif.: Prima, 1992.

Krantzler, M., and Krantzler, P. *The New Creative Divorce.* Avon, Mass.: Adams Media, 1998.

Kübler-Ross, E. *Death: The Final Stage of Growth.* Upper Saddle River, N.J.: Prentice Hall, 1975.

Lao-tzu. *Tao Te Ching.* (G.-F. Feng and J. English, trans.). New York: Vintage Books, 1989.

Markman, H., Stanley, S., and Blumberg, S. *Fighting for Your Marriage: Positive Steps for Preventing Divorce and Preserving a Lasting Love.* (New and rev. ed.) San Francisco: Jossey-Bass, 2001.

May, R. *The Courage to Create.* New York: Bantam Books, 1975.

McBride, J. *Encouraging Words for New Stepmothers.* Ft. Collins, Colo.: CDR Press, 2001.

McGraw, P. *Self Matters.* New York: Simon and Schuster, 2001.

Morrissey, M. *No Less Than Greatness: Finding Perfect Love in Imperfect Relationships.* New York: Bantam Books, 2001.

Newman, G. *101 Ways to Be a Long Distance Super Dad . . . or Mom, Too.* Tucson, Ariz.: Blossom Valley Press, 1996.

Notarius, C., and Markman, H. *We Can Work It Out.* New York: Perigee, 1993.

Parker, K., and Jones, V. *Every Other Weekend: Straight Talk to Divorced Men Who Love Their Children but No Longer Live with Them.* Nashville, Tenn.: Nelson, 1993.

Ricci, I. *Mom's House, Dad's House.* (2nd ed.) New York: Simon and Schuster, 1997.

Rosenberg, M. *Nonviolent Communication: A Language of Compassion.* Del Mar, Calif.: PuddleDancer Press, 1999.

Ross, J., and Corcoran, J. *Joint Custody with a Jerk: Raising a Child with an Uncooperative Ex.* New York: St. Martin's Press, 1996.

Satir, V. *Peoplemaking.* Palo Alto, Calif.: Science and Behavior Books, 1972.

Stahl, P. *Parenting After Divorce: A Guide to Resolving Conflicts and Meeting Your Children's Needs.* Atascadero, Calif.: Impact, 1995.

Tannen, D. *You Just Don't Understand: Men and Women in Conversation.* New York: Ballantine Books, 1991.

Teyber, E. *Helping Children Cope with Divorce.* (Rev. ed.) New York: Wiley, 2001.

Thomas, S. *Parents Are Forever: A Step-By-Step Guide to Becoming Successful Co-Parents After Divorce.* Longmont, Colo.: Springboard Publications, 1995.

Thomas, S., and Rankin, D. *Divorced but Still My Parents.* Longmont, Colo.: Springboard Publications, 1998.

Tolle, E. *The Power of Now.* Novato, Calif.: New World Library, 1999.

Trafford, A. *Crazy Time.* (Rev. ed.) New York: Harper Perennial, 1992.

Viorst, J. *Necessary Losses.* New York: Fawcett Columbine, 1986.

Worthington, E. *Five Steps to Forgiveness: The Art and Science of Forgiving.* New York: Crown, 2001.

# About the Authors

*Christine (Christie) A. Coates* is an attorney in Boulder, Colorado, whose practice now emphasizes alternative dispute resolution (ADR), processes for resolving disputes outside of court.

With a B.A. degree in psychology and sociology and an M.Ed. degree in adult counseling, Christie brought a rich and varied background in management and education to her law practice. Since opening her solo law practice in 1983, she has been active in local, state, and national bar association activities, which she sees as a way to bring about positive change in our legal system. She was named the Colorado Bar Association's Outstanding Young Lawyer in Colorado in 1986. She was also honored by the Colorado Council of Mediators and Mediation Organizations as the 1996 Mediator of the Year and was recognized by Voices for Children (CASA) for her advocacy for children in that same year. She received the 1999 Community Service Award from the Boulder Interdisciplinary Committee on Child Custody.

Coates has served as president of the Boulder County Bar Association, the Boulder County Bar Foundation, the Boulder Interdisciplinary Committee on Child Custody, and the Association of Family and Conciliation Courts, an international interdisciplinary organization. She is the past chair of the Boulder County Bar Association's Professionalism Committee and is a frequent lecturer, trainer, and speaker on family law, professionalism, and dispute resolution options. She has taught family law at the University of Colorado School of Law and family ADR at the University of Denver.

Coates is coauthor of *Working with High-Conflict Families of Divorce* (Jason Aronson, 2001). She has published articles on ADR in professional journals and appeared on television and radio.

*E. Robert (Bob) LaCrosse* is a licensed clinical psychologist who has been in private practice in Denver, Colorado, for twenty-five years. He has a B.A. degree *cum laude* from Harvard College and earned his M.A. and Ph.D. degrees from the University of North Carolina at Chapel Hill.

Work with children and families has been a constant throughout his career. In his private practice, he specializes in therapy with children of divorce, their parents, and divorcing couples. In addition, he offers services to help parents mediate parenting plans, to develop parenting plans, and to oversee the execution of parenting plans. He teaches classes for Parenting After Divorce-Denver, the four-hour course required by the court for all divorcing parents in the five-county Denver metropolitan area.

Bob started his career as an assistant professor at the Harvard Graduate School of Education. He then moved to California, where he was president of Pacific Oaks College in Pasadena. In 1976 he came to Colorado to head the Early Childhood Project of the Education Commission of the States. In 1978 he opened his private practice. He also has taught at Brandeis University, Regis University (Denver), Claremont Graduate School, and in the Colorado Bar Association's continuing education programs.

He has served as president of the Metropolitan Denver Interdisciplinary Committee on Child Custody. He also served as vice chair on the Governor's Commission on Children and Families under Governor Lamm and on the Fatherhood Initiative under Governor Romer. He was a member of the Board of the Day Care Council of America.

LaCrosse has appeared on numerous radio and TV talk shows, where he has discussed everything from the meaning of love to childrearing. Over the years he has authored sixteen articles, and most recently he coauthored *Working with High-Conflict Families of Divorce.*

# Index